THEY TOLD US
TO JUST BELIEVE

THEY TOLD US TO JUST BELIEVE

Critically thinking about the origins of beliefs
- ARE THEY REAL?

DANIEL FRIEDRICH

They Told Us To Just Believe

Copyright © 2024 by Daniel Friedrich

All rights reserved. No part of this book may be reproduced in any form or by any electronic or mechanical means, including information storage and retrieval systems, without written permission from the author, except for the use of brief quotations in a book review.

Cover design & typesetting by riverdesignbooks.com

ISBN 979-8-9920591-0-6 (Paperback)
ISBN 979-8-9920591-2-0 (Hardback)
ISBN 979-8-9920591-1-3 (Ebook)

This book is dedicated to my adult children. I wrote this book as much for you as for me. My wish is that I would have researched the origins of my own beliefs when you were younger. Fortunately, we were able to pass along the importance of critical thinking and intellectual curiosity which helped you to develop your own beliefs. I am so proud of how you treat others and yourselves with respect, kindness, and compassion. At the end of the day, this is what's most important.

Table of Contents

Introduction	What is This Book About? Where in the world did our beliefs come from anyway? Shedding the light on what is real and what is fiction.	9
Chapter 1	We're number one! Ranking the biggest organized religions in the world by the number of followers because everyone knows, superior numbers equal power. How can they all claim to be the best?	16
Chapter 2	Religious Auto-Enrollment How and when did most of us adopt our beliefs and make our religious choices? Often the answer is, blame your parents!	30
Chapter 3	Immaculate Conception Stories – How Could There Possibly Be This Many? Similar story, different Gods. The prerequisite to becoming a God – your father needed to be a God or spirit, because everyone already knew the identity of your mom.	42
Chapter 4	The Big Man Rules! The origins of ancient religions, including the beliefs in a variety of gods as a way to explain the world, and how these religions transformed as societies shifted from hunter-gathers to food producers.	52
Chapter 5	Religious Roots Sprouting in the Fertile Crescent A majority of current day religions all have roots in the same geographical area, specifically the Fertile Crescent. Why here? The abundance of food gave them a head start.	65
Chapter 6	The Many, Many, Many Gods of Hinduism An introduction to Hinduism, the oldest major religion in the world, having evolved over thousands of years - as much a culture	83

as it is a religion, made up of a web of customs, obligations, traditions, and ideals and not just a system of beliefs. And yes, there are many, many Gods.

Chapter 7	Buckle up – A Chronicle from Zoroastrianism to Abrahamic Religions	109
	Zoroastrianism? Never heard of it! And yet their thinking led to inventions of the Abrahamic religions – Judaism, Christianity and Islam.	
Chapter 8	A Who's Who of the Best-Selling Religion Founders	134
	Confucius, Buddha, Jesus, and Muhammad – founders of the best-selling religions of all time. Their life stories, as told through the verbal retelling over many generations, gives a glimpse into these men's lives, albeit with hardly any provable authenticating facts.	
Chapter 9	I Talked to God, and He Said to Tell You…	167
	The origins of many well-known spiritual world beliefs came from direct communication with God with no corroborating witnesses. We'll explore some of the explanations for these supernatural events.	
Chapter 10	I Know Math, So How Does 1 + 1 + 1 = 1?	195
	How do monotheistic religions, the so-called "one God religions," justify still believing in many gods? It's a mystery!	
Chapter 11	The Devil is in the Details	211
	Are there really supernatural devils lurking among us? A look at the origins of devils as well as our current visualizations of them – because including bad guys always makes for a good story.	
Chapter 12	Church Service – Rated R for "Intense Graphic Violent Images"	222
	How images of a man's death through cruci-	

fixion and the idea of eating God and drinking his blood became mainstream - perhaps a little inappropriate for young children.

| Chapter 13 | If You're Happy and You Know it, That's a Sin! | 231 |

Who is to blame for western Christian culture becoming so prudish and guilt ridden? Saint Augustine of Hippo, the first born-again Christian and the father of the Inquisition, is a good place to start.

| Chapter 14 | This Calls for a Celebration | 244 |

Some are joyous, some are somber – highlighting a few of the main religious holidays celebrated around the world; their origins, links to pagan festivals, ties to secular observances and related traditions, rituals and customs.

| Chapter 15 | Another Powerful Empire Bites the Dust | 308 |

Tolerance to people's beliefs and cultures is essential for survival of an empire, whereas, intolerance leading to oppression and subsequent economic decline can collapse even the mightiest of empires. The Roman Empire - here's looking at you!

| Chapter 16 | Does God Really Bless America? | 331 |

The founding of the United States was not supernatural, nor endorsed by God. Rather, the Founding Fathers used knowledge of history, reasoning, and philosophy to engineer this modern-day great empire.

| Chapter 17 | And Now, My Thoughts | 359 |

Time to share my thoughts – the things I "know" to be true about religion and then my "beliefs" in the absence of facts or proof. Just one man's beliefs.

| Reference Sources | 390 |
| About the Author | 393 |

Introduction

This book explores the difference between religious beliefs that are factual and those that are something else entirely—it combines religious history and critical thinking to help readers of all beliefs have "not-so-blind faith." More broadly, getting better at differentiating between what is real, what is fantasy, and what is unknowable makes us savvier about misinformation, less likely to be fooled or taken advantage of by others, and it makes us more tolerant.

A Catholic priest once told me about some of his most faithful parishioners who told him they had unquestioning faith. They were very proud of their commitment. He informed them that blind faith was no faith at all. He cautioned them that everyone should question what they believe, otherwise it is mere brainwashing and not actually faith. People who do not question their leaders and influencers can become very dangerous since the possibility exists that they will blindly do anything they are told. Although people with blind faith often think of themselves as good, righteous people, they can also be mobilized for very evil actions in the name of their religion or cause.

Typically, our beliefs are passed on to us from our parents, which had been passed on to them from their own parents. And so on, and so on. Over time, some of our beliefs may change as the result of fear, experiences either good or bad, pain and suffering. They may change because of the influences of the people we share our lives with. Or sometimes they change for no apparent reason at all other than we're merely navigating our way through everyday life and all that is thrown at us.

Beyond what we were taught and encouraged to believe as children, inexplicably as adults we have not analyzed enough why we believe what we believe. We're busy and we have many responsibilities, so we give more thought into selecting our cell phone plans. But having the courage to explore the origins of our beliefs can be interesting and make us more informed and tolerant. By studying the history related to beliefs, we begin to gain a deeper understanding of the origination of our own culture and other cultures, different ways of thinking, and why.

I wrote this book for people like me, raised in a religion, and for those raised in a non-religious family. We all "inherit" some beliefs and, to some extent, blindly believe or follow them. In my case, I always had some doubts - the sneaky suspicion that maybe this stuff, these beliefs, were fabricated. But I was persuaded to keep believing, with arguments such as: "You should believe just as an insurance policy, because what if you're wrong," or "If you don't believe, then you're on your own, and good luck with that!"

or "What about all the churches built and all the money spent on religions, isn't that enough proof for you?"

You have probably had some of these same reservations about your beliefs. Maybe, like me, you have asked yourself some of the following questions.

Questions such as...

— What do you believe in? Why? What *should* you believe in?

— Where/how/when did you form your beliefs?

— Are you devoting your life to beliefs you were taught as a child but never explored once you became an adult?

— Have you sought out any actual research before you chose to believe in something or before developing strong opinions? Are you confident you're right?

— Why do you feel so strongly about beliefs in which you have very little or no background information as to their origin? Are your beliefs based on actual facts or are they unable to be proven? Do you simply accept these "facts" as genuine? Could it be that what you assumed to be "facts" are nothing more than mere fictional stories?

— Are your beliefs based on knowledge and good reasoning, or emotions and superstitions?

— What was the bias of the religious history you believe in? Do you know who wrote that history? Do you know when it was written?

— Are you willing to die for your beliefs? Willing to kill for your beliefs?

— Do you have tolerance for those who have beliefs that differ or contradict yours?

For many people, including myself, the word "religion" can be a turnoff, which is why I like to use the word "beliefs" instead. Although the book is about the origins of our beliefs, it is not a boring religious history textbook, as it poses critical thinking questions and then answers them with facts, leading to learning and conclusions. It was written to be engaging and eye-opening and at times a little humorous. This book is also not a religious philosophy book as it primarily addresses the historical origins of religious beliefs and even some of the United States' constitutional beliefs from a history, archaeology, and science point of view.

Before we start philosophizing about how we should live our lives, our first goal should be to determine which religious stories we have been told are real vs those that are fantasy or unknowable. Only then can we really talk about how to act and treat one another.

The word belief in the Greek language is *pistis*, which means confidence or trust. Beliefs related to religious convictions are particularly tricky, because at their core is the need to trust and have confidence in the unknowns, the intangibles, the spiritual world – and often without the validation of any real facts or observable evidence.

I saw a quote on a t-shirt once that has stuck with me: "What you believe is not the problem. What you believe I should believe is the problem." Whether or not anyone's beliefs are changed, hopefully people will be encouraged to be more tolerant, kinder and respectful of other's beliefs.

Never in the history of the world have we had so much knowledge available, and such a high level of literacy. For people over 15 years of age, literacy is over 80% and growing, and for many countries is in the high 90% range. There is no longer an excuse for people to be blindly led by their leaders because of illiteracy and ignorance, which was a common occurrence for thousands of years. People can and should question and do research to determine if what they are being told by their leaders, both political and religious, is factual and based on reality.

Although most religions condemn killing, they support warfare and don't see it as immoral and destructive as long as their religion wins. This was less dangerous for the human race when people were fighting with swords and clubs, but now that we have nuclear weapons, chemical weapons, ballistic missiles, automatic high-powered guns, etc., wars have become extremely detrimental to the survival of human beings. In addition, some extremist true believers have been appallingly clever at turning modern technology into killing weapons through the use of cars, buses, trains, jet aircraft, and even the Internet.

Though the Internet is a great resource for distinguishing fact from fiction, a dangerous amount of misinformation also exists. It can be a very powerful propaganda tool, able to reach millions of people in seconds, thus enabling select groups to strengthen their power. Religious leaders and some politicians want you to be like sheep, which are easily led, or children who are overly trusting. When we see the Internet used for evil purposes, the best way to fight against all this power of misinformation is to debunk it through intellectual curiosity, research, and critical thinking.

Most books written on the topic of religion and beliefs approach it from a philosophy of religion point of view about what you should think, or from an atheist point of view trying to prove why religions are idiotic and evil, or from a theologian or world religions history professor point of view who teach how wonderful all religions are in their own way. This book is more pragmatic and primarily goes after the question – "What's real and what's not?" I have been unable to find any book on the market that takes this balanced approach, with an emphasis on critical thinking.

I emphasize critical thinking because I was a successful business executive who spent a lifetime perfecting and using critical thinking to grow businesses. I was often the one who questioned everyone and everything to make sure we were developing the best company plans for: growth, our consumers, employees, the communities where we were located, and of course to achieve a profit. I have no financial ties to any religion or the business of religion, but I am a longtime student of religion, history, philosophy, and personal development.

I felt somewhat embarrassed when I began questioning the beliefs I inherited, and realized many of the stories I was told about my own religion turned out to be made up. Many of them appeared to be nothing more than fantasy. I became more aware of the real history, and then started thinking about the billions of people living around the world, many of them also likely blindly following their inherited beliefs.

That is one of the main reasons I wrote this book – I felt compelled to share what I had learned. I also wanted to share my learning with my children and others to help people think more clearly about what they believe, which, hopefully in the long run, will lead to a better, kinder, and less selfish society. It is never too late to start on your own mission of fulfilling your intellectual curiosity and learning to think more critically. No matter when you start, you will get the benefits.

Chapter 1

We're number one!

Throughout history, religion has proved itself to be such a bewildering paradox - uniting us or dividing us, building communities of love or sowing seeds of hate, serving as a source of strength, or sadly, as seen all too often, an inexplicable justification for killing. Across the entire world's population, it's mind-boggling to recognize how extremely different everyone's level of interest in religion is; ranging from all-in church-goers, to the sometime attenders, to only on significant holidays, to the indifferent, to the outright rejecters. Thankfully, living in the United States, our constitution guarantees the right of freedom of religion for everyone – a right that is greatly appreciated, albeit sometimes taken for granted. This means, in theory, we're unequivocally free to choose any version of religion we want. Or alternatively, equally free to reject them all. Furthermore, everyone has the right to have their own beliefs. Unfortunately, as seen throughout history, this has not necessarily been the case, as religious freedom was not always tolerated. Today as Americans, we are fortunate to have choices regarding religion and our religious beliefs, and we certainly value having those choices. But what we don't have is the right to judge or discriminate others for the choices they have made. No one has a license to discriminate - in my opinion; discrimination based on religious beliefs should not be tolerated by anyone, anywhere in the world.

Understandably, just the mention of religion often evokes such diametrically opposing reactions, from those zealots to the apathetic and everyone in between. No wonder it has more and more become such an uncomfortable, touchy, delicate subject, even to the point of being branded with that lethal word of warning – it's taboo! Of course, we're all familiar with the advice to avoid broaching the subject of religion at all cocktail parties, casual neighborhood barbeques, the office water cooler (if there still exists such a thing), and especially first dates. It certainly does seem a bit safer to stick with bland chitchat about the weather, sports or favorite fried chicken recipes, rather than debating whose God is the best or if some version of God even exists at all. Well, next time you find yourself caught in one of those uncomfortable, water cooler religious tête-à- tête, feel free to lighten the mood by sharing one of my favorite quotes describing religion from Oscar Wilde – "Religion is like a blind man looking in a black room for a black cat that isn't there, and finding it." Yes, I think that pretty much sums up the essence of religion – end of discussion.

Some may argue that by its nature, all religion is mere

brainwashing – convincing you to believe in something akin to Oscar Wilde's black cat that may or may not be there. You really aren't sure what to think about it, and yet somehow you make the choice to believe or not. The same hesitancy might be true for your religion - you're not quite sure why, but you decide on one religion over another, or alternatively decide to reject them all. Some unequivocally put all their faith in their religion of choice, with the unquestioning belief that theirs is superior, the chosen one, the true one, and the morally right one. And when they imagine themselves standing at the pearly gates, although a smidgeon of doubt may creep in, ultimately, they sure hope they picked the correct one. Interesting to think, given how many different religions there are in the world, with billions and billions of people, and all of them have the same thought - their religion is the best one. The non-believers in the world must be shaking their heads at this notion, laughing because their belief is that there is nothing more than this one life that we're living during our brief time here on earth. It doesn't matter to them because they believe there will be no pearly gates pronouncing which religion was the correct one. But the reality of this entire discussion is that we don't know with certainty who's right or who's wrong. No one does.

One of the objectives in writing this book is for you to examine your own beliefs – I mean really examine them. Have the curiosity and the courage to ask yourself the uneasy questions. Like where did my beliefs come from?

Why do I have those beliefs? Are they based on facts or made-up stories? Do I judge others who have beliefs different than my own?

My intent is not to preach, not to tell you what you believe is right or wrong, not to judge you based on your choices. And I hope I won't be judged for my own beliefs and opinions either. Instead, I want to share some of the interesting research I came across in evaluating my own beliefs – especially the history behind many of the religious ideologies. Delving into my project, I can't tell you how many times I found myself thinking, "Hmm, I had no idea that story was made up – so that's where that belief came from!" I was surprised to find how many of the key religious stories are so remarkably similar across different religions, how some stories have morphed over time, and how some stories seemingly were quite simply just made up and literally voted on by regular, ordinary people. Through intellectual curiosity and critical thinking, you may either come to confirm or reject some or all of your beliefs. And that's okay wherever you end up landing – the important point is to genuinely give them some thought.

As a starting place, it's important to get an overall picture of the subject matter you want to explore, which is one of the first steps in critical thinking. This is analogous to getting lost in a forest and then climbing a tree or mountain to see the terrain so you can find your way to safety. Not an outdoor person? One of the best ways to see and understand the layout of a new city you want to explore is to first get a view of it from a really high point such as the Eiffel Tower in Paris or the One World Observatory in NYC. It always helps to be able to visualize the bigger picture as you explore both geographies and topics.

In this case, it might be helpful to have a foundation of what other people around the world believe. There are so many religions in the world, with billions of people thinking their religion is the best. But, did you ever wonder which religion is considered to be the best one? Or do you just assume your religion is the best? I was raised in the Roman Catholic religion, so of course, that's what I was taught to believe – ours was the best. Think about all the time and energy this saved me - there was no need to shop around the religions of the world for the "best one." There was no need – I knew, because I was told, just as my parents had been told, that ours was the best one. Unfortunately, this is what most people experience and most of us also do not use critical thinking skills early in our lives even if we do ask our parents lots of why questions. Early in my life, looking out over the landscape of religions in the world would have given me a much better perspective on what I was told to believe. It certainly would have encouraged me to ask many more critical thinking questions.

So which religion is the best? "Best" is such a subjective term, but we can look at popularity based on the number of followers of the biggest religions around the world. If this was a competition based on numbers, it appears Christianity was winning the numbers game in 2020, but Islam was coming on strong with faster population growth trending in Asia and Africa, which are primarily Islamic dominated religious areas. Based on 2020 population estimations of the world population, the following chart shows the ranking of the top religions. Of the total estimation of 7.7 billion people on earth in 2020, Christianity accounted for 2.4 billion people, Islam had 1.9 billion, unaffiliated had 1.2 billion, and Hinduism had 1.2 billion followers.

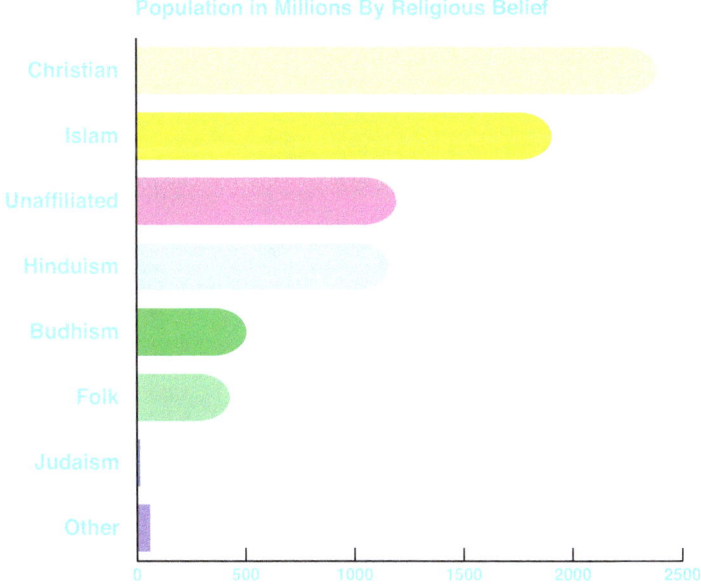

Source: Pew Research Center 2020 based on 2010 study projections, pewresearch.org

However, if you breakdown Christianity and Islam into their sub-religions, Sunni came out the winner with 1.7 billion believers of the total world population. Sorry Catholics - with only 1.2 billion followers, you had to settle for second place. Although Protestants are grouped as one religion, coming in third place, they are actually comprised of over 20 denominations including Anglican, Episcopalian, Baptist, Lutheran, Calvinist, Presbyterian, Methodist, and Pentecostal to name a few, which if broken out would have lowered each of their rankings.

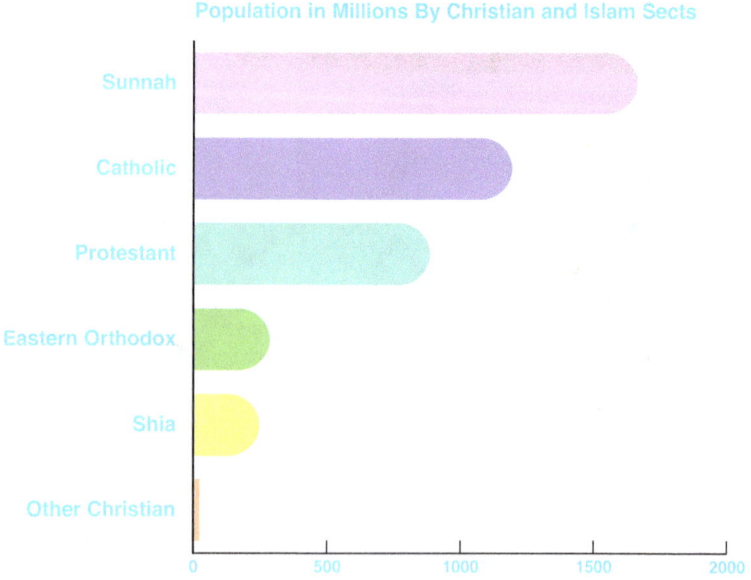

Source: Pew Research Center 2020 estimate based on 2010 study, pewresearch.org

Having been raised in the United States, my awareness of religions was largely focused on Christianity and Judaism.

I knew very little about the Islam religious denominations, and yet the Sunnis have the largest total world population of believers. And so, my intellectual curiosity was set in motion learning that Islam has two main denominations called Sunnah and Shia. The main Shia believing countries are Iran, Azerbaijan, Bahrain and Iraq. All other countries in the Middle East primarily follow the Sunni denomination, which is why the percent of Islamic believers following this denomination is roughly 87% and the Shia denomination believers only 13%. Part of the reason for the fighting and unrest in the Middle East today is due to intolerance between these two branches. Each group thinks they are the true Islam religion and theirs is superior to the other one. This is one of the reasons why Saudi Arabia (which is primarily Sunnah) is at odds with Iran (which is primarily Shia). Other reasons for this conflict are Saudi Arabia is home to the birthplace of Islam and it is a monarchy - they believe they are the leaders of the Muslim world. Iran on the other hand has a revolutionary theocracy form of government - they want to export their beliefs and ways of life as a superior society to the rest of the Muslim world. To increase their influence, it is also believed Iran is actively trying to establish a land corridor to the Mediterranean Sea. Religious infighting - this really begs the question: why can't we all just get along?

Of course, Islam does not have a monopoly on religious infighting as the Christian denominations have a long history of killing and torturing each other. However, the

Christian religions don't seem to be fighting each other as much anymore, as is happening with the current Islam denominations. Could this be because the Catholics outnumber the total of all the other Christian denominations, especially if you consider all the various subgroups making up Protestantism? Or perhaps it could be they all just got tired of fighting. Let's hope this tolerance and peace continues.

But how did religion popularity become a competition of numbers? Some religions have been accused of encouraging large families, even at the expense of the health of our planet – having more children means there will be more future members. I always cringed when I heard the Pope encourage Catholics to have large families and declare the use of contraception as "intrinsically evil". Encouraging Catholics to reproduce robotic-like, under orders from Rome. My cynical interpretation of this notion was more children meant more members, which in turn they hoped (but would never ever admit) would result in more money and power for the church. Cynical, I know. There were seven children in my family - a large Roman Catholic family, which was typical of my era. Such an awkward assumption - we had such a large family, so of course we must be Catholic! And the branches of my extended family tree were heavily drooping even more under the burden of Catholicism – 13 cousins in one family, 11 in another, 9 in another. Even my father recognized that their generation had been brainwashed by the church to have as many children as was God's will. Forget the fact most families, including mine, couldn't financially afford families this size. Forget the fact the world population was screaming, "STOP" our planet couldn't possibly sustain this level of population growth! Thankfully, the next generation has acted more responsibly and large Catholic families are becoming a thing of the past. But now the Muslims have accepted the procreation baton, becoming the world's fastest-growing religious group. Purposefully encouraging their followers to have a lot of children – because they recognize it's all about the numbers, and numbers are power. Interestingly, studies show that atheists and agnostics in general are having very few kids – so how is it that their numbers are increasing? The reason is simply there is currently a trend of many people leaving their faiths and not picking up a new one – quite an interesting phenomenon that will have an unknown effect on the future of organized religions.

Throughout history many empires and religions have come or gone, grown or dwindled in numbers, won or lost the popularity contest at any given point in time – and by the way, each had their own method of tracking those points in time and also their own approach to the numbering of years. Ahh, the battle of the yearly dating system. With so many variations throughout history, did you ever wonder why almost everyone in the world, regardless of what religion they believe, recognizes the yearly dating system beginning on Jesus Christ's supposed birth year? Even though adoption of this as the global standard was somewhat arbitrary, there has been no meaningful benefit to changing it, and so we continue to use it today.

Sharing the story behind our current dating system is a great example of this book's mission – bringing to light the origins of one of our most common beliefs. Agreeing on the starting point for this annual measurement was somewhat arbitrary and yet it still was adopted globally over time. With origins in the Western Christian foundation, the universally adopted yearly dating system is based on Jesus Christ's supposed birth year. Christianity obviously won the battle to set year zero, with some Christians using this as validation as to why their religion is the best. After you research this topic using critical thinking you find that despite its Christian origins, use of this annual dating system in fact transcends cultural, linguistic, religious and country boundaries.

This global standard of calendars is based on the "supposed" birth year of Jesus. Most of us are familiar with the abbreviations of BC and AD used in journalistic notations, with AD representing years counting up from Jesus' birth and BC counting down from it. While BC stands for "Before Christ," AD is an acronym for "Anno Domini" which means "in the year of the lord." Sure, this makes sense if you happen to be from a Christian denomination, but the message to the rest of the world is Jesus Christ is the implied "Lord" in question - perhaps a bit problematic for members of all other non-Christian groups.

Around the early 1700s, the abbreviations of CE and

BCE started to make an appearance to replace AD and BC respectively, where CE stands for "Common (or Current) Era" and BCE stands for "Before the Common (or Current) Era." The use of CE and BCE have been used in Jewish academics for the past 100 years, but recently have become more widespread, particularly in the fields of science and academia. Some people mistakenly refer to CE as "Christian Era," which is emphatically not correct. In an effort to be religiously neutral in this book, I have decided to use the notations of CE and BCE when referring to dates so as not to alienate or offend anyone.

As noted, many historical groups had their own idea as to when to start counting years – and of course, our current universally accepted system of keeping track of years was not the first approach. The Greeks started counting years from the first Olympic Games held in 776 BCE, and the early Roman Empire decided year one should be the founding of Rome in 753 BCE. The Byzantine Empire started year one in the year they thought creation occurred in 5509 BCE. (I'm not sure how they came up with 5509 and not just round it off to 5500, but whoever came up with this date must have been deemed a very detail-oriented person.) I could go on, but you get the point, there were many annual counting systems.

The change to our current system began in 525 CE by a monk named Dionysius Exiguous (which is a mouthful!). He decided the beginning of time should be more meaningful and, as a Christian monk, he picked the birth of

Jesus Christ. Unfortunately, his calculation was thought to be off by about four to six years. We know Jesus was born during the reign of Herod the Great who died in 4 BCE, so it is estimated Jesus was born sometime between 6 BCE to 4 BCE before Herod's death. Obviously, no one double-checked Dionysius' calculation even though it took some 300 years before his system was widely used. It was spread through the power of the Christian church in Christian territories and geographically outside of this area through missionaries. Using this AD year approach to dating, other monks and priests used this system in their writings as well - eventually over time, this calendar was adopted. It was not until the 1800s CE, over 1,300 years later when almost everyone in the world was using this system. I suppose over time so many writings used this numbering approach that it made no sense to change to something else. However, it is amazing to me that this universal annual counting system was a historical accident and not a conscious decision.

It's interesting to shine the light on something as simple as the dating of years we use every single day, learning where it came from and realizing it was based on the beliefs of one religion in the world - Christianity. The biggest religion? Yes, based on 2020 population numbers. But the best religion? No one knows. Hopefully by just simply acknowledging and being aware of the many religions in the world and their popularity, you will begin to have the courage to examine your own beliefs. Given all these variations in beliefs, how can all these religions be right? The good news of learning about other religions and their cultural differences is it can be very interesting. Each religion has its own orientation and personality as to explaining the world, and life and death. We can also learn new behaviors or thinking skills from each religion that help us become more peaceful and kinder people. Once you realize where some of your beliefs came from, you may become more tolerant of new ideas and better able to pick and choose those that are beneficial to your life and society. It may also open your eyes to beliefs that could be harmful and should be reexamined or discarded. However, we first need to start with critical thinking and intellectual curiosity to determine the origins of these religious beliefs.

By its nature, religion is largely based on the unprovable and yet it is still able to attract a large number of unquestioning faithful followers – it really is a bewildering paradox. It's appalling to witness when the ideology of religion is morphed into a political weapon and used to oppress marginalized people or punish people having different cultures. This is all so hard to fathom, since at its core, religions are based on the assumption of things that are unknowable and cannot be proven. As a result, the words, "just have faith" is used by all of them. In my quest to make some sense of it all, I came to the realization that there's not a single religion in the world that can survive two simple words – **prove it!**

Chapter 2

Religious Auto-Enrollment

Not to sound cliché, but it seems as if religion has been around since the beginning of time. Literally! And now here we are in today's world, living in a vastly different environment from that beginning of time, where volumes and volumes of information are at our fingertips. In the face of all this information, how do we possibly begin to explain our own religious beliefs? How did they start and where did they come from? Why did we choose to believe what we believe? Essentially religion, as well as non-religion, is often passed from one generation to the next, much like the transmission of a genetic disorder. Of course, this wouldn't be such an issue if people never discriminated against others on the basis of their divine birth, to a set of parents who just happened to believe in some faith they just happened to be born into. Yes, wouldn't it be great if we all could just be accepting of others who happened to be born into a religion different from ours - wouldn't that be a wonderful world? Live and let live, to coin a noble phrase. But sadly, in today's world, hate and discrimination based on inherited religious beliefs are all too familiar– and unfortunately, all too dangerous.

So why did we, which includes me, turn our brains off when it came to beliefs we were born into and just unquestionably accepted them as facts or truths? There are many reasons for this, but at the top of the list is we trusted our parents and close relatives since they were very influential in our lives. By the way, the same situation was true for them. Other reasons for not using critical thinking and questioning our inherited beliefs was we did not want to be alienated from our family and community since they were all strong believers in the same religion. And finally, many of us are just afraid, especially of death, and as a result, we just don't want to know if our beliefs are based on fantasy. More on this topic later, but from my point of view, removing beliefs in fantasy, superstition, and magic from our lives may actually reduce anxiety and help us be more at peace and focus on what's really important in our lives.

To give you a sense of my own religious auto-enrollment experience, I thought I would share my story. Through this narrative you will understand how beliefs were ingrained in me from an early age. As you read this, imagine if I or any of us had been born into a completely different country, culture, or religion. We would inherit totally different beliefs and we would think ours were the best. In my case, instead of being a devout Roman Catholic I could have been a devout Muslim. Or Jew. Or Hindu. Or Buddhist. From talking with other people, I know there are many similarities of auto-enrollment practices across different faiths. Hopefully, you'll be able to relate to my experience, especially if you also grew up in a religious family. However, even if you did not grow up in a religious family, my story will give you a sense for the strength of how these beliefs are deep-rooted in us from a very young age.

So, what's my story – where did my beliefs come from? I was born in the 1950s CE in the suburbs of Pittsburgh, Pennsylvania, USA and just happened to be raised in the Roman Catholic religion. I say I "just happened" to be raised Roman Catholic because that's what my parents were. Because that's what their parents were. And most likely, that's what their parents were. I didn't "choose" to be a Roman Catholic. But just like that, without my consent, my parent's religion was bestowed upon me. Quite simply – my religion was an accident of birth. My parents, my family, and by default me, were among the typically dedicated, staunch followers of the Roman Catholic faith – not just casual partakers, we were hardcore Catholics. Hardcore as evidenced by my large Catholic family filling an entire church pew every single Sunday, as well as every single one of those unbearably long holy day masses. We religiously (pun intended!) attended each and every one of the many mandatory masses, mindlessly reciting the prayers, standing, sitting, kneeling on cue, and basking in the spiritual blessings of the priest. We really did feel as if we were blessed. I had dirt smeared on my forehead on Ash Wednesday, ate my share of frozen fish sticks on Fridays, gave up watching *Star Trek* on television for the entire forty days of Lent, confessed my petty sins of brotherly fights to the all-judging priest in the creepy confessional, and said the four *Hail Mary's* and three *Our Father's* to satisfy the penance randomly handed out by that all-judging priest. I even served as an altar boy, but sometimes had to look extra angelic to distract the congregation from the black eye I earned during one of those brotherly fights. Sure enough, before being allowed to dive into any meal, we mumbled our way through a speedy rendition of the Catholic's "Bless us, O Lord, and these, thy gifts" prayer, which was preceded and followed, of course, by a lightning-quick Sign of the Cross. And every day, to punctuate this blessing of the meal, my dad always ended the prayer with his humorous little add-on, "He who eats the fastest eats the most-est!" Although I think he meant this to be funny, it really did hit the nail on the head – you know, because our typical Catholic family was so freaking large! So, eat fast we did!

From the day I was born until I went off to college, my exposure to the world didn't extend much further than the city and suburbs of Pittsburgh, a place that still holds some of my most vivid childhood memories. Pittsburgh is famous for its diverse European immigrant groups, with rich colorful ethnic neighborhoods and identities – a real melting pot of Italian sausage, kielbasa, sauerkraut, pierogies, and beer. There's Bloomfield, the old-world, working-class neighborhood with its Italian roots extending back more than five generations. Pittsburgh's very own "Little Italy" with shops and restaurants filled with the sights and smells of garlicky homemade pastas, stromboli and cannoli. And Polish Hill, a neighborhood settled by Polish immigrants working in Pittsburgh's booming steel industry. As a young runner in training, I remember the heart-pounding challenge of taking on the nearly vertical quarter-mile climb up to some of the best views of the city, with the historic and opulent "Polish Cathedral" perched at the very top. There were neighborhoods settled by German, Irish, Croatian, Ukrainian, and Hungarians – each with their unique cultural heritage, food specialties, famous people, customs, parades, festivals - all of it proudly on display. A real smorgasbord of sights, sounds, and smells – a place for anyone and everyone. That is, anyone and everyone who happened to identify with one of these narrowly concentrated European groups.

Many of those immigrating to Pittsburgh stamped their way into the United States through Ellis Island in the early 1900s CE. Naturally, as time went on, there was bound to be some intermingling of those ethnic neighborhoods. As I was growing up in the 1950s and '60s in the south hills area of Pittsburgh, I was always aware of where my friend's families were "from." "What are you?" was as common a question as "What did you have for breakfast?" Me? I always described myself as German and English (that is until *23 and Me* got involved, setting me straight about the bulk of my heritage coming from Ireland and England, with barely any German at all). Most of the kids I knew growing up were an ethnic dual-lineage fusion – Italian/Polish, Czech/German, Pizza/Goulash. It was that easy – you always knew. And with that ethnic awareness, came religion awareness - Ethnic roots often went hand in hand with religion, with generation after generation passing their religious beliefs on to the next. Based on my small world of Pittsburgh, I grew up with the impression that almost everyone in the world was Christian (Roman Catholic or Protestant), with just a smidgeon of Jewish thrown in for interest. That was it. There was no Hindu. No Islam. No Buddhism (although you would see a Buddha statue occasionally). These other large religions of the world were nonexistent in Pittsburgh – at least none that made it onto my radar. Thanks to those predominantly European origins, the traditional Christian faith groups were alive and well in Pittsburgh. It was a predominantly Jesus loving, Christmas celebrating, church-going society.

As I mentioned, being raised in this very traditional Roman Catholic family, my parents provided me with a strong religious base. Clearly, a generic public-school education was not considered to be good enough for me – no, the additional molding of my religious beliefs was far too important to be left to ordinary lay people. After all, my parents survived a Catholic school education, so of course that was my destiny as well. So, every day I put on my traditional school uniform of hand-me-down blue slacks, that always seemed to be too short, white button-down shirt, clip-on tie, grabbed my embarrassing plaid book bag and then walked or ran the several blocks to Saint Anne's, the local Catholic grade school. When I think back on this, I find it baffling that my siblings and I would carry on this Catholic school tradition, especially after hearing my dad's horrifying stories about the nuns whacking his knuckles with a wooden ruler until they bled. His crime? He was left-handed! Nope, back in his day, there was zero tolerance for left-handedness in his Catholic school upbringing. Thankfully, that was not my experience at all – most of the religious leaders and teachers I encountered during my youth were kind and even-tempered. Except for that one miserable priest who was loud, gruff, mean-spirited, preached fire and brimstone, and sang totally off key with an extremely loud voice. I had always wondered why this man became a priest, as he didn't seem to be very kind or caring. But I got what I needed from my Catholic School education – the four "Rs" – reading, (w)riting, (a)rithmetic and of course, religion.

First through eighth grade, every single school day, I clipped on that clip-on-tie and headed to school. I was so proud when the priest bestowed his blessings on the entire St. Anne's 8th grade graduating class, and then I was headed onward and upward to the local Catholic high school. Apparently, there was still plenty more of faith molding needing to be done. But attending Catholic high school proved to be quite a challenge as the "local" school was located way, way, way over on the opposite side of the city - just getting to school required an hour-long trek that included public trolley service, walking a long distance, and then, if I was lucky, being picked up as a hitchhiker to cover the last bit of the punishingly steep McNeilly Road hill. Each and every single school day. As you can imagine, I only endured that for one year before transferring to the closer generic local public high school. But fear not, I still was able to further my religious training by religiously attending weekly classes called CCD (Confraternity of Christian Doctrine) along with the other non-parochial school kids. This CCD association was established in Rome way back in 1562 CE for the sole purpose of providing religious education – with such a long and storied past, they surely were worthy of shaping my own spiritual beliefs.

Throughout my childhood, over the years as a devout Catholic I certainly logged in a significant amount of time in church. Not only was I a faithful church-attender, but serving as an altar boy for several years, I assisted the priests by fetching, carrying, ringing the bell, cross-bearing, candle lighting, all the while trying my best to look holy in that white robe and struggling not to fidget too much. To put your mind at ease – no, I was never abused by any priest or nun. Sad that would even be a question I felt compelled to address, but thankfully this was not the case for me.

Naturally, as a result of all this religious education, church going and family reinforcement, I was indoctrinated into all the Catholic Church stood for – it's beliefs, rules, dogmas, principles, philosophies, you name it. It was made clear, reinforced over and over and over again, how important it was to buy into the teachings and beliefs of the church in order to become a good person and ultimately be granted entry into heaven. Some might see this as a brainwashing of sorts. But I listened and understood the message loud and clear. All I had to do was believe. Not to question. Just believe.

And so, believe I did – sort of. Even as a small child, I uneasily had my doubts - something was definitely amiss. As a seven-year-old, I remember being taught about Holy Communion, which the Catholic religion believes is the reenactment of the last supper with Jesus. After a few magic words by the priest, the little disc shaped wafers and store-bought wine are miraculously transformed into the actual body and blood of Jesus. Not symbolically. No - the actual body and blood. This is known as transubstantiation, which has been the theological explanation supported by the church since the 16th century. Even at this young age of seven, this concept sounded absurdly far-fetched, but whatever, I opted to go along with it. I mean, I really wanted that tasty looking wafer and who knew, I hoped it might actually work to make me holy and good. During the teaching about this ritual, the Priest emphasized how important our belief in Jesus needed to be in order to accept this sacrament of Communion. He stressed there was nothing better in life than to give up your life and die for Jesus Christ because then you would go straight to heaven. He went on to remind us we needed to unequivocally tell people we were true believers, even if they were going to kill us for this belief. Up goes my seven-year-old hand – "What if I still believe in Jesus, but lie to the bad guys telling them I don't believe, so then they would not kill me and I would still be alive?" Hmm, quite the daring challenge from a little kid addressing the priest. He quickly responded this would be lying and I would go straight to hell – bam, just like that. Fire and brimstone, threatening an impressionable little kid in his parochial school uniform complete with that clip-on tie, with the torments of hell. Wow, even at this young age, this didn't make any sense to me. Was God really that ruthless and unforgiving? And yet again, I just let it drop. Fortunately for me, it was highly unlikely I would ever encounter this scenario living in a suburb of little old wholesome Pittsburgh, in the 1960s CE. Little did I know however, that this was in fact a very big issue for those people living in 600 CE who were persecuted for their beliefs, which I came to realize through my research as an intellectually curious adult. Reflecting back on my memories of this encounter with the priest, this notion sure sounded like the Catholic version of Islam's focus on wanting to die by fighting as a mujāhid on behalf of their Muslim faith to obtain paradise.

Yes, even at this young age, I was beginning to question some of the doctrines of the Catholic Church. Even though I was unable to get satisfactory answers to my seemingly simple questions, I just let it go. The possibility of my winding up banished to hell for eternity was a scary thought, and so for me, it was just easier to go along with the status quo. And so, I continued to cooperate with most of the Catholic dogma for about the next 40 plus years. Or perhaps, maybe it wasn't so much that I was cooperating, but instead I was just pretending. It continued through my college years, through my marriage, through the years as I raised my reluctant children in the Catholic Church, through many moves, many job changes – I guess it was just easier to go along with it all. For whatever reasons, my critical thinking skills concerning my religious beliefs were put on the back burner for many years. Not until I was in my 40s did my intellectual curiosity take over - when my small world eventually became larger and larger as I traveled more, read more and became friends with people from all around the world. It was then, the unthinkable happened – I really started to have doubts.

In my case, I started questioning my beliefs as a result of reading many history books - it was then that I began to connect the dots as to what was real and what was fantasy. In critical thinking, connecting the dots is a metaphor for having the ability to associate a mass of data or information into a big picture view or conclusion. Some people have this skill and some people have to go step by step to understand a concept or idea. An analogy would be when you were a kid and got a puzzle book with numbered dots in the shape of an animal or vehicle. If you connected the dots using a pencil, the picture is revealed. However, many of us can just look at the picture and realize it's a bunny or a firetruck as examples, while some people need to connect every dot first to reveal the picture.

The good news in this book is it doesn't matter if you can connect the dots easily or not, since critical thinking skill methodology was followed. This methodology begins with asking questions, then gathering, understanding, and interpreting information, and finally drawing conclusions based on this data. The dots have been connected. Using this methodology engages our brains by getting us thinking and then helps us address autoenrollment in a more informed way.

Chapter 3

Immaculate Conception Stories – How Could There Possibly Be This Many?

Having been raised in a very traditional Roman Catholic family, I am most grateful for the guidance and reinforcement I received from my parents, friends, educators and church regarding how to treat others. Compassion, kindness, honesty, and trustworthiness – these were all traits I acquired during my childhood and have continued to value throughout my life. When I was heading into my college years, I realized I was responsible for living my life as the type of person I wanted to be. Although I had been armed with everything the Catholic Church stood for – its philosophies, dogmas, rules and beliefs - I now had the opportunity to decide for myself what I chose to believe. Up until this time, I was told what to believe. Now the onus was on me to seek out answers to my questions: Were these beliefs even true? Real? Where did they come from?

In the quest to better understand my beliefs as to what

was real and what was fiction, I took a World Religions humanities course in college. Actually, it was in my junior year and I only needed three more humanities credits to get my degree. What better way to find out more about some of the other non-Christian religions, which I admittedly knew very little about? I always wondered how it could be possible that the religion in which I happened to be born into was the only true one - or at least that was what I had been taught. I was led to believe even those poor misguided protestant Christians picked the wrong religion since we all knew the Roman Catholic religion was the original Christian religion and therefore the best one. The only true one. Naturally we were urged to be nice to those poor unfortunate Protestants - sorry they happen to believe in an inferior religion. It seemed odd that everyone else in the entire world believing in some other religion would not be able to get to heaven just because they choose the wrong one. Why wouldn't they just pick the right one? Seems like a pretty obvious solution. But I assume every religion orients their believers from a very young age to think the same about their particular inherited religion – I had never considered they were feeling sorry for me! This attitude, that my inherited religion is the best one, is one of the reasons there is so much hatred in the world attributed to religious differences and beliefs. But seriously, how could it be possible for one billion people to get it right, but the other six billion plus people had gotten it wrong about their religious beliefs?

As I began to study other religions, the biggest aha moment for me was learning about the many similarities of the beliefs among the various religions. Some people focus on the differences, but there sure is much alike as well. For example, long before Jesus lived, the Hindu religion believed that Gods came down to earth as Avatars to help humans counteract some evil in the world. In the Hindu religion, these Avatars, or incarnations of a deity, would show up on earth in human or animal form. There are many of them in this religion but to illustrate, Lord Vishnu (the second God to the main God Brahma and also part of the Hindu Trinity of Gods) was born on earth as Krishna to help out the humans. It looks as if the Christian religion replicated this approach by making Jesus, the Son of God, a man or Avatar on earth, following the same story formula as Hinduism. Both Jesus and Krishna came to earth as humans to help humans, and both were also the number two God of a trinity of Gods, which both religions happen to count as only one God. (Note: More on this religious method of counting multiple Gods as just one God, later in chapter 10 entitled "I Know Math, So How Does $1 + 1 + 1 = 1$?")

As another example, are you aware that the Holy Ghost or Holy Spirit God that existed in Christianity was also present in Hinduism, Buddhism, Greek Mythology, and the Ancient Roman Religion as well? This was a new revelation to me in college, which also was somewhat troubling, as I believed the Holy Spirit was not only a real God, but was also unique to Christianity. Realizing this God was invented by many other people throughout the ancient world was one of the reasons that led me to question my religious faith and that of other people as well.

But the biggie for me was learning the similarity of the birth stories for a number of Gods, demi-gods, and prophets that walked the earth all having been born as a result of an immaculate conception to mothers who were virgins. Seems like a pretty specific unusual set of circumstances, but it turns out there were a number of different religions with different gods, all recounting that similar story regarding their birth. On a side note, I find it funny how the Catholic religion, who would never ever get anywhere remotely near the subject of sex education, threw around words such as "immaculate conception" and "virgins" but would never, ever attempt to define what those words actually meant to grade school children. We would sing songs that included those words, include them in our prayers, all the while having absolutely no idea of their actual meaning. Can you imagine seven-year-old me asking my nun teacher to please clarify the particulars behind the song, "The Virgin Mary Had a Baby Boy"? But seriously, are you kidding me that the concept of being born to a virgin was not unique to Jesus? Is it possible the whole Christmas Virgin Mary story was simply made up? Just so you don't think I was totally naïve to what I was taught by the priests, nuns, and my relatives, I did figure out Santa Claus was not real, despite the claims in all the Christmas movies.

The most likely impetus for these immaculate conceptions was the difficulty arguing these Gods could not have been born from mere human women. Because too many people at the time were witnesses to the pregnancy and birth, and therefore it was obvious who the mom was. Ah, but the identity of the father? So, one of the best ways to make them into a deity or a divine person was to have a supernatural power impregnate their mother. This approach was common with not only demi-gods (man gods), but with full gods and prophets as well.

One of the supernatural ways of impregnating these human mothers of gods was through the Holy Ghost. Of course, we're all familiar with the story of Jesus Christ, originator of what eventually became the Christian religion, being immaculately conceived. The Holy Spirit visited his mother, Mary, and impregnated her one evening in a dream. At least that's what she told her husband Joseph. However, Mary was not the only person to use and get away with this explanation, as you'll see in the similar accounts told by other religions. In today's world, I can only imagine the reactions by husbands, fathers, or friends after being told by their wife, daughter or friend that they had been immaculately impregnated.

In addition to Jesus Christ, there were many other gods and prophets who were believed to be immaculately conceived, including: Pythagoras, Zoroaster, Vulcan, Augustus Caesar, Krishna, Buddha, and Muhammad. Their stories...

The legend in ancient Rome claimed the mother of

Pythagoras was impregnated by the Holy Ghost of Apollo, the Greek god of the sun and light. Pythagoras (570 BCE to 495 BCE) was a Greek philosopher, mathematician, and founder of the Pythagorean religion or brotherhood that influenced Plato and Aristotle. He contributed to the development of mathematics and is credited with the Pythagorean theorem (remember this from geometry class?), as well as Western rational philosophy. He claimed to be semi-divine as he was related to the superior god Apollo. This, he claimed, is why he knew so much more than other people. He must have been really smart, but obviously had trouble with humility. At any rate, his religion believed in the reincarnation or transmigration of the soul, with the goal being to get nearer to the gods through purification of the soul. This was done through music, mental activities (later called philosophy) and rituals to reach higher incarnations or spiritual lives. His teaching influenced the Abrahamic based religions including Judaism, Christianity and Islam, as well as the religions of Hinduism and Buddhism.

Zoroaster was the founder of Zoroastrianism, which dominated ancient Persia before Islam took over around 650 CE. His mother was impregnated by a ray from the Divine Reason around 628 BCE.

And then there was Vulcan, the Roman god of fire. The immaculate virgin, Juno, conceived Vulcan by being overshadowed by the holy wind or ghost. Juno was the queen of the gods in the Roman ancient religion and was the wife of Jupiter, the king of the gods.

And how about Augustus Caesar? He was a Roman statesman and military leader who became the first emperor of the Roman Empire from 27 BCE to 14 CE. He was immaculately conceived in the temple of Apollo by the overshadowing of Jupiter's divine influence.

In the Hindu holy book, the mother of Krishna, a major deity in Hinduism, conceived him by being overshadowed by the spirit of the supreme god Brahma, the god of creation. Krishna is worshipped as the eighth incarnation of the god Vishnu and also as a supreme god. He is the god of compassion, tenderness, and love and is a very popular Indian divinity.

The mother of Buddha, Queen Maya, was impregnated in a dream by a white elephant with six tusks entering her right side. After ten lunar months she stood upright holding a branch of a Sal tree (Sal tree is a deciduous tree in India used for medicinal purposes and wood) and gave birth under her right arm. She died seven days after giving birth to Buddha (Could her death have been caused by giving birth under her right arm?) and then was reborn in the Tusita heaven, which is where divine beings live. Buddha is said to have been able to walk and talk at birth and he goes on to be the founder of Buddhism. Buddha most likely lived from 563 BCE to 483 BCE. About 500 or so years later, the Christians had Immaculate Mary ascend into heaven similar to Queen Maya. In addition to the immaculate conception story, it seems the Christian's knew the Queen Maya story was working for Buddhism believers so they incorporated a similar story for Mary too.

Islamic prophet and founder of Islam, Muhammad (570 CE to 632 CE) was born after his mother, Aminah, was visited by angels informing her she would give birth to a boy long after her husband Abdullah had died. To help with the birth of Muhammad ten lunar months later, three women appear with the same angels that got her pregnant in the first place. These women are Eve (from the Adam and Eve Judaism bible story), Asiya (Moses' adopted Egyptian mother from another Judaism bible story), and Mary (Jesus Christ's mother from the Christian bible story). As the story continues, immediately once Muhammad is born, all the pagan idols of Kaaba fall down and a bright light appears in the center of Mecca's great polytheistic religious mosque. Hmmm, not very believable, but extra points for creativity!

In fact, the belief in the immaculate conception of demigods, prophets, and full gods extended to every nation in the eastern world at the period of time from 600 BCE to 700 CE. An interesting facet is how these ancient people calculated the timing of their immaculate conceptions and resulting births. Many of the virgin mothers of gods and prophets such as Hercules, Sakia, Guatama, Scipio, Arion, Solomon, and Jesus Christ were reported to have been pregnant for ten lunar months from divine conception to delivery, which is 280 days or 40 weeks. By comparison, through medical research, the average gestation period for a human baby is known to be 268 days from conception. I'm guessing the purpose of these extra days could have been the gods and prophets needed a few more weeks in the womb to become divine.

I don't know about you, but learning about the many similarities across different religions, including the many immaculate conception stories, was somewhat disappointing to me at the time. After all, I had been taught Jesus Christ was THE GOD. And I believed it! Now I find out all these guys (yes, they are always men), have similar, dubious stories about their birth and where they came from. These stories have been around for thousands of years and yet each religion still not only teaches, but also truly believes, their god or prophet was immaculately conceived. I doubt a woman claiming to have been immaculately impregnated today would be believed, so why are people still believing these accounts from thousands of years ago?

Unfortunately, at this point in my life I did not act on this learning, even though suspicion was creeping into my beliefs. I suppose I just got too busy as this was the period of my life when I finished college, began my career, got married, got an advanced degree, and then raised a family involving many career-driven geographic moves. All this time I continued to follow the Catholic religion. It wasn't until later in life that I began to read more which included how religions started. Although my reading was primarily oriented to understanding the history of the world, during this process I began to uncover flaws in religious beliefs. It was during the pursuit of this I realized my belief foundation was most likely not based on reality.

To summarize, investigating and analyzing historical information on religions reveals many of them have similar stories about immaculate conceptions for their gods or demi-gods. To investigate and analyze information is the second stage of critical thinking. On to the third stage, drawing conclusions. So why did all these religions include immaculate conception stories into their beliefs? Once we know most religions have these stories, we realize this must have been how people justified that a seemingly ordinary person was to be viewed and treated as a god or a supernatural being. A logical conclusion based on critical thinking is these stories are based on total fantasy. And yet people still believe them to be real or factually accurate. It is interesting to me that these same people, after watching a crime drama on television, with less information than what we know about immaculate conceptions, would be able to identify the killer. This is why once you have this overwhelming evidence it becomes very difficult to defend these immaculate conception stories. Knowing the facts about immaculate conceptions and then using critical thinking encourages us to ask the next big question: Why was it so important to create these fantasy stories about the gods and demi-gods in the first place? The answer to this question leads us to researching the origins of religions and learning about the need for the "big man" to be a supernatural being.

Chapter 4

The Big Man Rules!

To better understand religions, it is helpful to know why and how they originated in the first place. To do this we need to go way, way back thousands of years to the origin of humans - way back before there was any understanding of science. No Internet, no Wikipedia, nada. Absent this knowledge we all take for granted, supernatural beliefs arose as a way to explain nature, including death. Initially the earliest human bands of people were especially interested in what happens when an animal or human died. They sensed a force or energy leaving the body and naturally wondered where it went. Remarkably, even with all the marvelous advancements in science that have transpired over time, this same question still remains a mystery to us, even to this day. So, what does happen to us when we die? Some people have grandiose ideas about what glorious or (inglorious) fate awaits them in their afterlife, some gratefully believe in getting a do-over in the form of reincarnation, while others are convinced this one short life on earth is all we get and still others believe we become one with the universe. I guess the bottom line is no one really knows for sure. But way back, to give meaning to the energy they sensed leaving a body at death, the concept originated as to the existence of a soul – the soul was thought of as a substance similar to an odor, smoke, or wind. It was there and it was real to them, even though they couldn't touch or contain it. Although the soul was intangible, to them it existed in their minds. It wasn't until much later that the teachings of certain religions included this idea in their beliefs, the concept of a tangible soul living on after death. Even today, we still often think of the soul as the spirit or essence of a person.

In addition to this fascination with death, early humans also came up with supernatural gods to explain nature. It was a means for them to explain all sorts of phenomena they didn't understand such as the seasons, weather, earthquakes, droughts, you name it. This explains the origins of gods for the sun, moon, rain, wind, growing food, health, water, wealth, etc. They also envisioned gods as acting like humans and having human vices. For example, when the ancient people encountered bad weather or a lack of food, they reasoned the gods were angry and were punishing them. When everything in their life was comfortable and rosy, the gods were thought to be very happy. Initially, ancient people across different parts of the world had similar thoughts regarding the spirit world and gods. People in the Americas had comparable nature related gods to those in Asia, Africa, and Europe. So, despite unrelated regions and vastly different cultures, it appears the concept of gods in ancient religions was a worldwide universal invention. Some of the most popular who's-who of gods during early civilization were the Greek or Roman gods. The Greek and Roman gods bore very similar purposes, albeit with different names. Of course, some of these gods most likely would have been shared or influenced by the interactions amongst these societies, which explains the similarities. Observing this interaction and then using critical thinking leads us to further explore the question, were most religious beliefs influenced by other societies through trade routes and conquering armies? We'll get to this analysis in subsequent chapters.

You're probably already familiar with many of these names, but here is a list of the top Greek and Roman gods along with their purpose - a chance to test your trivial god knowledge:

— Zeus (Greek)/Jupiter (Roman) - the king of the gods and controller of the weather, throwing thunderbolts at the earth when he was angry.

— Hera (Greek)/Juno (Roman) - the queen goddess in charge of marriage.

— Poseidon (Greek)/Neptune (Roman) - the god of the sea, causing earthquakes and rough seas when he lost his temper.

— Hades (Greek)/Pluto (Roman) - the god king of

the dead who lived in the underworld, ruling over the dead.

— Aphrodite (Greek)/Venus (Roman) - the goddess of love and beauty, as well as the protector of sailors. I am not sure of the relationship between love and the protection of sailors, both being included in this goddess' job description– could it have something to do with male sailors being lonely and missing the love and affection of women while at sea? Perhaps.

— Apollo (same for both Greek and Roman) - the god of music and healing.

— Ares (Greek)/Mars (Roman) - the god of war.

— Artemis (Greek)/Diana (Roman) - the goddess of the hunt and protector of women in childbirth.

— Athena (Greek)/Minerva (Roman) - the goddess of wisdom, who also helped with warfare strategy.

— Hephaestus (Greek)/Vulcan (Roman) - the god of fire and a furnace to make metal, called a forge.

— Hestia (Greek)/Vesta (Roman) - the goddess of the fireplace at the center of a home, called a hearth.

— Hermes (Greek)/Mercury (Roman) - the god delivering messages and causing fun and mischief. With his iconic winged sandals, this god could run really fast - still an inspiration for runners today.

— Demeter (Greek)/Ceres (Roman) - the goddess of the

harvest. Ceres is the root of the word cereal.

— Dionysus (Greek)/Bacchus (Roman) - the god of wine (my personal favorite!). It's not uncommon to find wine restaurants and shops using these names.

Ancient people believed in many different gods as a way to explain the world and what was happening to them. During their time, all of these civilizations believed these gods and myths to be genuinely real. Today through scientific discovery, we now have a much better understanding of much of nature and the world. As a result, we tend to view the Greek and Roman gods, as well as those similar gods in ancient civilizations, as merely mythical. But despite all our fancy scientific knowledge, some of the same relationships with gods continue even today. For example, for help with all kinds of topics, many Catholics still pray to various saints, who are recognized as deceased holy people with supernatural spiritual powers. There are literally hundreds of them, but some you may be very familiar with, even if you are not Catholic: St. Francis helping animals, St. Christopher helping with traveling, Joan of Arc helping soldiers, St. Jude Thaddeus helping hospitals, and St. Joseph helping workers. Some people even believe that burying a little St. Joseph statue (as in Mary and Joseph) in their yard will help them sell their house faster. No one knows exactly where or who started this practice, but I know real estate agents who are not necessarily Catholic, that practice this ritual frequently. Grown, educated adults digging holes near the "For Sale" sign then sticking St. Joseph inside the hole upside-down and facing the house in hopes of a speedy real estate transaction. Seriously?

As the population size of these ancient societies grew, in addition to the belief in gods to explain what they could not understand, religion in conjunction with the introduction of governments also became more and more important. The need for increased power to govern or control people was critical for society to remain somewhat peaceful and orderly.

Originally, people were hunter-gatherers and organized themselves in tribes for companionship, safety, and to share food and shelter. As with any group there was a need for a leader and these small groups were thought to have different leadership approaches. Some were led jointly by a male and female and others were either female or male. These different structures can also be observed with animals in nature. Wolves in the wild leave their packs when they mature to find a mate and then form a new pack co-dominated by both the male and female since they are the parents of the new pups. We also see examples of matriarchal species such as Bonobos apes, elephants, killer whales, hens, and of course lions have a dominant female leader of the pride. And finally, we observe the Chimpanzee following a patriarchal model and gorillas also have a dominant male leader of the band. Since there are different leadership models we observe in nature, we should not assume the primarily patriarchal based culture we currently experience in society as the natural state for human beings. Through research and critical thinking skills it appears our current, primarily male dominated social structure evolved when human beings moved from a hunter-gatherer form of existence to an agriculture and homesteading society.

With the beginning of agriculture estimated at about 10,000 years ago, people began to settle down and more effort was needed to defend themselves against other tribes attacking them to take their people, crops and living location. As a result, power shifted to males who were on average physically stronger than females – enter the "big man". The big man's position as leader was obtained through strength, personality, intelligence, and most importantly fighting skills. The strongest and most clever man tended to fight his way to the leadership position of a tribe, earning the title – "big man".

Over time, as human societies transitioned from hunter-gatherers to food producers, the tribes or groups got significantly larger. To maintain power, these bigger groups required the big man to be even bigger. As societies grew to thousands of people, it became necessary to have reasons other than family ties to keep the population from killing people from other bands or tribes. Authority needed to centralize in order to monopolize force and resolve these conflicts. Over time the "big men" became chiefs, often based on heredity, and ruled over groups numbering anywhere from thousands to tens of thousands. With such large groups, the chiefdom had to fine-tune its bureaucracy to maintain control and to distribute wealth as people began to specialize in trades. But of course, value or tribute needed to be paid to the ruling class to support them and their initiatives – yep, the introduction of the dreaded concept of taxes. Additionally, fighting groups were needed to support the chiefdom people, keeping them safe from invaders – yep, the introduction of armies. To unite the masses and ensure their continued allegiance to the elite group, various methods were used. One way was to make sure the elite were more heavily armed versus the average person. It was also necessary to keep everyone happy and comfortable, so wealth was redistributed in the community. Force was also used to maintain order and curb violence. And the final way – use of an ideology or religion to justify the elite people's power and gain public support.

These ancient religions, as well as current day religions, were very useful to the elite ruling class. By forcing the people to all believe in the same ideology or religion, they could unite large groups of people and gain their support. These religious beliefs helped unite people from many different families, giving them common beliefs. The leaders could then use this religion as a weapon to control the people. When anything bad happened to the masses, it was convenient to blame it on the unhappiness of the gods as opposed to their own actions or any perceived excessive greed. In addition, before the introduction of laws, religion was used to control the behavior of the masses. When a chiefdom conquered another chiefdom, they often required the conquered people to follow their religion by making it very painful for them not to conform. This is how religions have primarily been spread around the world. As chiefdoms grew into states, this power increased even more. These government groups were able to initiate conquests of other societies for power and greed, all the while justifying these conquests with religious beliefs.

Over time, societies became bigger and bigger. Of course, these bigger groups required that their big man now needed to be even bigger in order to maintain power – I'm sure you see where this is going - he needed to become a God. In some states, the rulers became gods themselves so they would not be questioned or challenged by the people they ruled. A good example of this was Alexander the Great during his conquest of the Persian Empire. He declared himself a god and would wear ram horns over his ears similar to the Egyptian god, Amun, whom he claimed was his father. Although the conquered people did not really buy into this, they went along with him to keep the peace. After Alexander's death, his Generals split up the kingdom, declaring themselves God Kings as well. Other examples of leaders ruling as living gods were the Pharaohs of Egypt and the Shahs of Persia. This approach was very effective especially when aided by a very loyal army.

Over time, tribes, groups and governments continued to grow through the conquering of other groups, whether peacefully or by force. Government and religion have been linked together throughout history in these conquests – in general, the government organized the conquest while the religion justified it. Today there is very little land in the world that has not been conquered by centralized governments and organized religion. Using gods and the threat of damnation for all time were very powerful incentives to control illiterate people. Unfortunately, it is still used today with both literate and illiterate people.

We certainly know a fair amount about the origins and beliefs of these ancient religions, but did you ever consider where this information came from? While it is common knowledge that much of what we know about religion and their beliefs comes from what was written thousands of years ago in so called sacred scriptures, what is less known is the fact that these writings were not actually made at the time of the events being recounted, but rather hundreds of years later in some cases. This pertains to the familiar religious stories as well, with the actual texts being based on the telling and retelling of events through many generations. The accuracy of the history of what happened, not to mention the potential for embellishment of the folklore, is suspect. As a kid, you may have played the "telephone game" at a party, where one person whispers a phrase to another person, who then whispers what they heard to the next person. And so on, it continues through several different retellings, until the last person recounts the message, as she heard and understood it, to the group. The funny part of the game was hearing how vastly different the message became as it passed through the group, often ending with nothing even close to the original phrase. And that was the result of retelling a phrase by only a handful of people.

As humans our brains are not wired like a computer, which can call up facts exactly as they had been first stored in its memory. Instead, when asked to recall something from our memory, depending on what that memory was or the purpose for recollecting it, these memories are rarely recalled with total exactness. Alterations may creep in due to emotions; hope, joy, fear, sorrow, anger, or shame. Selective recall and embellishments may also factor in. Sometimes we revise memories, whether intentional or unintentional, to make us look and sound better. As a result, memories over time can get further and further away from the original facts. As humans we are all probably guilty of some degree of memory revisionism. Think about this reality related to the telling and retelling of historic and religious events and stories over hundreds and hundreds of years.

Remember the Christmas story of Jesus' birth? The account we're familiar with was actually written several hundred years after he was born. Do you think the story captured the event exactly as it happened, or could there have been lots and lots of revisions as the story was retold and embellished over time? So, in thinking about the ancient writings used to support many of the religious beliefs, I have to wonder how many variations, changes, misinterpretations, and embellishments took place in the retelling of the stories through the many generations. And yet religious beliefs are based on these stories – they continue to be quoted, are thought to have been inspired or written by God, and ultimately, are considered to be "factual". For me, what I find really disturbing are those who develop, and then fervently hold onto, ultra-extreme opinions about religion, beliefs, and spirituality based on these writings to the point of being willing to die for them or even worse, kill for them.

Since much of what we know about the origins of religion and religious beliefs are based on experiences and events that pre-date written history, the subject is naturally open to continued debate regarding its veracity and accuracy. And yet, religion has continued to evolve over time – from that early quest to explain nature, the curiosity about life and death, to the big man, and all the way through to the billions of faithful followers today.

One thing is certain, we know civilizations developed as people evolved from tribes to larger and larger groups and from nomadic hunter-gatherers to farming and food production. As these societies got bigger, the big man or ruler needed religion ideology to maintain peace through common beliefs and the fear of eternal damnation if those beliefs were violated. The great thing about this set up for the ruling class is they got to establish the rules and the ideology to control the common people, which further strengthened their power base. This dynamic is how religions became so powerful over time and then when you combine these beliefs with unquestioning auto-enrollment of peoples' offspring, molding the thinking of eventually billions of people you can see why these religious beliefs are almost unbreakable.

Using critical thinking skills, it is obvious how religious beliefs originated and why they became so strong in people's minds. The authoritarian governments and their endorsed religion counted on the unquestioning belief of the people to protect their power base. Any critical thinking or questioning, often referred to as blasphemy, heresy, impiety, or lack of reverence for God(s) was met with severe penalties to discourage this activity. As a result, these authoritarian leaders were able to capture the total unquestioning commitment of the illiterate masses. Surprisingly this continues today even as literacy has dramatically improved. Thankfully, the notion of "illiterate masses" is an outdated concept no longer seen in the world today, and yet religious beliefs are still imbedded in our society dating back to these ancient civilizations.

Chapter 5

Religious Roots Sprouting in the Fertile Crescent

We've learned about the ancient religions of the world, where beliefs were dictated by the elite big men with the biggest armies. We now move on to the discovery of the early cultural and religious records obtained from archaeological texts, temples, and artworks dating as far back as 4000 BCE to 3000 BCE (remember to count backwards when in the BCE time frame). Based on these artifacts, it's astonishing to realize the majority of current day religions all have roots in the same general geographical area. Specifically, the Western side of Asia – and more specifically, the area known as the Fertile Crescent.

Think about it. Christianity, Islam, and Judaism originated in what we now call the Middle East. Hinduism, Buddhism, Sikhism, and Jainism originated in the Northern India area, including parts of Pakistan and Nepal. Noteworthy, as this Western Asia area accounts for the origin of religions followed today by over 5.7 billion people or approximately 80% of the world population. If you take out the 1.2 billion people that do not believe in a religion, then the people following religions originating in this area of the world is 93% of the world population. What produced this phenomenon? What about the rest of Asia, Europe, Africa, Australia, or North and South America – why not them? When you think critically your next step is to find out why this happened by digging deeper into what made this area of the world unique? Once you have this information you can then come up with plausible and logical reasons for this geographic concentration of religious inventions. For example, one simple answer is… this area of the world had the early support of the ruling class and the resources of an army, giving them an advantage in inventing religions. In other words, they were first and being first in anything is important - even true for launching religions. Marketing principle 101 – be the first to market and you'll have a huge advantage in capturing long-term market share.

But it wasn't just the rulers and the armies that gave the Western Asia area early head starts in the sprouting of religions - it also happened to have the widest availability of food in the world. This benefit enabled people living in this location to develop urban communities ahead of the rest of the world. As fewer people were needed to provide food for everyone, other people had time to innovate in areas such as writing, mathematics, agricultural growing techniques, cooking, animal husbandry, engineering, community organization, military defense, transportation, science, astronomy, and of course religion and philosophy.

When humans were primarily hunter-gatherers, they tended to move around searching for food and although they had villages, these were easily moved when the available food sources became scarce. This need for mobility and lack of permanence was not conducive to organizing in larger tribes and building urban societies. Once humans transitioned to food producers, they were able to stay in one place, begin building urban communities, and could support people who then had the time to innovate.

The first detected evidence of domesticated plants and animals in the world was found in Western Asia in the region known as the Fertile Crescent, dating to around 8500 BCE to 8000 BCE. The validation of this evidence was done by radiocarbon dating small archeological samples using an Accelerator Mass Spectrometry device. It was during this time period the people living in the Fertile Crescent area began transitioning from hunter-gatherers to a food production society. To be sure, a very slow transition because it would take thousands of years for more sophisticated civilizations to develop.

The Fertile Crescent was a crescent shaped region of moist and fertile land from the Nile River in Egypt to the Tigris and Euphrates Rivers. This area included current day Iraq, Syria, Lebanon, Israel, Palestine, Jordan, Egypt, southeastern Turkey and western Iran. The rivers in this region provided much needed water to irrigate the crops. As you probably know, the Fertile Crescent is no longer fertile as much of this land is now a desert. This was caused by over farming, and dams being built throughout the area causing erosion and the loss of topsoil. Sadly, in more recent times this area is getting even more inhospitable and less conducive to growing food due to climate change.

Map of Fertile Crescent Shown in Red

© Shutterstock

Back when this area was very fertile, the earliest crops grown in this area included cereals such as emmer wheat, barley, and pulse crops such as sesame and lentil. These crops existed in the wild, were easy to grow, could be harvested in a few months, and could be stored for eating later. The combination of growing and eating cereals with pulses provided a balanced diet of carbohydrates and proteins, the grains providing the carbohydrates and the pulses the protein. By domesticating these crops, people were able to establish more permanent villages. In addition to having available crops, the people of the Fertile Crescent also had domesticated animals such as sheep, goats, and pigs as early as 8000 BCE. There is also evidence they had cows as early as 6000 BCE.

Once people had the means, the desire, and commitment to living in one place, they were able to cultivate other foods such as fruit and nut trees. As an example of how long it actually took to master food production, it wasn't until around 4000 BCE that we find olives, figs, dates, pomegranates, and grapes cropping up. Although the original fruit and nut trees were fairly easy to grow from cuttings or seeds, it took years until the plants actually produced food to eat – in general it would take three to ten years to establish a productive grove of these trees.

The next food growing stage was the addition of fruit trees including apples, pears, plums, and cherries. The only way to get good consistent fruit from these trees was to graft them from a fruit tree that had produced fruit you enjoyed eating. Grafting was invented in China most likely from experimentation as early as 1560 BCE. This knowledge spread over time to the Fertile Crescent area. To produce fruit, these early farmers not only had to use grafting, but they also needed to plant trees that were genetically different varieties of the same species in their orchard for cross pollination. All these requirements are what delayed domesticating these types of fruit. In fact, it took until 200 CE for the Roman Empire to learn grafting techniques. The point being, food production was critical to establishing an urban civilization but it took a long time to perfect.

Much of what we now eat around the world originated in the Fertile Crescent and was exported over time east and west toward Europe and Asia, and south toward Egypt, Africa, Pakistan, and India. There are foods that are indigenous to other areas of the world but no area had the breadth of crops, fruit, nuts, and domesticated animals as the Fertile Crescent. Contrary to what you see in movies like Indiana Jones' "Raiders of the Lost Ark", "Mummies", and "The Exorcist" to name a few, the Fertile Crescent area was not a supernatural hot spot for gods and demons, it just had an abundance of food.

In ancient times, what if you lived in areas such as North and South America, Africa or Australia and didn't have all the advantages as the Fertile Crescent area? You didn't have an abundance of available agricultural and animal foods? You weren't connected geographically to a large innovation pipeline spanning east and west? Short answer – you were unfortunately not quite so fortunate. You see, plants and animals are more easily produced in similar climates, which tend to be along the same latitude band when traveling east and west. It was much more difficult to grow plants to the north or south of this band because the climate was so different. This is why civilizations in Africa had a tough time bringing in new plants and animals because it required connecting through the equator area and the Sahara Desert. Even the great civilizations of Mesoamerica had limited influence on North America and South America for the same reason. In the case of the Fertile Crescent area, these ancient people benefited from an 8,000-mile connection between the east coast of Ireland and the west coast of Japan. Think about it, the Fertile Crescent connected across all of Asia and Europe including India, Egypt and Ethiopia. What an advantage! In other parts of the world, without the abundance of food production and innovation, it was very difficult to advance your civilization.

In Western Asia, between 6000 BCE and 3000 BCE, gradually humans changed from living in villages to urban communities. The evolution of urban centers coincides with the development of settled agriculture, animal husbandry, and the beginning of fruit culture. It is not a coincidence that the three earliest and most significant ancient civilizations, Mesopotamia, Ancient Egypt and Indus Valley, all originated from this general region.

Mesopotamia was considered to be the first civilization and is located in the northern part of the Fertile Crescent. It was a fairly large civilization with a population of about 800 thousand to 1.5 million people. This civilization's written history began around 3100 BCE showing it was responsible for developing much of what we eat today.

These Mesopotamian innovations traveled south, creating another civilization during this time period called Ancient Egypt beginning around 3100 BCE. This civilization benefited from importing crops and animals from the Fertile Crescent, which was not difficult because the Nile River Valley was also extremely fertile during this time period. The Nile River Valley was excellent for growing crops and provided the means to feed a significant population that grew to an estimated 2.5 to 3 million people.

The third major civilization during this time period was the Indus Valley civilization located in the Punjab region of Pakistan and North East India. The people in this area were also able to import the innovations and foods from the Fertile Crescent and were able to develop a very large civilization. It is estimated that one to five million people lived in this civilization from 3300 BCE to 1300 BCE. Unfortunately, the fertile Indus River Valley dried up first out of the three civilizations causing the people of this area to move east and south into current day India around 1500 BCE.

Map of Mesopotamia, Egypt, and Indus Valley

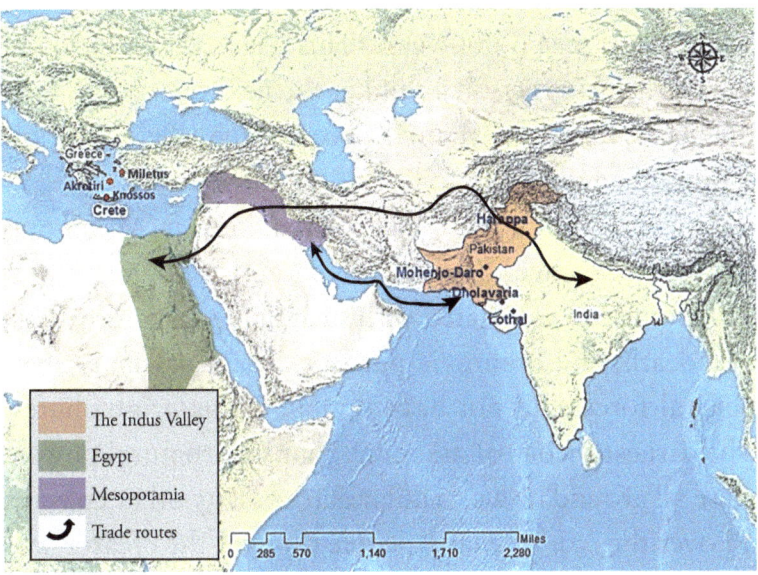

© Shutterstock

Not only had the Fertile Crescent led to the development of urban centers through new innovations in food production, but it also led to flourishing innovations across all disciplines, especially in the areas of religion and philosophy. In fact, when we look at where current religions originated, they all have roots in these early civilizations and more specifically the Fertile Crescent area. The Mesopotamian civilization is where we have the earliest records of religions, which were obtained from those archaeological texts, temples, and artworks dating as far back as 4000 BCE to 3000 BCE. Much of what people currently believe about their religions started here a very long time ago - apparently many of our beliefs have not evolved all that much in the past 5,000 years. This seems very logical but then as a curious critical thinker the next question is how did beliefs evolve to eventually become the religions people around the world still follow?

Very much like those ancient religions, in Mesopotamia the first stage of belief was in gods or supernatural superior forces associated with such things as nature, birth and death, and economic pursuits. These original supernatural forces did not have human forms or attributes. The earliest theory of assuming that supernatural powers were all around us was similar across many other cultures all over the world. Many people thought the creator was present in nature and our environment. Others thought the wind or the warmth of the sun was a manifestation of the creator's presence. Other manifestations of supernatural powers were fire and smoke, fertility for producing food and infants, and death. The gods of these powers were different depending on where you lived and what you did for a living. For example, the fertility god did different things for the orchard growers versus the farmers versus the animal herders. But the ideas of supernatural forces were similar.

The second stage of supernatural god development was the visualization of God as human in shape, with each deity having specific functions. Mesopotamia invented many gods during this time period, building temples for these gods including pantheons, which were dedicated to all the gods. Some of the top gods they believed in were:

An	God of heaven and responsible for the calendar and seasons
Enlil	God of winds and agriculture and creator of the hoe - obviously a very important invention for planting crops.
Ninhursag	Goddess of stony ground including both mountain ranges in the east and the desert in the west. She was also the goddess of the animals that inhabited these areas and the goddess of birth.
Enki	God of sweet waters of rivers and marshes. He was a troubleshooter solving problems for both the gods and people.

During this second stage, humans thought of themselves as powerless and totally controlled by the gods. They just lived without taking any responsibility for their actions (sadly, some people living today still seem to be stuck in this same stage of human development!). The people during this time period praised the gods for good things happening to them while blaming the gods for bad things happening to them or for their own cruel behavior. Demons played little or no role in their god stories during this time period but they did influence people's lives. Demons were mainly viewed as outlaws causing diseases and bad storms, damaging crops and property. You could even blame your own wickedness on one of these demons in court. So basically, the gods were all powerful, the demons caused mayhem and people were just their pawns.

The third stage of God and religion invention evolved in the 2000 BCE to 1000 BCE time period. During this stage people became more of participants in their religious beliefs. They believed they had some free choice in their behavior and were therefore responsible for both good and bad behavior. The concepts of sin and forgiveness were invented and the role of the gods became similar to the actions of a ruling monarch - more of a judgment type of role. This is when the concept of free will was originated. As religious thinking evolved it put more emphasis on man-made evil as opposed to blaming everything bad on demons. However, fear of the unknown increased. As a result, when pain and suffering occurred, the people attributed it to some magical force and they often blamed it on witchcraft. The people accused of being witches, primarily woman, didn't have a chance of surviving. I guess human nature to blame someone or something for painful experiences or misfortune was strong back then and unfortunately still seems to exist today.

Religious thinking continued to evolve in Mesopotamia and these ideas heavily influenced the foundation of current religions. In Mesopotamia the earliest beliefs of creation presumed heaven moved away from earth after the gods created human beings. They assumed the gods dug out the Tigris and Euphrates River for agricultural irrigation and then made people out of wet clay. These stories, both the river creation story and the human creation story are similar to the ones in the Hebrew Bible, the Old Testament Bible, and the Quran believed by Judaism, Christianity, and Islam, and also in the Hindu sacred texts.

The Mesopotamia religion had humans created from a mixture of clay obtained from an underground wet area and the blood of two slain gods. This made human nature part earthly with the clay and part god-like with the divine blood. However, the god part was powerless because it came from slain gods. This is where the soul invention came from since the god part of a human lives on after death in the netherworld according to this religion. So, your soul is not really a god but it is immortal because it came from a god, at least that's what they believed.

In the Hebrew Bible and Old Testament Bible this story was changed slightly to have God making man out of dust and breathing a soul into him. The human in these bibles was a little dryer than the Mesopotamian human maybe because of erosion or desert conditions. The only difference between the Abrahamic religions and Hinduism is where the soul goes after death. The Mesopotamia soul lived on after death in the netherworld, Abrahamic religions had your soul going to heaven, hell, or purgatory, and Hinduism had your soul transmigrating to a different body after death and eventually joining or merging with God. I always thought the Hindu religion was an early identifier of genetics playing a role in human beings. I realize they did not know about genes, but they probably noticed offspring had similar traits to their deceased relatives and then invented reincarnation as an explanation. As mentioned earlier, religions often used religious beliefs to explain what is now known through scientific discovery.

The building of temples and statues to gods also started in Mesopotamia and this custom lives on in current day religions. In Mesopotamia, humans believed they had to get a god or goddess interested in them to survive. They believed humans were created to work for the gods by providing them with food, clothing, housing, and services. As a result, in people's minds, the gods lived as nobility relieved of all manual labor now done by humans. People wanted the approval of the gods, so they provided them with a great place to live. This is why people built fabulous temples or pantheons including vast tracks of cultivated land. People still have this same mentality today as evidenced by the elaborate churches and temples they build and continue to maintain.

They also made statues of the gods and took care of them like real people. In addition to providing food and drinks for the statues, they would give them a bath periodically to keep them happy and clean. Overseeing all of this activity were the kings, priests, and prophets. The kings of each city were more than administrators since they also were thought to possess magical powers to create prosperity and fertility for the people. The prophets and priests interpreted what the gods wanted.

Keeping the gods happy and having someone communicate with the gods was very important to the people of Mesopotamia. This is because when anything happened to them, they assumed it was the divine will of God. You hear people say the same thing today when someone dies unexpected or bad things happen. They will say, "It was the will of God" or "God works in mysterious ways". They also assume God will take care of them as they say things like, "I am putting my trust in God to take care of me". It seems to me that taking some action might be a better plan! But when things do work out for these people, even if they did nothing, they are vindicated that God helped them out. When they don't get help and end up in misery, they either get disgusted with God or say God had a different plan for them. People had this same mentality over 3,000 years ago, so this is not new.

The Mesopotamians believed God(s) lived in these great estates (temples) similar to people's beliefs today. It was very popular for people to sleep in the temple hoping the god would send them an enlightening dream so they would become a prophet. Everyone wanted to be a prophet, as it was highly desirable both economically and spiritually. It was like winning the lottery in ancient times if you were not fortunate enough to be born into nobility and so the desire to becoming famous as a prophet encompassed their lives. In addition to interpreting what the gods wanted, prophets also predicted future actions by the gods. The Mesopotamians would even look for divine indications of what was about to happen in their lives to gain prophet status. As an example, if a desert plant grew in the city center, they would interpret this as a sign from God that the city was about to be destroyed. I suppose that since there was frequent fighting for control of neighboring cities, this destruction prediction could happen frequently reinforcing the divine sign. In addition to divine signs like the plant, they also used astrology. Astrology and horoscopes became especially popular as divine predictors of a person's fate. This was based on the constellation of the stars at a person's birth. Sound familiar? It is amazing horoscopes have been used for over 3,000 years and people still believe in them as supernatural predictors of their lives. I guess people still want to be prophet-like, although I don't think there is much status or money in it today. Well, except for the horoscope writers.

The religion business has always been lucrative for both the priests and the ruling class since ancient times. These groups of people benefited the most from the labor and gifts provided by the people for their god(s). This is still true today especially if God is somehow connected to your organization or government. What comes to mind are how wealthy some of the current religious organizations are such as; the Catholic Church is thought to be valued at over a trillion U.S. dollars, Islam is also in the trillion-dollar range, Televangelism is estimated in the billions, Church of Latter-Day Saints in the tens of billions, and the list goes on and on – of course, these valuations could be much higher as much of the wealth is thought to be hidden. To say the business of religion is financially lucrative is quite an understatement.

In summarizing the evolution of religions, they all started with gods and spirits as a way to explain nature, birth and death, and the world around them. This was true in ancient Mesopotamia, Egypt, and the Indus Valley. In later years other religions had similar evolutions; the Chinese developed folk religions that focused on honoring ancestors. Africans invented their nature gods along with ancestral spirituality similar to the Aztec and Mayan religions in Central America. The religions that eventually dominated current society were the ones that were written down and had political or ruling class military support. They also tended to include philosophies of life developed over time. The religions where the rulers added themselves as demi-gods in addition to the nature gods, tended to die out over time as the power of the ruling class was lost. Examples were the Pharaohs of Egypt, Alexander the Great and his subsequent Generals, and early Roman Emperors. In addition, Greek mythology lost its following as the early philosophers realized these gods were fictional. It seems odd that mythology in other religions was not questioned as well.

In today's religions, most of the religious foundations evolved directly out of Mesopotamian religious inventions, including Vedic and Zoroastrian. This evolution of religious thinking can be traced to these two religions, which predated Hinduism and the Abrahamic religions of Judaism, Christianity, and Islam. As the oldest current day major religion, Hinduism can connect itself the closest to the ancient Mesopotamian beliefs. Hinduism also had a strong influence and is closely connected to Buddhism, Sikhism, and Jainism. The next oldest religion coming out of this region and still in existence in a significant way was Judaism. Both Hinduism and Judaism were invented over a long period of time and were followed verbally for thousands of years until they were documented. And finally, the next two large religions still in existence today with their roots in Mesopotamia are Christianity and Islam. To think, all these religions have roots sprouting from the Fertile Crescent. From Mesopotamia to Vedic and Zoroastrianism, then directly into Hinduism to Judaism to Christianity to Islam with a little Greek and Roman cult beliefs added for good measure - every current day major religion seems to have been influenced by other religious beliefs in some form or other and all of them sprouted from the Fertile Crescent.

Chapter 6

The Many, Many, Many Gods of Hinduism

The invention of religion leading to current day religions didn't happen overnight – it would take thousands of years in fact, as innovation and communication flourished along the various trade routes as a result of travel and interaction between tribes and civilizations. Over these thousands of years, religious thinking and beliefs were established that many people today still consider being credible and real. As discussed, the Fertile Crescent area and what eventually became the Mesopotamian civilization was where religious thoughts leading to the current day largest religions originated. It was here that Vedism got its start, which in turn led to the formation of Zoroastrianism. Both of these religions influenced, and were influenced by, religions in both the Greek and Roman regions. The Vedic and Zoroastrian religions spread to the Indus Valley civilization, where their own innovations were added, creating what is now known as Hinduism. Of course, the Greeks and Romans also had their own direct influence on Hinduism. It was the early Greeks who referred to the Indus Valley people as "indoi" in their Greek language, now written as Hindu in English. We also observe many similarities between the Hinduism god and goddess stories and the Greek Mythology stories. Yet very few people today believe the Greek Mythology stories are real but there are many Hindus that believe their mythology is based on real facts and sacred truths from supernatural gods and goddesses.

In this chapter we'll take a look at a few interesting beliefs found in Hinduism, one of the oldest current day large religions. In the spirit of critical thinking, we'll now begin to connect the dots, so to speak, from the Mesopotamian civilization beliefs to Hinduism since it predates the other large current day religions still being practiced. It will be far from a complete review of their belief structure but it will give you a flavor for some of the thinking they developed and the influence they used to control their people. It will also show how many of their beliefs and traditions were later adopted by other religions. And yes, we'll also introduce a few of the many, many gods of Hinduism. Multiple research sources point to 33 core gods of Hinduism, although you'll also discover some sources mentioning 33 million as the number of gods. However, I've yet to come across anywhere that attempts to list that many. The point is Hinduism has a lot of gods.

As mentioned, Hinduism can trace its roots to the Vedic religion, which began in the present-day Iran region. The western fringes of current day Iran were part of the Fertile Crescent area, lush with food resources and prosperous urban civilizations, the perfect environment for innovation. Vedism gradually expanded from this area south into India around 1500 BCE. This religious expansion resulted from the migration of Indo-Aryan tribes from the general area of the Fertile Crescent into the Punjab or northern Indian subcontinent between 1500 BCE to 500 BCE. They brought with them the Vedic religion, considered to be the oldest religion with written records of its beliefs, traditions, and rituals, which were documented in an archaic Sanskrit language. These writings became the foundation for the beliefs and traditions that over time shaped the Hinduism religion.

Vedism was a polytheistic sacrificial religion worshiping primarily male gods, however there were also a few goddesses. Most of these gods helped explain the sky and the natural world. The priests led ceremonies, which included the singing of hymns from the Rigveda (the earliest sacred book written in Sanskrit), sacrificing animals to the gods, and drinking the sacred, mind-altering liquor pressed from a plant called soma. These rituals were all done around a sacred fire. Worshippers offered sacrifices to the gods hoping to improve their lives and believed singing hymns or songs of praise made their sacrifices more acceptable, enhancing their chances of success. This singing custom has continued today as almost all of the major religions in the world include singing or chanting as part of their rituals. Personally, I do enjoy singing and listening to some modern religious songs, provided excellent musicians and singers lead them - otherwise not such a fan. However, I never believed the act of singing would get God to help anyone be more successful. Maybe this only works if they sing really, really, really well.

Directly influenced by the original Vedic rituals, Hinduism continued the practice of sacrifices by offering things to God in a sacred fire called "homa". Other religions copied the practice of sacrifice from the Vedic rites as they also have offerings to God in their rituals. For example, as part of their Eucharist ceremony, in the offertory portion the Christian religion offers bread, wine or grape juice, and even money to God. Just to be clear, the priest or minister eventually eats the bread, drinks the wine or grape juice, and of course, keeps the money! I guess this is because no one knows how to physically get the food to God and no one seems to have god's bank account number. This is a great perk for the priest or minister and their churches and temples.

In addition to the practice of sacrifice coming from the original Vedic rites, the homa or sacred fire is also an important element of not only modern Hindu worship, but other current day religions as well. This reverence for fire can be seen in the Christian religion with the lighting of candles in their ceremonies and as an offering in a church. One specific example is the lighting ceremony of the Easter candle in both Catholic and some Protestant Christian religions. Buddhism is another religion that has a fire offering ceremony similar to Vedic practices where candles are lit in respect for Buddha. Buddhism also views fire as a symbolic way to burn away suffering to liberate oneself from the negative aspects of life. Judaism also used fire in their ceremonies and even has an entire holiday devoted to lighting candles for eight days called Hanukkah, which commemorates the Maccabean (founders of Judaism) victory in Judea and dedication of their temple in 164 BCE. The only current day major religion that does not have any rituals associated with fire is Islam. In their Quran, Islam associates fire with the devil due to his claims of being created from fire. According to the Quran the devil claimed he was superior to humans because they were created from clay-mud and he said fire is superior to clay-mud. This sure sounds like a game of rock paper scissors where fire beats clay. Anyhow, as a result of his views, the devil was banished from heaven. It seems the devil should have kept his opinions to himself. Nevertheless, the Islam religion does not use fire in ceremonies because they associate it with the devil.

Another example of how Vedism influenced Hinduism was its adoption of the four social classes of people, which in practice is still followed by many Hindu believers today. These four Vedic, and now Hindu social classes, were the Brahmins (priests), Kshatriyas (warriors or rulers), Vaishyas (traders), and Shudras (servants). Those people who were not part of these four groups were called Avarna or no classification. Initially, this classification system was based on a person's work function and abilities. Over time it became a social hierarchy based on birth lineage similar to royalty practices around the world. Imagine the arrogant joy for the people fortunate enough to be born into one of the four classifications, especially the Brahmins. But of course, not quite so lucky for those not classified, now called Dalits or "untouchables", as the caste system is still inflicting pain on these people.

As if their lot in life wasn't bad enough, to make matters worse, untouchables had to marry other untouchables, keeping their descendants in misery for generations. No marriage was allowed between the poor side of town and the rich side. Nevertheless, Hinduism, similar to many other religions, wanted to give the oppressed a glimmer of hope. They came up with the belief that if you were a good untouchable in this life, then there's a chance you could be reincarnated into one of the four superior castes in a future life. It is hard to fathom how people continue to believe this to be true as it is so cruel and was based on a total fabrication by religious leaders thousands of years ago. In India, where the majority of the population believes in Hinduism, the constitution now guarantees equal treatment of all citizens as the government also realized this social class discrimination was mean-spirited and brutal.

The good news today is the Dalits or untouchables group have become a more powerful political force in India and have obtained more access to education. As a result, many of them have become very successful without needing to be reincarnated. They just needed to get a good education and be offered a chance to succeed. However, discrimination among Hindu's still exists in India and in other countries including the United States. Although many Hindus no longer believe in these caste levels, considering them to be unjust and cruel, they still seem to know in which group they reside. I guess some fictional religious beliefs are just hard to break, similar to racism based on skin color or shape of facial features.

During the period from 800 BCE to 400 BCE, the Vedic Brahmanism religious thinking merged with preexisting religion cultures in the Northern India area, eventually becoming Hinduism. This is when the concepts of reincarnation of the soul, karma, and the release from the cycle of rebirth through meditation rather than sacrifice were developed, as the Vedic religion had not included the reincarnation belief. It's unclear exactly where these ideas originated, but we do know they evolved in northern India as semi-nomadic pastoral communities transformed into more urban communities. We also know sixteen kingdoms, named the Mahajanapadas, ruled in northern ancient India when Hinduism was created during this time period. Influential priests in addition to a military commander supported each of the Mahajanapadas kings. It is presumed the priests and kings invented the ideas about reincarnation and karma and then shared them across the kingdoms. The Persians and Greeks who invaded northern India in this general time period could also have influenced these ideas.

Although the beliefs about reincarnation are different across the many sects of Hinduism, they all basically believe that in the afterlife, based on your karma, the soul is reborn as another being in heaven or hell, or a living being on earth as a human or animal.

To explain what happens when you die, Hinduism determined your immortal soul went on a journey. They taught people the concept of reincarnation, with your soul moving to a new body after you die. The way it works is your karma, or your actions accumulated in previous lives, determine the kind of body the soul will inhabit next. The core belief of karma is that for every action there is a reaction, if you are kind and compassionate to others you will get this in return, if you cause others to suffer then you will eventually experience suffering. Hinduism believes your soul lives on after death in another body called the astral body which is made of astral matter and lives in the Devaloka or second world. Even the ancient philosophers Plato and Aristotle in the time period of 427 BCE to 322 BCE were believers in this soul matter as they taught that the stars were composed of a type of matter different from the four earthly elements. They claimed it was a fifth ethereal element and the astral mysticism people believed the human soul or essence was made of the same material. We are not sure if these philosophers got these ideas from northern India or the other way around, if they influenced the northern India Hinduism beliefs.

Through reincarnation, the ultimate goal of the immortal soul is to realize it is part of Brahman through unconditional surrender, which releases it from the cycle of death and rebirth. Hinduism teaches that your objective is to unite your soul with Brahman. Just to be clear, your soul is trying to get to Brahman not Brahma (the creator god). Brahman is present everywhere and in everything, it cannot be seen and can only be experienced. Death is only meant for the body and not the soul. The soul's goal is to get rid of the body and become one with Brahman. Most religions have an end game for when you die and Hinduism is no exception. In Hinduism it's all about needing to keep doing it over and over, until you get it right. The great thing about this belief is it cannot be proven or disproved, giving the leaders of the religion ultimate power. What a great invention! This is especially true if you are part of the group in charge.

Throughout the years, Hinduism continued to evolve primarily in the Indian subcontinent as a combination of religious beliefs, traditions, and philosophies. It became a very multilevel religion, as its followers in addition to believing in reincarnation of the soul, believed in both pantheism (one true God, Brahma) and polytheism (many gods and goddesses who personify aspects of this one true god). Pantheism believes there is only one true god, who signifies all things in the universe, including reality and truth, with no form or limit. As Hinduism was created, the decision was made to have only one God, similar to Zoroastrianism. Judaism, followed by Christianity, and then Islam later adopted the concept of believing in one God as well. However, all these so called one-God religions seem to hedge on this topic as they all have many supernatural characters or demi-gods performing supernatural actions, including Abraham, Moses, Noah, Immaculate Mary, Saints, Angels, and Muhammad as examples.

On the other hand, Hinduism was, and continues to be, more lenient as it also allows for the polytheism belief, allowing people a large variety of ways to worship based on family tradition, community, and regional practices. The way I think about this contradiction of Hindu's believing in one god but having many gods is the many gods are personalities or roles that Brahma is playing. To me, this is similar to one actor playing many different roles in a play. As with many religious beliefs, I find this concept difficult to understand, let alone try to explain.

The main Hindu god is called Brahma or the creator. He is the first member of the Hindu trinity. The trinity god - the three gods in one concept? That sure sounds familiar! Of course, it does if you are familiar with how the Roman's chose to treat Jesus and the Holy Spirit in the Christian religion - unifying the Father, Son and Holy Ghost into one God. Yes, the Hindu religion included the concept of a trinity of Gods long before the Roman Christian's adopted it, although it's unclear how or why this trinity notion was invented. What we do know is Hinduism harmonized the old Vedic religion belief in Brahma with two other main groups around 0 to 300 CE. One group believed in the god Vishnu, who was also incarnated in human form as Krishna. The other group believed in the god Shiva, along with his avatars. The Shiva group had been around for a long time as coins were found with Shiva on them as early as 100 BCE. The Hindu holy trinity was comprised of these three gods; Brahma, Vishnu and Shiva. In addition, once they were combined, they also added in some wives as goddesses. Brahma's spouse is Saraswati, Vishnu's spouse is Lakshmi, and Shiva's spouse is Parvati. Incorporating women into the god mix was a very enlightened addition at this time period, since almost all religions were primarily male oriented. There was also a sun god during this time period in Northern India named Surya. He had roots in the Vedic beliefs similar to the sun god Sol Invictus, who was worshipped in the Syrian area and then the Roman Empire. However, Hinduism stopped recognizing this god similar to the practices of the Abrahamic religions stopping their recognition of Sol. Instead, they adopted one true god and rejected the sun god. In any case, Hinduism embraced Vishnu and Shiva, by including them into a Hindu god trinity, possibly to make it easier for the people to accept Brahma as the one true god.

Hinduism also has many other deities, which is why it is so hard to keep track of them. All these deities start with the holy trinity but then each of these three Gods have many avatars. An avatar is the incarnation of a deity in human or animal form with the purpose of counteracting some particular evil, solving problems, or sharing knowledge.

They help humans, which is why people like them so much and there is much to be learned from each of their stories.

Although there are many, many others, here is a brief list of some of the main Hindu Gods and their related Avatars...

Brahma – The Creator

Saraswati – Brahma's Spouse

The Hindu God Brahma, or the creator, is the first member of the Hindu trinity and the main god. Brahma is associated with creation, knowledge and Vedas, which are the religious texts. Brahma has four heads signifying the four Vedas Scriptures. His multiple arms and the multiple arms of other gods shown in pictures illustrates their supreme power over humans.

There are seven main avatars of Brahma who appear on earth with the purpose of sharing knowledge of the world:

1. Valmiki (compiled the Ramayan Sanskrit epic that provides knowledge of dharma/moral law)

2. Kahsyapa (father of various species including humans)

3. Dattatreya (first teacher and uses knowledge from nature)

4. Vyasa (put together the Mahabharata history about fighting for the throne and teaching moral law)

5. Kalidasa (poet and playwright)

6. Chandra (the moon deity)

7. Vikahanas (teaches mystery of worship at Naimishayana – a sacred place near Lucknow, India which is about 500 km southeast of New Delhi)

Vishnu – The Protector

© Shutterstock

Lakshmi – Vishnu's Spouse

©Shutterstock

Vishnu is the second member of the Hindu trinity and he maintains order and harmony of the universe, which is created by Brahma. Vishnu also has avatars or saviors to intervene on earth whenever help is needed to restore the moral order and peace. Vishnu sure sounds like an early version of Jesus who was also a savior and a promoter of peace. His avatars follow the stages of human evolution and include:

1. Marsya (a great fish with a horn that pulled a boat carrying all the creatures of the world to safety during a flood that destroyed the world)

2. Kurma (a giant tortoise that helped churn the ocean to release the nectar of immortal life by holding up a mountain)

3. Varaha (a giant boar that carried the earth between his tusks from the bottom of the ocean to save it)

4. Narasimha (a half man and half lion that killed the evil Hiranyakashipu and ended his persecution of human beings for their beliefs)

5. Vamana (a dwarf turned into a giant god and then with two steps saved the world and heaven, and then with a third step he made the evil Bali ruler of the nether-world)

6. Parashurama (a warrior with an axe ended the rule of unrighteous kings and unchaste women and also used his axe to create the Indian southwestern Arabian Sea coastline)

7. Rama (a prince who killed the demon king and saved Sita, he represents good over evil and is celebrated in the festival of Diwali)

8. Balarama (elder brother of Lord Krishna)

9. Krishna (usually shown with a flute in his hand, he is frequently worshipped as the hero of various legends and represents love, duty, compassion, and playfulness)

10. Kalki (final incarnation of Vishnu visualized on a white horse with his sword blazing like a comet, he will start another cycle of existence for human beings)

Shiva – Destroyer / Renewer

© Shutterstock

Parvati – Shiva's Spouse

©Shutterstock

The third God of the trinity is Shiva, the destroyer, and his task is to destroy the universe so it can be renewed at the end of each cycle of time. Hinduism teaches the universe is created for a certain period of time and then rejuvenated. The only things not able to be destroyed are Brahma and certain Hindu scriptures. I'm sure the priests dreamed this rule up because if the scriptures were destroyed, and subsequently rejuvenated, this would result in the invention of a new religion. The nature of Shiva's destructive power is more regenerative, as a necessary step to renewal. This idea was most likely inspired by watching the seasons play out from winter, when the crops are dormant or have died, to when growth begins in the spring season. The 19 main Avatars of Shiva, whose purpose is to sustain the law and balance of nature or existence, include:

1. Piplaad (stopped Shani Dosha from causing pain and suffering for those under the age of 16)

2. Nandi (the great bull god, gate keeper of Shiva's home and protector of the herds)

3. Veerabhadra (destroyed King Daksha for his sacrifice of Shiva's first wife Sati)

4. Bhairava (punishes greedy, lustful, and arrogant people)

5. Ashwatthama (a warrior in the Mahabharata story where he killed the oppressive Kshatriyas)

6. Sharabha (a lion bird that killed the demon Hiranyakashipu)

7. Grihapati (conquered death predicted by astrology at age 9 and became the lord of directions)

8. Durvasa (to maintain discipline in the universe, this short-tempered god demands respect)

9. Hanuman (great monkey god of wisdom, strength, courage, devotion, and self-discipline)

10. Rrishabha (bull god that killed the cruel sons of Vishnu to save creation)
11. Yatinath (tested the hospitality of a couple by appearing as a guest resulting in death)
12. Krishna Darshan (taught the importance of worship sacrifice and rituals in a person's life)
13. Bhikshuvarya (a beggar that got a woman beggar to raise an orphan, protection from danger)
14. Sureshwar (tested devotion to Lord Shiva)
15. Keerat (hunter along with Arjuna killed the demon, Mooka, and then rewarded him for valor)
16. Suntantarka (asked Himalaya to marry his daughter Parvati, a reincarnation of Sati-first wife)
17. Brahmachari (tested Goddess Parvati's love for Lord Shiva)
18. Yaksheshwar (took away false ego and pride through divine grass that could not be cut)
19. Avadhut (crushed arrogance of Lord Indra – God of rain and sky similar to Zeus and Jupiter)

Shiva is also believed to help people overcome obstacles by destroying their life problems. For some reason Shiva needs to stay incognito, so as a way to accomplish this task for people, he appears as his son, called Ganapati or Ganesh. Ganapati is portrayed as the god with the elephant head and you will see his statue in many Hindu homes or cars because he helps people. It's also a cool statue. Shiva does have some similarity to the Holy Spirit in the Christian trinity in that both are associated with rebirth or renewal, with the spring season being their favorite season. The Holy Spirit is believed to help people through difficult situations similar to Shiva's son dressed up as Ganapati.

Ganapati or Ganesh aka Shiva's son

©Shutterstock

Some current day Hindus refer to Hinduism as a way of life and not a religion, even though it does have gods and mythology similar to other religions. Accordingly, Hinduism describes itself as a web of customs, obligation, traditions, and ideals and not just a system of beliefs. It was developed over time and not attributed to one founder as was Christianity and Islam.

As with other religions, Hinduism includes basic scriptures, called Shastras. These scriptures were based on people memorizing verbal stories from saints and sages, passing them along throughout history, and eventually being written down. Of course, these stories were told and retold for hundreds if not thousands of years before they were actually written - this is similar across all current day major religions. It's important to be mindful of this when regarding the accuracy of events as they relate to the origins of ideas leading to beliefs. The person who eventually was tasked with writing the story or the person in power paying for it to be written ultimately had the final say as to what was recorded. Again, this is similar to other religions. Whoever wrote the final version must have been really proud of his work because he and his priests decided these Shastras were immortal.

Hopefully you can understand why this religion or way of life attracted so many believers as its history is over 3,500 years old and it was practiced for most of those years by a majority of people who were illiterate. This religion has been passed down through about 150 generations primarily through word of mouth and the priest's lectures, making the strength of this culture and belief incredible. The brainwashing of illiterate people is, and was, almost unbreakable.

Similar to many religions, this religion has many beautiful teachings especially with regard to karma, which deals with how you treat others and yourself. However, at its core it doesn't seem to be very compassionate to over 200 million people in India living in poverty. They are living on less than $2 per day, approximately half of these people are illiterate according to the World Bank, and they are mostly considered untouchables. The Hindu religion magnifies this suffering by making these people feel even more inferior and bad about themselves since their soul was obviously horrible in a previous life to end up in such misery. The wealthy presumably feel very smug because their soul is doing quite well, making Hinduism a great religion for them. Moreover, this religion also promotes the caste system, which further prejudices people based on their ancestry. Most religions seem to feel the need to make people feel bad about themselves and Hinduism is no exception. The most likely reason for this is it provides a way to control people by promising redemption through strict adherence to their respective religious rules.

It is easy to understand how this religion got to be so large with such a long history in the Indian sub-continent combined with an unprecedented Indian population growth to approximately 1.4 billion people. The majority of the population, almost 80%, believes in Hinduism with Islam as the second most followed religion having 15% or 210 million people. This Islamic population dates back to the 1200s CE when Islamic conquerors forced the people to convert from Hinduism to Islam. Unfortunately, the current minority Islamic population in India is being attacked and marginalized by the majority Hindu population. Payback I suppose based on holding a grudge for such a long period of time. So much for a religion that encourages tolerance.

In closing, although Hinduism is one of the oldest cultural religions in the world, with teachings intended to help people improve themselves, it is also very much connected to stories which were invented thousands of years ago and can often be cruel or unhelpful even though that may not have been their intent. Using critical thinking you can now appreciate how this religion originated and evolved from the influences of Mesopotamia with the Vedic Scriptures, Zoroastrianism, along with Greek Mythology, and innovation by people living in Northern India. My hope after reading this is you realize these concepts and ideas were most likely dreamed up by many ancient priests, kings, or philosophers and not gods. In addition, the people who wrote these stories and invented these beliefs did not have a monopoly on how people should be treated and how you should treat yourself. I look at these guiding principles as I have for my own belief system – I choose to include only the parts that are helpful, kind, compassionate, and unselfish and reject the rest. Remember, just because something is ancient does not make it wise or insightful, it just means it's old.

Major Religious Belief Development

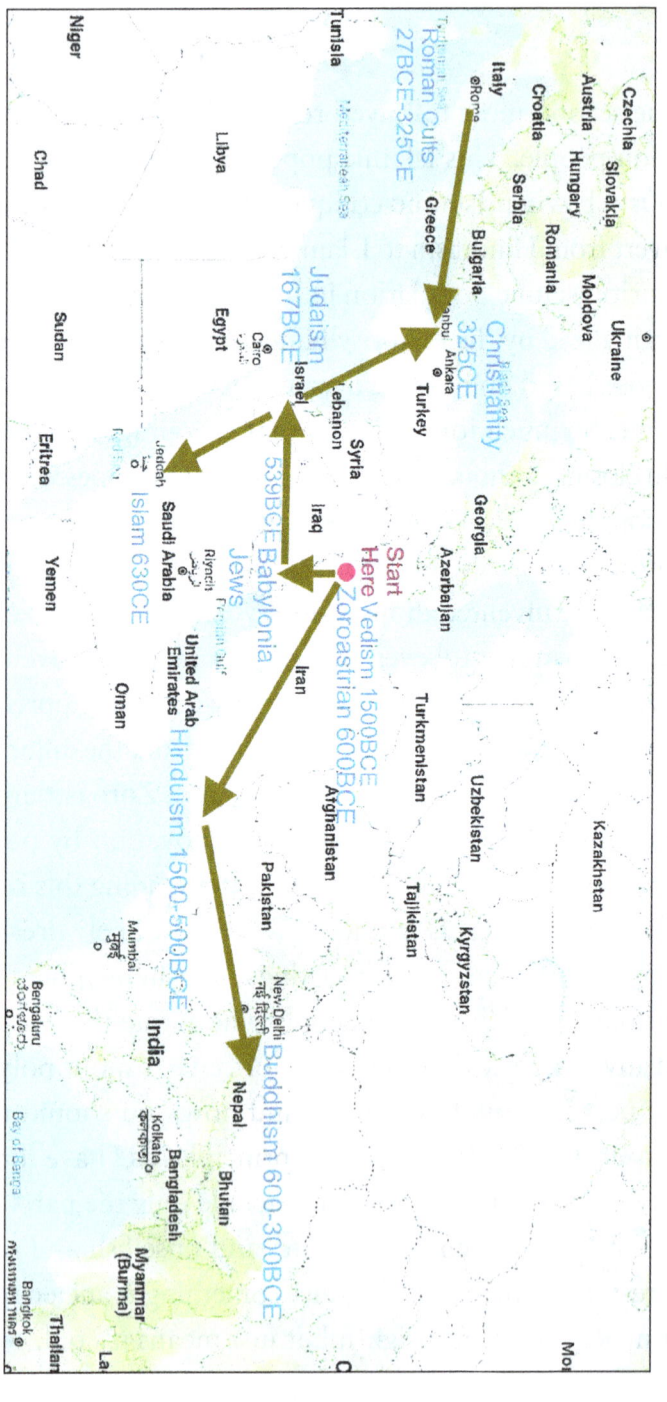

Chapter 7

Buckle up – A Chronicle from Zoroastrianism to Abrahamic Religions

Living most of my life in the United States of America, where much of our history is biased to the west and heavily influenced by Christian Protestant religions, I wasn't all that familiar with the history of other religions around the world. Much of what I was taught centered on Christianity and why it became so popular. The World Religions humanities course I took in college opened my eyes to some of the other non-Christian religions. However, it wasn't until many years later, when I had the time, curiosity, and motivation, did I take a deeper dive into learning more about these religions; their origins, history, and beliefs, and especially how their beliefs compared to my own.

As an example, I had always thought Jesus Christ was the first person to understand and preach human beings determined their own destiny by their decisions and actions. This concept had been a huge philosophical change in the thinking of people over 2,000 years ago. We take this for granted now, so it doesn't seem like such a big deal, but it clearly was a huge change in thinking back at that time. Remember those ancient Greeks? They had previously believed humans had little or no ability to change their fates as they were totally at the mercy of their many gods. To make it even worse for people, these gods often acted haphazardly or whimsically. People at that time period truly believed if something bad or good happened to them personally or to their town, it was caused by the gods. Clearly, humans' determining their own destiny was seen as a novel belief.

However, if Jesus originated this change in philosophy, "to take responsibility for your own life", it unquestionably would have made him God-like. Sorry to say, he wasn't the inventor of this philosophical thinking – it actually originated in the Iran area with a religion called Zoroastrianism in the 600 BCE time period. In my American ignorance, I had never even heard of this religion, even though it is still somewhat in existence today. The last chapter introduced you to the Hindu religion, with its roots stemming from the Fertile Crescent and the influence of the Vedic Religion coming out of this area. Continuing on our critical thinking journey, this chapter will explore the other significant religion coming out of the Fertile Crescent area – the Zoroastrian Religion, which also evolved out of the Vedic Religion. So, if you are like me, clueless as to those influential Zoroastrians - buckle up, you're in for a whirlwind tour of that religion spanning the past few thousand years. It begins with the Zoroastrian beliefs, which eventually led to the introduction of the Abrahamic religions. Along the way we'll weave through the many, many wars between the Romans and the Jewish sects, and finally land on where they stand today. We need to connect many dots to understand how and why these religions originated and evolved, so I'll take you through the chronological development of these Abrahamic religions, but keep in mind that Zoroastrianism also influenced Hinduism. To help you keep the story straight in your mind, you may want to periodically refer to the map at the beginning of the chapter for a visual view of the Zoroastrian belief migration influence leading to the development of these new beliefs and subsequent religions.

    The best estimates have the founder of the Zoroastrian religion, Zoroaster, being born in 628 BCE in the Iran/Persian area. Although the dates of when he lived are a little fuzzy, it is widely accepted that he was an ancient Iranian spiritual leader. Prior to this religion getting under way, the Persians worshipped the deities of the old Iran-Aryan religion, which would later come to be known as Hinduism. Zoroaster wasn't a fan of worshipping multiple gods. He preached only Ahura Mazda, the lord of wisdom, should be worshipped. And yes, in case that name sounds familiar, Ahura Mazda is the namesake for the Japanese car company Mazda. Amazing there were no objections in the boardroom to using an obscure religion's god as the namesake for this car company. I have to wonder if there would be an uproar from religious people if a car or truck company were to be named after the better-known figures like Jesus Christ or Muhammad. Imagine the "Jesus Christ Coupe" or the "Muhammad Mini-van" – that would probably be a marketing nightmare and drive extreme outrage among hard core Christians or Muslim believers. Outrageous!

So, getting back to Zoroaster and his one God, Ahura Mazda – his influence was key to launching the concept of this monotheistic faith. He must have been really onto something, because this belief was eventually copied by the new religious inventions referred to as the Abrahamic religions; Judaism, Christianity, and Islam. And it wasn't just the one God idea, other Zoroastrian concepts were copied as well by these three current day religions including the notions of heaven and hell, angels and demons, and judgment day. Like I said, he must have been a really influential salesman! Zoroaster's faith focused on the struggle between God and Ahriman. Not familiar with Ahriman? While God embodied the forces of goodness and light (represented by the Holy Spirit called Spenta Mainyu), Ahriman ruled over the forces of darkness and evil. This is the introduction of the idea of Satan as a polar opposite to God. Not surprisingly, this religion teaches that ultimately God, along with goodness and light, will eventually win the struggle. Of course, he wins! It wouldn't make for a good inspirational story if that weren't the case. Zoroaster also preached that people are responsible for their own actions and decisions, which will influence their life and ultimate destiny. Hmmm, interesting idea – personal responsibility with no one else to blame but oneself. I wish some of our politicians and business leaders would embrace this concept. The Greeks, after spending time in the Iranian area and learning of Zoroastrianism, eventually changed their own philosophy to reflect they were the masters of their destinies and their decisions were in their own hands. Now we know Zoroaster should get the credit for the notion of personal responsibility and not Jesus or the famous Greek philosophers.

As a fun fact, even within our current pop culture, some of today's popular books and movies have been inspired by this relatively unknown Zoroastrian religion. George RR Martin's book called *A Song of Ice and Fire,* which was adapted into *The Game of Thrones* series, includes a demi-god similar to Ahriman who rules over darkness. Of course, *Star Wars* is a very close copy of the cosmic battle between the forces of light and darkness. And who can forget *Harry Potter* with its good and bad magicians; the bad ones being dark and menacing while the good ones are represented by bright lights and a unicorn. Like I said, good vs. evil always makes for a good story.

Over time, the Zoroastrian concepts of a single god, heaven and hell, judgment day, and a self-determination philosophy continued to catch on. Eventually these beliefs were introduced and adopted by the Hebrew community of Babylonia, where people from the Kingdom of Judea had been living in captivity for decades. The Hebrew's had been deported from the Judea area and then held captive in Babylonia when Nebuchadnezzar the Great (second king of the Neo-Babylonian Empire) destroyed Jerusalem, estimated to have happened between 597 BCE and 586 BCE. Before this period the Israelites or Hebrew people believed in polytheism or multiple gods. In fact, some of the ancient Israelites believed the goddess Asherah was the companion or spouse of their god Yahweh.

When Cyrus the Great, a king of the Persian Empire, conquered Babylon in 539 BCE he liberated the Babylonian Hebrew people from their captivity. Remember, these were the people who had already embraced the Zoroastrian beliefs. Many of these liberated Hebrew people returned to their homeland in Jerusalem, taking with them their newly adopted Zoroastrian ideas. Over time, their descendants helped create their own religion, founded by writing the Hebrew bible, which was later revised to also become the Old Testament Bible in Christianity. This shift to monotheism took hundreds of years, as the worship of one God alone, called Yahweh, did not become universal until the second century BCE, beginning with the Maccabees. Who are the Maccabees you ask? The Maccabees were a group of Jewish rebel warriors who took control of Judea and founded the Hasmonean Dynasty. The Maccabees ruled from 167 BCE to 63 BCE and forced the Israelites to convert to the monotheistic Jewish religion, which remember, was heavily influenced by Zoroastrian. The rule of the Maccabees ended when Rome conquered Jerusalem and became the new ruling empire with General Pompey capturing Jerusalem in 63 BCE. And the trail begins - Zoroastrian to the Babylonian Jews to the Maccabees to the Israelites – quite a convoluted path to follow!

Eventually the beliefs of Zoroaster were adopted by all the new Abrahamic religions - Judaism, Christianity, and Islam. To give context as to how both Judaism and Christianity got their starts, it is important to understand what was happening in Palestine during the time when these religions evolved. As previously mentioned, the Romans led by General Pompey, conquered Jerusalem in 63 BCE, ending the rule of the Maccabees. This eastern Mediterranean area was strategic to Rome as it was between Syria and Egypt, which were both keys to trade. Rome sourced grain from Alexandria, Egypt, and silk, textiles, and spices from the Syria Silk Road, which connected China in the east and India in the south. This geographic area was also important to the coastal sea trade routes.

Those initial years of the Roman rule beginning in 63 BCE were fairly stable for people living in this area. Rome used a puppet government to rule Judea, which was relatively gentle since they were already overextended and really couldn't afford a Jewish revolt. The rulers of this puppet government were Arab allies of Rome called Herodians. The Herodians weren't concerned with changing or influencing the culture or religions during this time period - they didn't care what people believed as long as they did not revolt against them. Their goal was to just keep life stable. Consequently, Judaism developed new or different beliefs which varied depending on the area they occupied. The result was the Judaism religion splintered into many sects, the largest of which were the Pharisees, the Sadducees, and the Essenes, in addition to many other smaller sects.

The Pharisees were a progressive group that was actively reforming Judaism while being passively opposed to Roman rule. It is thought the Christian god Jesus belonged to the Pharisees group as his teachings contain Pharisaic doctrine. Another group, the Sadducees were the wealthy land-owning class that cooperated with the Romans and were therefore disliked by most of the common people. And the final group, the Essenes lived lives of manual labor and seclusion and believed that denying themselves physical or psychological desires helped them attain spiritual goals. They were also known to be very good at healing illnesses and injuries. The Christian biblical character John the Baptist happened to belong to this Essenes group, described in bible stories running around in camel hair clothes, eating locusts and wild honey, and not shaving or bathing except for baptism rituals.

Although these were all different sects of Judaism, they shared one important common belief - they believed they were the chosen people of God and thus felt superior. They looked down on the people such as those following the Greek or Roman religions, who continued to believe in multiple gods. Even though life was fairly stable in this area of the world, there still was friction due to the Jewish sects' belief in one God and the gentile people's belief in multiple gods. Both groups thought they were right and each disrespected the other group's god(s) belief.

The Jewish sects also shared the expectation that a messiah would lead them out of Roman domination. In Judaism, the term "messiah" referred to a king belonging to the Davidic line that would deliver Israel from foreign bondage into the Messianic Age. In Abrahamic religions, the Messianic Age is the future period of time on earth when the messiah will reign and bring universal peace and brotherhood without any evil. Oh, and everyone will believe in the one true religion, which at that time was Judaism since Christianity and Islam had not been invented yet.

Life continued to be somewhat stable – that is, until 6 BCE when the Roman Emperor Augustus appointed General Varus as the governor of Syria and Palestine. General Varus was a very harsh and high taxing leader, putting even more pressure on the suffering Jewish people. The Jewish people were ruled locally by Herod the Great, Roman client king of Judea, who reported to General Varus. Herod the Great, who was also a tyrant ruler even though he financed many building projects, died a few years later in 4 BCE. Under Herod's reign the Jewish people suffered extreme economic hardship, so they were not all that sad to see him die. However, when he died there was no local leadership to control the people resulting in chaos, and in addition people working for

Herod's projects lost their jobs. The result was even more people became impoverished. His death and this situation led to riots and unrest by the Jewish people who had endured enough of the Roman regime's abusive and absentee leadership.

To stop the unrest, General Varus occupied Jerusalem in 4 BCE and proceeded to crucify 2,000 Jewish rebels. Following the massacre in Judea, Varus and his army traveled back up the Mediterranean coast to Antioch in current day southern Turkey. Once he was gone, his cruelty resulted in Jewish boycotts against Roman goods and began many years of protest against Roman rule. The next 130 plus years became very tumultuous and violent for both the Jewish people and the Romans. This painful environment heavily influenced the beliefs of the various Judaism sects, including a forthcoming new sect, which was to be started by Jesus.

To appreciate what happened next, it's important to understand that Rome still wanted to control the Judea area since it was a key trading area as earlier mentioned. As the Roman Empire grew, the rulers wanted more of the money coming out of this region to fund their aristocracy lifestyle, army, and empire expansion plans. To accomplish these goals, they sent the governor of Syria, Sulpicius Quirinius, into Judea in 6 CE with his military force to combine Sumaria, Idumea, and Judea into one province under direct Roman rule, which was then called the Roman Province of Judea (basically all the land located directly below Syria- see map at end of chapter). In order to raise more funds for Rome, Sulpicius' next move was to take a census, which would then be used to increase the taxes on the Jewish people.

In response to the new harsh Roman leadership and the increased taxes, a rebel group rose up under the leadership of Judas of Galilee and supported by Zadok, who was a popular Pharisee. This group urged the Jewish people to resist the census and taxes since they preached this was a sin against God and Jewish law; plus, they wanted to keep their money. It's always about the money! As you probably guessed, the Roman's killed Judas to stop his group's influence, causing his gang to scatter to avoid persecution and death. In addition, the Jewish temple was plundered and defiled, and heavy taxes were imposed anyway. To keep the population under control, torture was frequently used and Jewish people were sold into slavery; this sadly led many to commit suicide. However, the young people became even more embittered as to how the Jewish people were being treated and unrest grew even stronger over the coming years.

Contrary to biblical impressions, life did not get better when Pontius Pilate was appointed the procurator of Judaea in 26 CE. A very cruel and corrupt man, he perpetuated the abuses of his predecessor, Herod. He was able to dominate the area with 3,000 Roman soldiers under his command living along the Mediterranean, only about a two days march to Jerusalem.

As you can imagine, this time period from 26 CE until the end of Pontius Pilate's governorship in 36 CE was absolutely terrible for the people living in Judea. During this period, they desperately were looking for a savior and along came Jesus who looked like a very good candidate. Not only was he from the Davidic line, but he also was charismatic and a good teacher. Jesus offered hope to the downtrodden and the oppressed. He began to unite the people in a common cause, which was both ethical and political. The bad news, he was identified by the Romans as a rebel and a threat to their dominating rule. Of course, you know it didn't end well for him – he was crucified similar to the other rebels before him.

Although Jesus was not able to be their savior, it did not stop Jewish communities within Judea from continuing to plan another revolt in their attempt to set up an independent Jewish state totally free of Roman control. Over time the Jewish people organized themselves and then revolted again in 66 CE to 70 CE. This war was extremely savage and brutal and did not turn out well for the Jewish people - the result of this Jewish revolt was a significant number of them were killed by the Romans. During this war the Romans destroyed the Herodian Temple, as it was thought to be the focal point for Jewish nationalistic pride. The Romans had enough of the Jewish sects and their intolerance with the Roman religion. Seeing the Jewish religion as the source of the unrest, naturally they wanted to destroy it. However, the Roman's destroying the temple made it worse, as intolerance often does. At this time, all the Jewish people living in Judea, Syria, Cyprus, and Egypt including Alexandria became very angry and distraught by the destruction of their temple. As expected, this led to even more revolts.

The next Jewish revolt against the Romans was called the Kito's War (115 CE to 117 CE) and took place primarily in Cyrene (near current day Shah hat, Libya) as well as in the area of Egypt. The Jewish people started this war by destroying Roman temples and government buildings as payback for the Romans destroying their Jewish temple. Keep in mind, during this time the Jewish people were very outspoken against people who believed in multiple gods. Initially the Jewish rebels were successful and significantly depopulated many Roman and Greek people from these areas. But once again, the Romans sent several legions of soldiers and were able to stop this rebellion. The Romans further encouraged people from other Roman occupied areas to repopulate Cyrene and towns in Egypt, because the Jewish rebels had killed most of their people who had been living there.

Not done yet! The third war was called Bar Kokhba (132 CE to 136 CE). The main reason for this war was the Roman Emperor Hadrian decided to integrate Jewish people into the empire by establishing a Roman colony in Jerusalem. He also had a temple built to Jupiter on the ruins of the Jewish temple and restricted Jewish religious freedom and observances. Why he thought this was a good idea can only be attributed to his belief that he was the emperor and therefore he was divine. His assumption was that of course everyone would want to become good Romans. After all, they were the greatest empire! Arrogant nationalism on full display, which unfortunately is still happening today around the world.

It was 132 CE and the Jewish people decided this oppression was too much. How to respond? Revolt of course, which was led by Simon bar Kokhba who was thought to be the Messiah and also Son of the Star. There were three beliefs associated with both Simon and Jesus that were most likely shared by the many Jewish sects, including the Christian sect. One belief was that the Messiah would be born in Bethlehem, which was the birthplace of King David. Secondly, there would be a new king from the Davidic ancestry line. And thirdly, a star would appear to indicate the birth. This is most likely the source for calling Simon the "Son of the Star" and also for the Star of Bethlehem included in the Jesus birth story. Interestingly, although Jesus predated Simon by more than 100 years, both Simon and Jesus had similar birth stories since this was the requirement to be the Messiah.

The Jewish sects under the leadership of Simon bar Kokhba acted as a unified group, with the exception of the Jewish Christian sect. The Jewish rebels attacked the Roman colony successfully and continued to rule Judea for several years. Although the Christian Jewish sect was also oppressed by the Romans, they refused to join the revolt. In

134 CE Rome started sending legions of soldiers to retake Judea and eventually amassed over 120,000 soldiers. The fighting was fierce, with both the Jewish rebels and the Romans suffering serious casualties, but the Roman soldiers finally won this war in 136 CE. By the end of this war, more than 580,000 Jewish people had been killed or sold into slavery, and the Messiah Simon bar Kokhba was killed as well. Although Rome won this war, their military strength was dramatically reduced. The small population of Jewish people remaining were barred from Jerusalem and sent into exile. In 138 CE, the intolerant and oppressive Emperor Hadrian died, which gave the persecuted remaining Jewish people in exile some degree of relief.

This Bar Kokhba revolt greatly influenced the course of Jewish history and the philosophy of the Jewish religion. Their philosophy became more politically cautious and conservative as they had suffered and caused tremendous losses of life by persistently fighting for their freedom and religious beliefs. They also had been exiled out of Judea and forced to establish their lives in smaller Jewish communities. In addition, the idea of a Messiah liberating them changed, becoming more about spiritual freedom and less about delivering them physically from oppression. Some of them viewed a Messiah as a charismatic teacher who would give the correct interpretation of Mosaic Law. This law, which was in the first five books of the Hebrew Bible and also the Christian Old Testament Bible, was believed to be god's revealed guidance for humankind. After the

Jews were exiled from Jerusalem, they also began to view Simon bar Kokhba as a false Messiah since he only freed them for two to three years. Obviously, not exactly what they were expecting from a true Messiah.

This Bar Kokhba war, over 100 years after Jesus lived, was also among the key events differentiating Christianity as a religion distinct from Judaism. Although Jewish Christians regarded Jesus as the Messiah and did not support Bar Kokhba as the Messiah, they were barred from Jerusalem along with the other Jewish sects. The Jewish Christians most likely felt very superior to the other Jewish sects since they had rejected Simon bar Kokhba as the Messiah from the beginning. They also did not want to participate in the fight with Romans as they anticipated terrible losses of life. Two, "I told you so," opportunities. I'm sure there was no love lost between the Jewish Christian sect and the other Jewish sects who had fought so hard for their freedom and lost so many of their friends and family members, with no help from these Jewish Christians. And I suspect the Christians most likely reminded them every chance they got that those who fought were unsuccessful in their attempt to gain their freedom from the Romans. However, now the Christians were exiled just like the other Jewish sects giving them the opportunity to start spreading their beliefs to others outside of Judea and develop a larger movement.

As you can appreciate, saying Judaism got a rocky start is a massive understatement. So where did they end up after all of their struggles? How is their religion described today?

Judaism is a religion similar to Hinduism in that it evolved over time and was not influenced by one founder. Both Judaism and Hinduism are viewed as a cultural identity and way of life, in addition to having religious beliefs. The big difference is Judaism only has one God and Hinduism has one God with many, many god and goddess manifestations. We know the one God idea started with Zoroastrianism and then Judaism decided to adopt this thinking. They all decided one God was enough. Anyhow, the Hebrews became zealots on this topic and decided everyone else was wrong and they were right. They also got out of the god or idol statue business. Could this have been because a non-Hebrew tribe had a monopoly on the manufacture and distribution of statues? The people believing in Judaism had a boycott on statues and even included it in their Ten Commandments by forbidding the worship of these objects. This directive actually makes sense since treating a god statue like a real person seems a bit much. If you think this custom went away entirely, think again as Catholic, Hindu, and Buddhism use statues in their churches, temples, and their celebrations. They also like to parade around town with them. To be fair, most religions with statues and pictures view them as mnemonic devices to focus their thinking and prayers and don't actually worship these objects. And similar to Hinduism, Judaism evolved over thousands of years and was documented much later based on memorized verbal information. Again, I doubt these memorized ideas were very accurate after thousands of years of retelling and were more dependent on the beliefs, prejudices, and bias of the person and ruling class at the time they were written.

Although, Judaism is a one God religion primarily for the Hebrew people, it has similarities to Hinduism in that it is also a total way of life, combining theology law, and cultural traditions. Judaism is one of the main descendants from original religious beliefs and philosophy originated in Mesopotamia roughly 4,000 years ago. Considering the population of the whole world, Judaism has a fairly small number of followers, 14 million, in relation to the largest religious groups that have over a billion followers. However, as a cultural and religious society, it drives an enormous amount of attention in the media world. If you were not aware of how small their numbers of followers are in a world of 7.5 billion people you would think it was one of the larger religions. You have to give them credit, the one God people certainly punch way above their weight on attracting attention. One of the reasons this religion seems so important could be it is the foundation for Christianity and Islam, which are two of the biggest followed religions in the world.

Sadly, the people believing in Judaism have been continually persecuted and killed throughout most of history, significantly reducing the number of followers. Without this extensive killing, you have to wonder if the number of people following this religion would have been competitive with Christianity and Islam. It is also not a mystery why fighting persecution is a major part of their current religious beliefs.

To illustrate, this listing comprises some of the major Judaism persecutions throughout history. These persecutions begin with the Seleucid Empire (Greek) 312 BCE to 63 BCE and then continued with the Roman Empire (4 BCE to 138 CE). During the Middle Ages in Europe, Christians believed Jews killed their God, Jesus Christ, so they felt obligated to murder these people every chance they got. Then during the Crusades, Christians decided to not only kill Jews but Muslims as well. Although this killing was justified based on religion, it was really more about wealth and power as the Judea area was still economically strong and a major trading hub. Since Christian people did not know the origin of the Black Death or bubonic plague (1346 CE to 1353 CE), they needed to blame someone and the Jews were an easy target resulting in more widespread killing. Of course, this did not seem to stop the plague nor did it stop the murders. Even when the Jews showed kindness, they were killed; for example, the Jews of Medina gave refuge to Muhammad and in return he had them killed when they would not swear allegiance to him and his new religion. These examples of killing Jews goes on and on throughout Europe, and the Middle East culminating with the Nazi Germans, who by the way, mostly belonged to Christian religions. The Nazis murdered approximately six million Jewish people between 1941 CE and 1945 CE. It's no surprise the Judaism religion is paranoid and tries to stay isolated. It also explains why Israel has such a strong and fearsome military and is quick to retaliate to protect themselves from further persecution.

Getting back to the original topic of this chapter, the Zoroastrians - what were they doing while all this fighting and revolting was happening between the Romans and the Jewish sects? Zoroastrianism continued as one of the main religions in the Persian area. Continued that is, until the Muslim conquest between 633 CE and 651 CE. After 1,000 years of popularity, this Muslim conquest led to the fall of the Sassanian Persian Empire and the decline of Zoroastrianism in Iran. Like most changes in religion, the conquering force tends to dictate the new religion. In this case, the Muslim invaders chose to do it more persuasively rather than destroying temples and killing people. The Muslim invaders took the passively aggressive approach and charged Zoroastrians living in Persia extra taxes and implemented laws to make life difficult and miserable for them to retain their religious beliefs and practices. Over time, most Iranian Zoroastrians converted to Islam. It was just not worth it to remain a Zoroaster.

We already know what became of the Jewish, Christian and Islam religions – they continue to be alive and well, and are among the current most popular world religions. But how about those Zoroastrians, whom I had never heard of until I dove into their history? What became of this religion, which was so influential in the development of Judaism and predated both Christianity and Islam?

Zoroastrianism is thought to be one of the world's oldest continuously practiced religions, and surprisingly, still in existence even today. Today, it is estimated there are only around 110,000 to 120,000 Zoroastrians, with most of them living in India, Iran and North America. But their legend lives on with the concepts of one God, heaven and hell, angels and demons, judgment day, and being the master of your own destiny. Oh, and don't forget the Mazda car company – think of them next time you see a Mazda on the highway!

And on a side note: All the religions coming out of the Mesopotamian Vedic and Zoroastrian religions invented a creator God; they just call him different names, including Ahura Mazda, Brahma, Yahweh, God the Father, and Allah. What's interesting is that both Judaism and Islam decided to prohibit images of their creator god as they consider this a sin of idolatry. Instead of an image of their God, their symbols include only the God's name. I guess they just don't like God pictures. However, the Zoroastrians, Christians and Hindus each have cool pictures of their creator god, which are shown on the next pages.

Zoroastrian Creator God
Ahura Mazda

© Shutterstock

Hinduism Creator God
Brahma

© Shutterstock

Christianity Creator God
God the Father

© Shutterstock

Islam
the symbol for Allah in Arabic

© Shutterstock

Judaism
the symbol for Yahweh in Hebrew

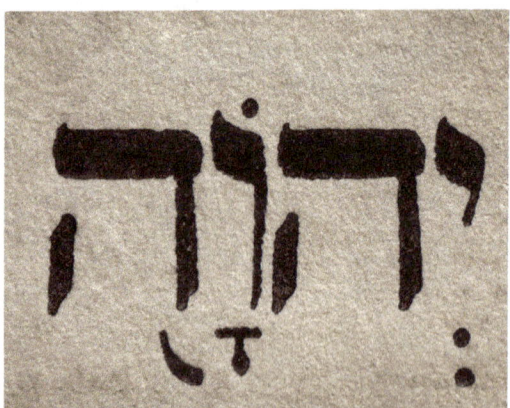

© Shutterstock

Roman Empire shown in Red
(Judaea Province located below Syria)

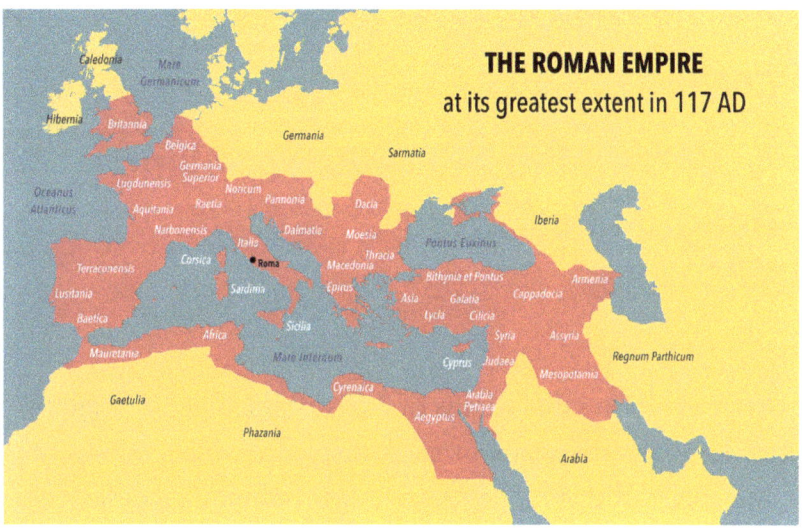

© Shutterstock

Chapter 8

A Who's Who of the Best-Selling Religion Founders

After exploring the origins of a few of the biggest religions in the world in terms of geography, influence, evolution and their followers, there are a few individuals deserving of attention. Four of the greatest religious leaders in history still recognized for starting a religion or quasi religion are Confucius, Buddha, Jesus, and Muhammad. Much has been written about each of them however we have very little information about their lives. You have to wonder if this was by design since it would be hard to think of these men as gods, divine prophets or demigods if we were overly familiar with their lives. Think about it, if we knew too much about their flawed lives as human beings it would take away from their aura, especially if they were bratty children or rebellious teenagers. This is why most of what we know about them is baked in fables and mythology to make them bigger than life. In fact, with the exception of Confucius, we aren't even sure if the lessons and philosophy for which they were attributed actually originated with them, or if they were just given the credit to make them appear God-like. Considering all of the followers of Confucius' philosophy, which number over one billion people, Confucius would rank very high in popularity although most of his followers do not consider Confucianism a religion. In this chapter I will continue to use a critical thinking approach in reviewing a high-level summary of these men's lives. Keep this in mind as I evaluate both the facts and mythology critically while interjecting my own thoughts about why these stories were invented. In the end, this evaluation will give you a more realistic picture of these men's lives. So, what do we know about these men?

Confucius

Let's look at Confucius first as he is considered to be the oldest of these four religious prophets, philosophers, or gods. Buddha could be older but since we are not sure exactly when he was alive, we need to give the oldest award to Confucius. We do know Confucius lived from 551 BCE to 479 BCE and that he died from natural causes at the age of 72. He must have taken good care of himself and was fed properly because this was a long life for the average person at that time. Some ancient Chinese texts describe Confucius as being nine feet six inches tall – a slight exaggeration perhaps? In reality there is absolutely nothing known about his actual physical appearance, but

I'm sure most people are familiar with the visual interpretations created by sketch artists with that iconic Fu Manchu mustache and long, luxurious beard. Of course, Confucius had to have a mustache as he allegedly said, "A man without a mustache is a man without a soul." I'm assuming he did not think women had souls except if they had a mustache, yikes!

Some people consider Confucianism a religion, while most consider it a philosophy. The seven million people that are recognized as following a Confucianism religion, primarily in Asian countries outside of China, consider him a demi-god and they worship him in temples. In total, over one billion people embrace Confucianism philosophy, as it is the official ideology of the Chinese state. However, it never existed in China as an established religion with temples and priests. His teaching initially became the state philosophy of China during the Han Dynasty from 206 BCE to 220 CE. The invention of paper in China during this period (beginning as early as 100 BCE) was also thought to have contributed to the spread of Confucius philosophy.

The thought of people worshiping Confucius would have appalled him, as he did not view himself as a prophet and certainly not a demi-god. Although we know very little about his childhood, we do know he was born in the state of Lu (located in the eastern coastal province Shandong, China). His father was a soldier named Kong (as in King Kong, but no relation). Sadly, Kong died when Confucius was only three years old. As a result, he spent the rest of his childhood in poverty being raised only by his mother. The man we now refer to as Confucius was named Kong Qiu as a child and early adult. Later in his life, people called him Kong Fuzi, which means Grand Master Kong. However, it wasn't until over 2,000 years later that Jesuit missionaries in China during the 1600s CE changed his name to the Latin-based word, Confucius.

Confucius' family was part of a growing middle class of people in China. Even though they were poor, their social status was above common peasants but not part of nobility. In this social class he was educated in schools for commoners where he learned the six arts: archery, mathematics, music, calligraphy, charioting, and ritual. As a result of his education, he was a strong supporter of teaching people to read and write. His social position and education gave Confucius a different outlook on life compared to the majority of people who were poor, uneducated, and illiterate peasants.

Confucius strongly believed ability and strength of character should be how people advanced in society and conversely, incompetent and morally corrupt nobility should lose their titled positions. The American culture also favors achievement versus hereditary titles as a way to improve oneself, consistent with Confucian teachings. Naturally, this achievement-based advancement orientation versus hereditary advancement put Confucius at odds with the ruling class. And yet, he believed in a strong central government authority, which is why the modern-day Chinese government continues to approve of Confucian teachings. The idea of abolishing nobility was way ahead of its time, considering it was not put into practice in a major way globally until the 1790s CE in both France and the United States. It wasn't until after World War 1 when the world finally experienced a significant decline in nobility and aristocracy.

Confucius was married at the age of 19 to a woman with the family name Qiguan and they had one son and two daughters. He worked in many jobs to support his family as a bookkeeper of the Lu granary, a supervisor of the fields, shepherd, cowherd, and clerk. He eventually moved into government, becoming a governor of a small town before working his way up to advisor roles at the top levels of Chinese government. In this capacity he started developing his philosophies. Basically, Confucius functioned as a professional advisor in politics. His coaching intent was to help make rulers great by encouraging hard work and moral decision-making. After many years he left his government job at age 51, either because the rulers did not appreciate his advice or he got frustrated with them for not implementing his recommendations. Apparently, age discrimination existed even thousands of years ago. To continue to be relevant, at this point in his life he traveled around China for the next 14 years teaching his philosophies, along with three disciples. He was searching for a feudal state in China that would utilize his services. As he travelled, he was given much respect and admiration but the people were not readily implementing his philosophies, with the exception of his disciples. On a positive note, his disciples wrote down much of what Confucius had to say during these traveling years and then they helped him get rehired back in Qufu near the end of his life.

Most of what we know about Confucius comes from his disciples' writings, which are called Analects. The Analects are records of his life, organized into 20 sections, which describe his character, behavior, manners, life in exile, and conversations with his disciples and other people. Initially these documents were not organized very well and therefore, it took two to three hundred years of refining to make them usable. In 1973 CE the Chinese actually found an early Analects text in a 55 BCE gravesite. These writings are thought to be fairly accurate as the text they found was written on bamboo strips that corresponded with the contemporary standard writing material in existence around 500 BCE. In addition to the Analects, Confucius worked on transmitting his wisdom by writing various other texts with his disciple's assistance, including the Five Classics (The Book of Changes, The Book of History, The Book of Poetry, The Book of Rites, and The Spring and Autumn Annals). These classics are often described in terms of five visions: metaphysical, political, poetic, social, and historical.

Confucius was a very honest and humble person. He never claimed to be an original thinker and gave credit to the sources for some of his philosophies. He is quoted as saying, "I transmit but do not innovate, I love antiquity and have faith in it." According to Confucius, the inspiration for his moral thinking came from the Zhou dynasty 200 years before he was born. He obtained this knowledge from reading the speeches these rulers and counselors gave on how to guide moral decision-making.

Although Confucius claims to have obtained much knowledge from others that came before him, he is still credited with providing some of the earliest records on philosophies that continue to be followed today. The most famous was his Golden Rule: "Do not impose on others what you do not want others to impose on you", (Analects 15:24). If you are a believer in Christianity then you will most likely be thinking that Jesus invented this rule. It certainly sounds a lot like Jesus' Golden Rule: "Do unto others as you would like others to do unto you" (gospel of Matthew 7:12). It's a good rule but not original to Jesus as Confucius came up with the Golden Rule almost 500 years before Jesus was even born. Of course, Jesus expressed it using slightly different words than Confucius – perhaps that's why it was thought of as "original". But the main difference between these two phrases is that Confucius prioritized the other persons' needs first rather than oneself by stating the rule in the negative. By contrast, the Christian Golden Rule is self-centered since it is dependent on what kind of person I am. The bottom line is that one of the core maxims claimed by the Christian religion, the Golden Rule was invented 500 years before this religion even existed.

Overall, Confucius was a big believer in being humane

to others, which in the world is still a work-in-progress. He was a very practical person and taught that we should be humane and thoughtful, motivated solely by the desire to do good rather than for personal profit. He believed in honoring one's ancestors and showing respect for age and authority but not necessarily requiring agreement. Confucius was not a god or prophet but a very influential person dispensing excellent advice. Perhaps with the exception of how he viewed women as subservient to men, as he definitely was not progressive regarding gender equality. This treatment of women reflected the prejudice of this time period, which was common in most ancient religions. In general, his quotes were very enlightened and by reading them you can understand why Confucius' philosophy and advice continues to be such a popular influence - even 2,500 years later.

Buddha

According to Buddhism scriptures, there are many Buddhas in the history of the world. The Buddha described in this chapter was either the fourth, the seventh, or the twenty-fifth one to live - the next one will be called Maitreya, who will show up when everyone forgets about the current Buddha. Really?

The historic Buddha we currently refer to as Buddha Gautama, is thought to have lived sometime between 600 BCE to 300 BCE. He was born in the Lumbini Province, in southern Nepal, which was originally considered the northern India civilization. Buddha was not his birth name as this word means the "enlightened one." Being enlightened indicates you have awakened from the sleep of ignorance and achieved freedom from suffering. Becoming enlightened seems like a noble goal for everyone in the world. Although Buddha Gautama has many names, he is often referred to as Shakyamuni, which communicates he was the sage of the Shakya clan. Thanks to those tacky souvenir statues, we often wrongly think of Buddha as a smiling, obese, bald-headed man sitting cross-legged and wearing an open robe that shows his enormous belly. Actually, with the help of historical texts he was described as being six feet tall, good looking, with dark hair and blue eyes. More accurate images still show him sitting yoga-style in a lotus position, but much thinner with tightly curled hair and a topknot.

As with other religions, the legends or mythology about Buddha are incredible in an obvious effort to make him larger than life. Although Buddha (the Shakyamuni guy) is credited for the scripture current Buddhists follow, it's not known who actually wrote them but it wasn't Buddha. However, it appears he and his monks invented this religion with a combination of some Vedic and some Hindu beliefs. Similar to other religions it was not documented until hundreds of years later, so we really don't know if it came from Shakyamuni himself or if the mythology was created later.

Basically, all the stories about the different Buddhas' lives begin before birth and extend beyond death. Each Buddha lives millions of lives trying to achieve Buddhahood which is when he passes into nirvana, or said another way, reaches a state of being with the absence of suffering. There are many legends about Buddha Gautama's last earthly life but the following one is the most popular.

In this popular version, Buddha began his life as the son of a king even though his mother conceived him through immaculate conception in a dream with a white elephant. He then was birthed ten lunar months later from under his mother's right arm. Whoever envisioned this scene must have decided that giving birth the conventional way was somehow not appropriate for a Buddha and decided coming out of an arm pit was more palatable. Sounds like the people who wrote this would have been members of the St Augustine anti-woman's anatomy club, more on that in a later chapter. Continuing with the story, Buddha plopped out of his mother's armpit and immediately started talking and walking around. Walking and talking at birth – incredible! He informed everyone this would be his last lifetime on earth and while he was walking around talking to everyone lotus flower blossoms sprang up from his every step.

If this scene wasn't already loaded with fantastic special effects happening, the King gathered his astrologers together to predict the Buddha's future. This story does not address why they didn't just ask him, you know, since he could talk and knew he was Buddha. When the astrologers got together, seven of them were unsure if this child would be a universal king or a Buddha, but one astrologer was absolutely sure the walking, talking infant would be Buddha. Buddha's mother died seven days later (which is so sad) and he was then raised by his mother's sister. As an observation, there seems to be a logic issue with the part of the story where the King questioned if this child was Buddha or a universal king – remember, the concept of Buddha did not even exist until after Shakyamuni (Buddha) founded the Buddhism religion. So how can you predict a person is a Buddha before anyone knew there was such a person as a Buddha? Hmmm. What a minute, I forgot that in the realm of religion anything could be written as long as it was justified as divine.

Did you happen to notice the repeated use of the number seven - the reference to seven astrologers and his mom's death after seven days? Even the Lotus flower on Buddha's pedestal has seven petals. The number seven was likely chosen because it was the most used number in Hinduism and was recognized as a spiritual and sacred number representing both divine concepts and philosophies. Seven appears universally in our everyday world as well, with the number of days in a week, colors in a rainbow, chakras, etc. One thing is certain, whoever wrote this story was partial to the number seven. Oh, and the number one as well. It was significant that only one astrologer recognized the child as Buddha. The number one was associated with

Brahma, the one true god in Hinduism who is the creator and all-knowing. So, the number one is considered to be the all-knowing number. It seems the people who wrote religious mythology and legends insert as much symbolism as possible into their stories to make them seem more credible and awe inspiring.

The story continued with Buddha living an opulent life as a Prince. His father, the King, shielded Buddha from seeing or experiencing any suffering whatsoever. At the age of 16 he married a beautiful Princess named Yashodhara, although he also had 40,000 beautiful woman attendants. He really enjoyed the good life until he turned 29 when his life totally changed. Could this be where the phrase you're not 29 anymore came from? At age 29 he left the palace and for the first time in his life, observed people who were suffering from being poor, sick, and old. Feeling distraught, he wanted to search for a way to help people overcome their suffering and also stop them from being reincarnated into these same conditions over and over. I find this part of the story very compassionate, portraying Buddha as a kind and caring human being/demi-god.

However, seven days before he left the palace on his search, he was informed his wife had given birth to a son. I find it odd that he was not aware his wife was pregnant and due any minute, but I guess with 40,000 women taking care of him, this sort of detail might have been easy to miss. Before he left, he named the baby Rahula, which means, "fetter." Okay, a little ironic since a fetter is a chain or manacle used to restrain a prisoner. Despite having a newborn, it did not stop Buddha from leaving the palace to pursue his very important mission of finding a way to end suffering and establish a new religion called Buddhism. I guess you could say he broke free of the Fetter, which was so unfortunate for his son and wife.

Fast-forward six years and Buddha was meditating to free himself from being controlled by the evil god, Mara, the god of desire or craving. This god does sound evil and is probably the reason you crave chocolate, ice cream, pizza, and nachos. I don't think they had these foods in 600 BCE to 300 BCE, but Mara must have evolved into the 21st century to taunt us with these cravings. So, you're probably wondering why Buddha waited six years and not seven years to free himself from Mara, since we know numbers are symbolic in religious stories. Well, it turns out six is also an important number and its significance is actually very beautiful. In Hinduism, the number six represents unconditional love and the ability to support, nurture, and heal. When associated with a person, their role is to use their heart and soul to be of service to others. Mara did not know about the number six - perhaps this was his downfall.

As Buddha was meditating, Mara attacked him with everything he could think of. He attacked with wind, rain, rocks, weapons, hot coals, burning ashes, sand, mud, the kitchen sink, and darkness. Okay, I added the kitchen sink just to see if you were paying attention. To fight back,

Buddha meditated on love and all these things magically turned into a shower of soft, sweet smelling, blossoms. This of course made Mara really angry and so he sent his three beautiful daughters: Lust, Thirst, and Discontent. This didn't work either. Of course it wouldn't work, since Buddha already had a wife and 40,000 women attendants. So, he easily walked away as there was no way these three daughters were going to be able to tempt him.

Now even angrier, Mara told Buddha he couldn't sit there anymore because that was his seat. Buddha then said the famous line "on your feet lose your seat", which has stood the test of time and is respected by people worldwide as truth. Not really! What Buddha did was he touched the earth with his right hand and the earth goddess said, "Buddha can sit here under this tree". Mara then left in a huff! Later that night after Mara left, Buddha kept meditating and he officially became Buddha, "the enlightened one". It sure seems like the Christian writers used the same plot line with Jesus being tempted in the desert by the devil. Jesus wins this temptation and proves he is God by beating the devil. The main difference was Buddha was not made a God whereas Jesus was made God, despite the Buddha story having more compelling details and a better devil battle scene than Jesus' story.

Buddha hung around the tree for seven weeks after being enlightened and then the God Brahma came down from heaven and asked him to teach humans for the rest of his life on earth. Accordingly, the rest of Buddha's life on earth was spent teaching and founding Buddhism. He had many monk followers or disciples and also coached some of them to become arhats. An arhat is enlightened, much the same as a Buddha, except that a teacher guides the arhat, whereas the Buddha becomes enlightened on his own. Women can be an arhat, as Buddha's wife Yashodhara became one. However, a woman can never be a Buddha, as she would need to be reincarnated as a man to achieve this status. Being born female is considered bad karma. So much for equal rights back in the 600 BCE to 300 BCE time period. During Buddha's older years, Buddhism became popular and he had groups of monks and nuns teaching Buddhism.

When Buddha reached 80 years' old, he told Ananda, his attendant and one of his main disciples, on three separate occasions that if Ananda would make the request, a Buddha could extend his life span for eternity. However, the god Mara appeared and reminded Buddha that he had agreed that when his teaching was complete, he would pass away in three months into nirvana. Buddha agreed with Mara and then the earth quakes. Ananda then asked why they were having an earthquake and Buddha told him there were eight reasons for earthquakes, one of them being when a Buddha decides to leave this world. Ananda begged him to stay but Buddha said it was too late – Ananda should have requested him to stay before he made the promise to Mara, as he could have stayed for eternity. I am assuming the moral of this story is we must learn to take a hint, or pay attention.

In another similar storyline, the Christian writers also had an earthquake happen when Jesus died on the cross, similar to the Buddha story. However, the Christians improved their story to be more spectacular than Buddha's by including darkness coming over the land in the afternoon, and the temple door curtain ripping in two along with the earthquake.

The end of Buddha's life story used several references to the number three - three occasions and three months. It seems both Hindu and Christian writers also liked the number three. In Hindu, three represents the divine trinity that includes Brahma, the creator, Vishnu, the preserver, and Shiva, the destroyer and Christianity has the holy trinity of God the Father, Jesus Christ, and the Holy Spirit. Three also represents all things: the beginning, middle, and end. It represents heaven, earth, and water; body, mind, and spirit; past, present, and future. These religions considered the number three to be a perfect number and liked to use it in the stories they wrote, to give them more significance and mysticism.

Not unlike other religions, Buddhism continued verbally for a very long time (300 to 500 years) after Buddha left the physical world without being written. The first Buddhism texts were written on palm leaves during 29 BCE in Sri Lanka. In addition, no pictures of Buddha exist and we have very little information on his life as most of what we know is based on verbally passed on legends or fables. We do know he lived, was a prince, got married, had a son, and taught the beginnings of Buddhist thinking, but the rest of the stories were most likely created by people's imaginations. Once again, I find it incredible that someone who supposedly lived millions of lives and reached the pinnacle of spiritual thought and meditation skill, did not write or could not write anything down.

Although Buddha founded Buddhism, the person responsible for expanding this religion was Ashoka the Great (265 BCE to 238 BCE) who became the emperor of most of what is present-day India. He spread Buddha's teachings in India after feeling devastated from witnessing the killing and destruction he caused when he conquered a region of India. He also sent missionaries to Sri Lanka, China, Korea, and Thailand. Without his support, Buddhism would have most likely died out.

In the 600 CE time period, some Chinese Buddhists gave Buddhism a boost in popularity when they traveled to India, translated the Buddhist texts into Chinese and took them back to China. In 868 CE these texts were then printed on paper and distributed in China and began growing this religion even more. As a result, Buddhism definitely had a good head start on Christianity since it took another 587 years before the Christian Gutenberg Bible was printed on paper in 1455 CE.

Jesus

As with Buddha, we know Jesus was a real person but know

very little about his life. And also similar to Buddha, much of what we know was written hundreds of years after he died from stories that were told verbally by his disciples and followers. By contrast, Confucius could read and write and had disciples who were able to write things down while he was alive. We do not know if either Buddha or Jesus were literate and there is no indication that they were educated men. There are also no records of anything Buddha or Jesus wrote. You would think that as the founder of a religion and a god-like person, you would have written some of your instructions for people to follow.

The Jesus image commonly seen is the one portrayed in Western cultures, with fair skin, long wavy brown hair and a neatly trimmed beard. And always wearing a flowing robe and trendy strappy leather sandals. But based on archeological and historical evidence, it is more likely that his skin was a darker hue, with dark hair that was woolly in texture. It is speculated that he was likely to be a little over five feet tall, which was typical for a Jewish male during his time period.

Jesus' life is full of myths, legends and contradictions. He was born sometime between 6 BCE and 4 BCE before the death of Herod the Great and he purportedly died in his 30s sometime between 29 CE and 33 CE. He went by many names; during his childhood he was known as Jesus, son of Joseph, later he was called Jesus the Nazarene, Jesus of Galilee, Rabbi, and then Jesus the Messiah or Jesus the Christ. The word "messiah" just meant an anointed king or the anointed one - it did not refer to a god. The Greek word for Messiah is Christ and was not a new title or uniquely associated with Jesus. When David, from the house of Judah, was made king, he was called Messiah or Christ and so was every king after David. In fact, even during the Roman occupation of Judea, the appointed high priest was known as Priest Messiah or Priest Christ.

As mentioned, Jesus did not write anything down about his life, so most of what we know is from gospels written after the Jewish uprising of 66 CE to 70 CE when thousands of Jewish people were killed by crucifixion for rebellion and their temple was destroyed by the Romans. Tension between the Romans and the Jews continued so this situation shaped the writing of these gospels about Jesus. In order for the documents and Jesus' teachings to survive and be accepted, these stories needed to be pro Roman and show them to be guilt free of Jesus' death. In addition, the actual New Testament bible was not put together until the late 300s CE – it was clerics and their rulers who ultimately decided what to include and what to omit. It was an arbitrary selective process, as most of what was written before this time period had been destroyed.

What we know from these writings was often contradictory, incomplete, and mythical. We know that Jesus' mother was called Mary and his father was Joseph. Jesus was born in Bethlehem, but one story has him born poor in a manger, while another describes him born wealthy in a house. The most popular story told today is the version having him born poor in a manger and visited by shepherds and kings. The alternative wealthy story has kings coming to visit Jesus at his house. Also, there is a disputed story of a pregnant Mary and Joseph traveling from Nazareth to Bethlehem for a census, however historical records do not support a census happening. Therefore, in all likelihood they had always been living in Bethlehem, so the riding on the donkey trip, although it paints a romantic story, is seemingly a myth.

Most likely the affluent house story is the more plausible one, as Jesus was thought to be the legitimate king of the Jewish people as a descendant from King David via Solomon and then Joseph. Apparently, the kings did not know about the immaculate conception of Mary, as this element of the story was not asserted until later after Jesus' death. Rather the kings had assumed Joseph was the father. Even the gospels reference Jesus' ancestry as going through Joseph. This storyline sure implies Joseph was his biological father. It is doubtful Jesus was the son of a poor carpenter, as kings would only have come to visit a potential newborn king. As a result of being a potential future king, the new family fled into Egypt to evade Jesus being killed by Herod the Great. This specific element of the story evidently is based on historical facts.

If you ever wondered why Herod had male infants killed in Bethlehem, the simplest answer was because he was mentally unstable. He suffered from arteriosclerosis, which caused him great physical pain and mental instability. He was also extremely paranoid of people trying to overthrow him. This was due to many factors including the mental impact of his disease, being deceived by family members, being the target of several revolts, and losing the confidence in his leadership abilities by the Roman Emperor Augustus. As a result, Herod had family members killed, changed his will several times, and even had his first-born son, Antipater, killed. When Herod was told a new future king was born in Bethlehem, he ordered the killing of all males under two years of age in that area to stop any potential future uprising. Shortly after doing this, he unsuccessfully committed suicide but then died anyway soon after this failed attempt. Once Herod died in 4 BCE, Jesus and his family returned from Egypt to live in the town of Nazareth.

We know almost nothing about Jesus' adolescent and teenage years. We don't know if he was educated and literate and nothing has been discovered having been written by him. We also do not know if Jesus was married but it is highly probable that he was since according to Judaic custom at the time, it would be mandatory for a man to be married at his age. In fact, celibacy was condemned and therefore, if Jesus had been celibate, no one would have followed him as it would have certainly caused controversy. He was also called "Rabbi" which is a self-appointed teacher; under Jewish Mishnaic Law, "an unmarried man may not be a teacher". These facts would indicate that he was both married and most likely had children, especially since he lived into his mid to late thirties.

It is also feasible the wedding story at Cana may have been Jesus' wedding. It doesn't make sense for him and his mother Mary, to be in charge of the wine at someone else's wedding, or have them manage the servants. Moreover, Jesus and his family had to be wealthy to even be in attendance at this wedding as it was an aristocratic affair. This wedding was extravagant for the time period as it had several hundred guests, many servants, and a master of ceremonies (similar to a chief butler). Furthermore, there was an enormous amount of wine. Jesus miraculously or mythically transformed six hundred liters of water into wine. This is equivalent to 800 bottles (750ml) of wine or four bottles per person – this supposedly happened after they had already consumed a fair amount of wine. This was a serious party! There is no way a poor carpenter family would have attended or hosted this kind of a celebration indicating Mary, Joseph, and Jesus were probably members of the aristocratic caste. In all likelihood, they had money!

There was also a good possibility Jesus could have been the universal king of the Jews as this title was used in many of the gospels. As a member of the tribe of David, if Jesus married Mary Magdalen, who was a member of the tribe of Benjamin, this would have united the Jewish people. This marriage would also have created a serious political threat to the Romans as Jesus was in a position to unify his country, mobilize the people to support him, drive out the Roman oppressors, and restore the monarchy as it was under Solomon. If Jesus did have a legitimate claim on the

Jewish throne, it was initially only supported by a small group. This is why to increase his following; he began to preach a message offering hope to the poor and oppressed. He was attempting to unite his people in a common cause that was both ethical and political.

It is unclear which Jewish group Jesus was associated with, as there were many and he may have been able to straddle several of them. What we do know is Jesus' lifetime spanned the first 35 years of the turmoil between Roman and Jewish people that lasted for 140 years. The Jewish people were not united during this time period. As a reminder the three biggest Jewish groups during the time of Jesus included the Sadducees, the Pharisees, and the Essenes. In 6 CE when Rome took over direct control of Judea, a Pharisee rabbi known as Judas of Galilee, created a highly militant revolutionary group of Pharisees and Essenes. Although Judas of Galilee was killed in 6 CE by the Romans, people with the same thinking continued to assemble and eventually became known as Zealots. These people were very much a part of the political situation during most of Jesus' life and they continued their activities after his death until they organized a massive revolt against Roman rule of Judea in 66 CE.

There was a good chance Jesus took part in this movement. He most likely belonged to either the Pharisee or Essene groups as many of his philosophies and teachings were not original and could be traced to both groups. For example, his healing skills definitely came from the Essene sect. We also know he was charismatic and had skill at teaching people through parables. We're not sure what his personality was like as he is often described as meek and lamblike, as well as powerful and majestic. During Jesus' lifetime, the people were looking for a "lost king" descendant of the house of David to free them from the Roman occupation. Anticipation of this person was at a near mass hysteria level that continued even after Jesus' death.

As to Jesus' death, he was undoubtedly killed for crimes against the Roman Empire. If it were for crimes against Judaism, he would instead have been stoned to death. Also, it was unlikely someone as ruthless as Pontius Pilate (Procurator of Judea) would order the killing of Jesus solely because of pressure from a Jewish mob. Although the gospels claim Jesus was not a political person, he must have been organizing a rebellion against the Roman occupation of Judaea since punishment by crucifixion was used only for crimes against the Roman Empire. Even during that time period, they did not kill people without a reason or merely for being disliked by someone or a group of people. As a reminder, the gospels had to make sure Jesus was portrayed as friendly to the Romans so these teachings and this new religion would be accepted by the Roman people and ruling class. This is why the Jewish people were made to be the scapegoats for Jesus' death, however the reason they invented for the Jewish hatred of Jesus was extremely vague and also a very weak argument. The bible story says the Jewish people accused Jesus of blasphemy or disrespecting god or sacred things, which were really weak arguments for capital punishment when you consider the Jewish people had been living among Roman gentiles who believed in a polytheistic religion for hundreds of years.

Christianity did not grow strongly until the Roman Empire made it the official religion in the late 380s CE. Thereafter, this religion spread throughout the Empire. Many of the tribes such as the Goths, Vandals, Franks, and Huns that bordered along the Roman Empire wanted to be like Romans and so with the help of missionaries, they were convinced to adopt Christianity. This further increased the popularity of this religion providing a strong base for growth. Similar to other religions, it promoted that the belief in Jesus Christ was the only way you could get to heaven, as all other non-believers were destined for hell. Obviously a very powerful message, especially for the illiterate, uneducated masses.

Muhammad

Our final religious founder was the Prophet Muhammad. He was born in 570 CE in Mecca, Arabia (now Saudi Arabia) and died June 8, 632 CE in Medina. Compared to Jesus, we know a little more about his life due to historical records of military battles in which he fought. However, similar to the other one-man religious founders, there is very little biographical information available and most of it is not included in the Quran. Much of what was written about Prophet Muhammad's life was completed hundreds of years after his death. Once again, similar to the other founders, Muhammad wrote nothing himself about his religious beliefs or his life and thus we are not sure he was literate.

I can't recall ever seeing an image of Muhammad and so I'm at a loss for words as to how to give any description about his physical appearance. Research on the subject didn't get me any further as the Quran prohibits or strongly frowns upon visual images of the Prophet. But here's the best I was able to find – he was average. Not too tall and not too short. Skin was fair, not very white and not dark. His hair was not very curly and not too straight. Quite the average mystery figure!

The first book about Prophet Muhammad, written in the mid to late 700s CE by a person named Muhammad ibn Ishaq, is primarily about his military expeditions. Other various versions of the Prophet's life were written in the eighth and ninth centuries and even later. One of the things that was obvious about the intent of these writers was they wanted to portray the Prophet Muhammad as being better and more magnificent than the previous other religious founders or leaders. To accomplish this, they incorporated supernatural stories into Muhammad's life; some stories being similar to other notable religious founders and some that were original. For instance, one story had Muhammad's father almost killed and sacrificed to God by his grandfather, similar to Abraham almost killing and sacrificing

Isaac to God as written in the Hebrew Bible or Christian Old Testament. They also wrote about Muhammad being born as a result of immaculate conception, having divine markings on his body to be recognized by other religious people, communicating interactively with angels and God, traveling magically through space and time, talking with Jesus, Abraham, Mary, and others, and having angels help him win battles against non-believers. Even though much of the biographical information on him is fabled or mythical, some of it is historically accurate.

Muhammad was born in 570 CE in Mecca, the same year Abraha unsuccessfully attacked Mecca with elephants. Abraha was a Christian viceroy for the Saba Empire centered in Ethiopia at this time period. Muhammad's early life must have been tough, which most likely influenced his outlook on life, as warfare was vital to the culture since the threat of being conquered was always a possibility. In addition, he experienced many tragic events in his early life. His father died before he was born, his mother died when he was age six, his grandfather, who was raising him, died when he was age eight, and he then went to live with his uncle Abu Talib. This last change in his living arrangement was positive, as Abu Talib was the leader of the Hashim clan, which was part of the Quraysh mercantile Arab tribe that controlled Mecca. As a result, Muhammad gained status from this association.

At age 25, Muhammad was employed as a merchant by a wealthy woman named Khadijah, selling goods to

Syrian towns. He married Khadijah even though she was 40 years old - hopefully they were able to ignore the cougar jokes from their friends. They got to work quickly after the marriage and had two sons, who sadly died, and four daughters who did survive.

His career as the prophet of Islam did not start until he was 40 years old. This is when the trouble started since he was at odds with the religious beliefs and practices of the ruling tribe in Mecca called Quraysh. He and his followers were fanatical about only accepting Allah as the true god and denounced all other gods. The Quraysh people couldn't accept the constant criticism and so they banished Muhammad and his followers from Mecca and wouldn't associate with them anymore.

Muhammad then took his entourage to Ethiopia, as they were a very tolerant people. Ethiopia at this time was primarily Christian, but accepted people practicing other religions. They did not know Muhammad was not tolerant of any other religions but he must have restrained his rhetoric in Ethiopia because he lived there peacefully for five or more years. Nevertheless, over time, the people of Mecca must have forgotten why they didn't like Muhammad's attitude and teachings and he subsequently was able to return there with his followers.

However, in 619 CE life changed dramatically as Muhammad's uncle died and the new leader of the Hashim clan stopped his protection of Muhammad and his followers. To make matters even worse, Muhammad's wife died about the same time. As life in Mecca got more difficult, Muhammad focused on convincing the people of Medina to protect and support him. In 622 CE he moved with his followers to Medina and was accepted by the people living there, including the Jewish tribes.

Once living in Medina, Muhammad was able to build an army and use it to attack and rob Meccan trade caravans to provide for his relocated community. Everyone who was a believer in Muhammad's messages and teaching became part of his community, benefiting from his fortunes. He was very skilled at using his belief system, coupled with forming alliances with clans and tribes, to expand his empire. He connected the material success he provided and nurtured as proof of divine favor from God, which encouraged loyalty and solidified his followers' belief in his message. This approach was not new as the Israelite leaders, leveraging their Judaism beliefs and culture, had used these same tactics successfully on their people. The true Muhammad believers were heavily rewarded, thus inspiring others to follow. This could be compared to the current day pyramid scheme approach to gaining wealth. He would have been an awesome Amway salesman! As he continued to build his army of believers, he caused friction with the Jewish population by forcing everyone to face toward Mecca for prayers instead of Jerusalem, and he began to exile Jewish people who were non-believers. Who didn't see this coming?

Muhammad was also able to build alliances with neighboring tribes through his expert tribal relationship skills, along with sharing his war spoils and caravan raiding fortunes. To strengthen his empire even further he used marriage for himself and his key followers to unite tribes and strengthen his influence. After his first wife died, Muhammad married another 11 wives for various reasons over the remainder of his life. In addition to annexing tribes, other reasons he married were to spread his beliefs to other clans and for compassionate reasons. Aisha, the daughter of Muhammad's best friend Abu Bakr, was the one wife he married for love at the age of 53, while she was only age 10. Apparently, she did not have a problem with the age difference and since Muhammad was both the military general and the moral leader of the Muslims, no one dared ask him if he thought she was a little too young for him. Regardless of the age difference, she proved to be very intelligent and continued to spread Muhammad's message for another 44 years after his death. All of his other wives were widows, divorcees, or captives. According to legend, Muhammad kept all of these women happy at the same time, so in addition to being a famous prophet, he was also quite the lady's man. All the women happy at the same time? I find this part of the story to be even more unbelievable than his supernatural visions and encounters.

When the Meccan people tired of Muhammad and his army attacking and robing their caravans, they retaliated by attacking Medina unsuccessfully in 625 CE. Muhammad's army of believers continued to get stronger and he led a three-pronged campaign against non-supporters in Medina, the Quraysh tribe in Mecca (even though he technically was a member of this tribe), and against surrounding tribes even in southern Syria. In 627 CE the Meccan army attacked him again and he defeated them for the second time. When the remaining Jewish people in Medina would not help him in this battle against Mecca, he had all the men murdered and he enslaved all the women and children. I guess he forgot these people were the ones who gave him a place to live when Mecca threw him out.

In 630 CE, Muhammad and his powerful army marched into Mecca and overtook the town. He then continued to overtake other towns in Arabia and Syria building his empire through war. He died in June 632 CE in Medina shortly after returning from another trip to Mecca. This trip to Mecca is now celebrated as the last pilgrimage of Muhammad. Unfortunately, Muhammad must not have realized he was old and at risk of dying, as he made no arrangements for his succession. This is why it is advisable for everyone to make sure they have a will. This forced the leaders of Muhammad's empire to elect Abu Bakr, best friend and father-in-law of Muhammad, and father of Aisha, as caliph and ruler of the Islamic community. Fast-forward to today, and the Sunni Muslims continue to believe in this election approach to leadership. However, the Shite Muslims prefer the royalty approach and believe the leaders should all be royal descendants from Muhammad. The leaders wanted Ali to be caliph since he was Muhammad's cousin and son-in-law by being married to Muhammad's daughter, Fatimah. The one thing the Sunni's and Shite's have in common is they did not respect woman at all since neither group even considered making Aisha or Fatimah the caliph.

The Islam community spread quickly after Muhammad's death through warfare and a focus on missionaries spreading the message. During this growth period, the dominating Islam community was tolerant of religions such as Christianity, Judaism, Zoroastrianism, Hinduism, and Buddhism, as long as these people paid a tax for protection. This worked well for a hundred years, but the practice over time made the non-Muslim people socially and legally inferior, which caused extreme inequality and subsequent suffering. The belief that all Muslims go to heaven, while infidels and non-Muslims are destined for hell, is still prevalent even today and is similar to the beliefs of other religions.

Confucius, Buddha, Jesus, and Muhammad are all considered to be among the greatest religious leaders in history. At the beginning of the chapter, I had posed the question, what do we know about these men? Other than they were very influential as founders of the largest current day religions – it's now apparent we know very little about them that is historically factual and verifiable. What we read about them was written many, many years after they lived, filled with stories, fables and mythology to make them bigger than life. It is implausible to even think this stuff was invented or inspired by a god, since it is very apparent how their stories originated. However, not all of it should be discarded, as included in all these religions are some good teachings and powerful life lessons. They just need to be carefully identified and selected with critical thinking. Much of what was written thousands of years ago reflects the prejudices of that time period, a high level of acceptable cruelty, limited scientific knowledge, and the constant need to establish a power base through warfare. Oh, and lest we forget, they were based on the telling and retelling of accounts over the period of many, many generations before anything was written. Verifiable and filled with actual facts? No. Just really compelling supernatural stories

Chapter 9

I Talked to God, and He Said to Tell You...

It's been quite a journey from those early ancient religions led by the "big man" to the founding and evolution of today's largest religions in the world. So here we are today, with billions of people believing in some sort of God – this can hardly be considered a marginal condition. No, with billions of believers, this is definitely a mainstream phenomenon. People believe in supreme beings, in angels, in spirits and ghosts. They believe in the soul and karma. In a heaven and reincarnation. They pray and carry good-luck charms. They worship, light candles, and sing. In this and the next several chapters we'll explore some familiar spiritual world beliefs, including their origins, reasoning, adaptation, and similarities or dissimilarities across religions.

The important thing to keep in mind about spiritual world beliefs, is no one can claim with certainty their spiritual beliefs are right. But by the same token, no one can tell you yours are wrong either. One thing is certain

- no one has ever been able to prove spiritual beliefs or support them with facts. We only know these beliefs have been invented over time. It's true, spiritual beliefs seem to offer some help for people coping with life and death, which is a positive reason for holding onto them. But even with the best of intentions, no one should ever insist they know their beliefs in the spiritual world to be right or even real and then force these beliefs onto others. In my opinion, spiritual beliefs causing pain and suffering to ourselves and others shouldn't have a place in our society and should be abandoned. After all, these beliefs have merely been invented and perpetuated in our minds.

Yes, that's the essence of spiritual beliefs – they're all in our hearts and minds. Based on something we were taught, saw or heard, we choose to simply believe. But one of the things I found very suspicious about many of the well-known spiritual world beliefs was where and how they originated. Many beliefs were established by religious people deemed to be gods, demi-gods, prophets, and saints, through direct communication verbally or visually with other gods or angels. It sure seems suspicious that they all were always alone during the experience – there was never anyone else around. This communication always took place while they were alone in some remote location and then they later told people about their experience. The other thing that is suspicious is these people never documented their experience by writing anything down, but instead only verbally told other people. Don't you think it absurd that these gods, or prophets supposedly chosen by god, were not able to or decided not to write anything down? Not only do we not have anything they wrote, but we also are not sure any of them were literate. I would hope at a minimum God would be literate, or someone who was handpicked by God to be the earthly representative on earth would be able to write down these valuable messages.

In today's world, someone claiming to see or speak directly to gods, angels or deceased famous people would be perceived as suffering from mental illness. We would not believe these stories if people said they experienced them today, yet we believe the accounts from thousands of years ago. It's doubtful these people from long ago had any special connection to supernatural experiences versus people living now. This is an example of thinking critically about fantastic, magical stories from the past that were portrayed as real by religious and political leaders. And, just because people believed things from ancient times doesn't make those beliefs accurate, correct or even real, it just means they were really old beliefs that were not challenged. When you look at these stories from a critical perspective, you suddenly realize how absurd these stories are at the point of being humorous if not for what they achieved. These stories were very effective at dividing people into groups or tribes insuring them that their heredity and beliefs were superior to all the other groups of non-believers. They also were used to achieve loyalty and control since the people were told they would be rewarded in heaven as long as they followed and believed in the fantasy stories created by their leaders. I find the power of this strategy incredible to have lasted thousands of years.

It is noteworthy how prevalent the direct-to-God encounters are in the foundation of religious dogma. It is also amazing we are taught to believe these stories to be categorically true. Here are just a few examples, although there are hundreds of these encounters across all religions.

The earliest available writing we have related to supernatural encounters is from ancient Mesopotamia in a poem called "Epic of Gilgamesh", which was written around 1800 BCE in the Sumerian language. According to the people's beliefs at that time, Gilgamesh was thought to be part divine and part human. The real Gilgamesh was a young ruler of the Mesopotamian city-state Uruk, sometime between 2800 BCE and 2500 BCE. He was a great builder, a warrior, and knowledgeable of all things on land and sea, according to the writings. However, he forced his subjects to work too hard and so they prayed to the gods for help to get Gilgamesh to ease up a little.

As described in Gilgamesh's story, he began interacting with many gods and goddesses who were directing his actions. No one at this time period even questioned Gilgamesh's claims that he was best of friends with these gods, seeing and talking with them regularly. Remember, during this time period, leaders had significant power over their subjects. In one of Gilgamesh's adventures, directed by God of course, his friend Enkidu died. Gilgamesh became terrified of his own inevitable death and began searching for eternal life. In this search, he met up with a couple, Utnapishtim and his wife. These two people are significant because they had built a great boat at the request of the gods. In the great Babylonian flood, the couple became the only human survivors and were credited with saving all the animals. To give you an idea of the geographical area where these stories came from, Babylonia was located along the Euphrates River in Iraq about 94 kilometers (58 miles) south of current day Baghdad and Uruk was a little further south about 250 kilometers (155 miles) of Baghdad. It makes sense they would have flood stories along this river as it still floods today, primarily in the spring.

Following the flood, as a reward, the god Enlil made Utnapishtim and his wife gods, giving them eternal life. Gilgamesh met up with the immortal Utnapishtim and his wife asking them to bestow eternal life on him as well, but they could not give it to him. However, they told him where a plant was located that would make him a child again or youthful. Gilgamesh followed their directions and found the plant, but on his way back home he became hot and went for a swim. While he was in the water, a snake came out of a hole and ate his plant. As a result, Gilgamesh returned to his home in Uruk as a mortal man without the plant, and concluded that eternal life was beyond human grasp.

Gilgamesh's story must have been liked so much as some of the poem was mimicked in the Hebrew Bible. For example, Noah (easier to pronounce than Utnapishtim) was instructed by God to also build a great boat called an ark. The Hebrew Bible has essentially the same story, although with a few twists - Noah and his wife were not made into gods. However, Noah is considered to be the originator of vineyard cultivation, so if you like wine as I do, you may consider him God-like or maybe a demi-god.

Another part of the Gilgamesh's story surely sounds similar to the Adam and Eve story, although with a little different approach as to who ate the fruit or plant. In the Adam and Eve story, they were the ones who ate the forbidden fruit in their pursuit of making them immortal or Gods, instead of the serpent eating the plant in the Gilgamesh story. However, even though Adam and Eve ate the fruit, they weren't able to achieve their goals either since they were banished from the Garden of Eden and had to remain as mortal human beings similar to Gilgamesh. This story along with the Noah story reinforced the Judaism belief there is and can only be one God. In their adaptation of the Gilgamesh story, Adam and Eve and Noah could not become immortal gods since the early writers of the Judaism religion remained adamant there was only one God. This is why the followers of Judaism were called the one god people during their early years since most people at this time believed in many gods. The founders of Judaism also decided they were the chosen people of their one God, Yahweh, naturally since they sort of invented him or at least in their minds made improvements to the Zoroastrian one God idea.

They were confident they were right and everyone else believing in more gods was wrong.

The Abraham bible story is another influential story coming out of Mesopotamia about the same time period regarding communications with supernatural angels and God. Abraham lived in early 2000 BCE and is the first patriarch recognized by the three biggest monotheistic (one God) religions – Judaism, Christianity, and Islam. He reported to have had a discussion with angels and God telling him to establish a new nation in a land eventually called Canaan. So, he traveled with his tribe from where he lived in Ur, Mesopotamia (at the time this was a port city on the current day Persian Gulf in southern Iraq) to Canaan. This trip took him 2,200 miles north and west to prime real estate on the eastern coast of the Mediterranean Sea in current day Lebanon, Israel, northwestern Jordan, and some areas of Syria.

During his life, Abraham had many supernatural visions and dialogues with angels and even his Egyptian servant Hagar, had a supernatural experience. She saw God and he insisted that she and Abraham have sex. What a great story for people to use when they want to cheat on their spouses. But as a word of caution, using God as your excuse to cheat may not work as well in today's world. As the story continued, with God's help, Hagar became pregnant and birthed Abraham's first-born son, Ishmael. For some reason, God kept appearing to Abraham and told him to also have sex with his wife Sarah and as a result he eventually had a son with her called Isaac. Both Abraham and Sarah were really old so this was considered a miracle. You can't make this stuff up...oh wait a minute, apparently you can.

This story is important because it provided one of the reasons why the Islam people don't get along with the Judaism people and why the Christian people don't really approve of either of these religious groups. To explain, Ishmael is recognized as the Islam genetic lineage, which is why they think they are the true religion since Ishmael was the first son, even though he was the maidservant's child. Alternately, Judaism thinks they are the true religion since Isaac is recognized as their genetic lineage as he was Abraham's wife Sarah's first child. Also, Christianity thinks they are the true religion since Jesus was a descendant of Isaac, so of course this proves Judaism was the correct choice of religion. Too bad for the Islamic religion – they picked the wrong child. Oh, but it doesn't stop there - the Christians believe Jesus is far superior to Isaac, making their religion an even better choice than Judaism. Too bad for the Judaism religion, although they were apparently the correct choice, that is until Jesus showed up. Who knows what these religions would have done if Hagar and Sarah would have had girls first? Interesting they both had a boy first or at least that's how the story was written. I guess God at this time didn't like girls as much, at least when it came to starting religions.

Abraham kept having God visions and discussions, but no more about sex or having more kids. In one of his visions, God told him to sacrifice Isaac when Isaac was just a little boy to prove Abraham's loyalty to God. However, as Abraham was beginning the motion of plunging the dagger into Isaac's heart, God stepped in and stopped him from killing his son at the last second. This plot tension technique is very effective at getting people emotionally involved in the story and is still used today in many books and films because it works.

All the angel and God visions and dialogues always happened for both Abraham and Hagar when they each were alone. In addition, neither of them wrote anything down and these stories weren't written until over 1,000 years later. Yet people believe them to be factual and 100% true. We can't even get accurate stories about events that happened yesterday in the news the following day. And yet these stories telling of supernatural events from thousands of years ago are thought to be real and totally accurate even though they were based on the recounts through many generations by word of mouth.

Let's take a quick time out and recalibrate what these tribes of Abraham, called Israelites were doing after Abraham died before we go on to their next fantastic story. Basically, these people were living in the Canaan area along the Mediterranean coast in and around the location of current day Israel. They were seminomadic herdsmen and occasional farmers, and their religion was similar to all the known religions of this area – just another of the Mesopotamian religion du jour. The Judaism religion believing in their one God Yahweh was not invented yet and was not even universally adopted by these tribes until the Maccabees influence in 167 BCE. The Hebrew Bible was a collection of writings from 1200 BCE to 100 BCE and was assembled and written into its current form between 100 CE to 200 CE. The Christian Old Testament Bible was both translated into Greek from this Hebrew Bible version and revised in the 100 CE to 300 CE time period. The takeaway from this explanation is the stories compiled in these books were communicated over thousands of years, some written and some verbal, and then assembled into a cohesive story line. What we ended up with was some serious history revisionism.

Abraham did not invent or discover Yahweh as the god of Israel and creator of the world as the Bible suggests. Until Zoroaster founded the belief in one God and the Maccabees started Judaism, the theme of these old Israelite tribal stories was not about Yahweh as the one true god. Instead, they followed another theme focused on their patriarchs and the popular gods in this region. These patriarchs of the Israelite tribes were described as having the gods' blessings along with their protection and care for the tribes' wellbeing. In return, the gods required loyalty, obedience and the providing of prayer and sacrifices to them. There is evidence this Israelite cult had sacrifice rituals supporting this, usually on or around an altar, stone pillar, or a sacred tree. Another aspect of the Israelite cult was circumcision, which was a distinctive ritual in their community versus other tribes in the area. The ultimate goals of their belief system and rituals were that this faith in the gods would result in gaining more land and the population growth of their tribes. All of these beliefs were included in the Hebrew Bible with the exception of their belief in many gods. They just made revisions to synch their stories up with the belief in one God, Yahweh, as opposed to what they had believed before the Maccabees established Judaism.

Getting back to the ongoing story of the Israelites. The next big change for these descendants of Abraham's tribes happened approximately 700 years after Abraham's life, when they migrated from Canaan to Egypt most likely because of famine. Although they found food in Egypt, this turned out to be a devastating move as they were then enslaved by the Egyptian rulers. The good news was a new patriarch called Moses apparently led them out of Egypt and back to the Israel area.

Moses is another person who saw angels and talked with God. Living around 1300 BCE, Moses was considered the greatest Judaism prophet (remember that Judaism did not exist yet but this is not an important detail in the nebulous religion world). He was famous because he led his people out of Egypt, established laws as well as the Ten Commandments, and was the founder of the religious community in Israel that eventually became current day Judaism. Moses first encountered God in the form of a burning bush that did not get consumed. In this experience, God told him his name was Yahweh, which meant "he who makes that which has been made", basically the creator of the universe. Yahweh told Moses to lead his people out of Egypt. Of course, no one else was around to see or experience these visions or dialogues. Only Moses. Also, this god had not been introduced yet, and therefore this was a prime example of history revisionism. It makes sense, since if you start a religion over 1,000 years later and you only believe in one god, you need to go back to make all the gods be this one in your old stories so they are consistent with your new beliefs.

Moses' next big god encounter was on Mount Sinai in the desert, where he received two stone tablets from Yahweh (or whatever this god's name was at the time), with the Ten Commandments. Again, no one is around to witness this transaction so we are not sure if these were all the rules he received. A funny example of how these stories can be viewed in a ridiculous manner is in Mel Brooks' comedy movie "History of the World Part 1". In this movie, he shows Moses receiving 15 commandments on three tablets, but just as he is ready to announce these rules to his people, he drops one tablet and breaks it, so he is forced to settle on Ten Commandments. Getting back to the encounter, once again, Moses wrote nothing down even though he supposedly was in direct communication with God. Even God did not write anything down, well except for those Ten Commandments according to Moses, but those stone tablets were destroyed after he came down from the mountain. Surprising?? Don't you think if God wrote something down you would do whatever it took to protect this valuable item? The stories about the Ten Commandments and the burning bush eventually were written in the final version of the Hebrew Bible over 1,400 years later along with the Abraham stories. It should be noted that some of the bible stories were written earlier in rough form in the Hebrew language and some in the Aramaic language and then they were compiled and revised into the final Hebrew Bible between 100 CE to 200 CE.

Daniel, another heroic figure who lived around 600 BCE, was also written about in the Hebrew Bible. In this bible story, Daniel was portrayed as an upstanding person who was persecuted by being put into a lion's den but was able to survive because of his righteous behavior. This story also introduces a new character, the angel Gabriel, who will be repeatedly used in both Christian and Islamic stories. Gabriel was God's messenger to Daniel who showed up to help explain Daniel's visions about the future of the people of Israel (of course, only Daniel saw and spoke with Gabriel). With Gabriel's help Daniel was able to assure the people they would eventually overcome all their hardship and persecution. As you would expect, this made everyone feel better including Daniel since the lions did not maul him with Gabriel's help. For some reason this lion's den, with Daniel in it, was isolated from any other people witnessing what was happening to Daniel. You don't need much critical thinking to realize this is a farfetched story.

*

Fast-forward to Christian supernatural encounter stories. The first one was angel Gabriel appeared to Zechariah announcing the birth of John the Baptist. Yes, the same Gabriel angel as in the Daniel story. Zechariah was a priest preaching in Solomon's Temple and saw Gabriel in the incense smoke. Gabriel told him he would have a son with his wife Elisabeth, who was Mary's cousin, the future mother of Jesus. Of course, no one else in the temple witnessed this interaction. Although, Gabriel did say no one would remember this encounter. This seems similar to the way memories of aliens are erased in the "Men in Black" movies. Gabriel never explained why only Zechariah's memory was the one remaining intact, but of course all the Christians believed it when it was eventually written in the Greek language 330 years later.

*

While Gabriel was in the area, he showed up again appearing before Mary, to inform her she would be impregnated by the Holy Spirit. No one was around, not even her husband Joseph for this dialogue nor for the impregnation act. Of course, by all indications Joseph was okay with all of this. Can you imagine telling this story to your spouse today? I doubt you would be married very long or at least you would be encouraged to seek out mental illness therapy or couple's therapy.

*

When Jesus was a grown man, he was baptized by John the Baptist and saw the sky open up. At this time period, it was thought the sky was like a big astrodome, with water above it and stars hanging down like lights. When they said the floodgates opened, they thought gates in the sky opened up, allowing the water to pour on them. There was no scientific understanding of clouds, condensation and weather patterns with high- and low-pressure systems. In this case, another gate in the sky opened up without water behind it and the spirit of God landed on Jesus as a dove and then a voice from above said, "This is my son." The writers of this story were not very creative as they copied the dove imagery from both the Greek and Roman religions. In Rome and throughout the empire, goddesses such as Venus, Aphrodite, and Fortuna were often depicted in statues with a dove resting in their hand or on their head, since the dove was a symbol of divine presence. So, it makes sense that the Jesus story tellers used this symbol since people were familiar with it. However, the story gets even more unbelievable since no one else witnessed this happening except Jesus, even though other people were around. You would think this would be big news during this time period, but according to the story, Jesus just left and went into the desert. In the desert he had many discussions and encounters with the devil, but of course no one else was around to witness these events either. Oh, did I mention Jesus did not write any of this down? These stories don't get written until over 300 years after Jesus died.

No religion has a monopoly on supernatural stories but the last religion written does have the advantage of making their stories better than the previously written religions. So of course, Muhammad the Prophet and founder of Islam living 570 CE to 632 CE in Mecca, Arabia, had his supernatural encounters too. Mecca is a city in a dessert valley located in western Saudi Arabia about 90 kilometers or 55 miles from the Red Sea coast. When he was 40 years old, the angel Gabriel (yeah, the same angel from Judaism and Christianity) appeared to Muhammad. All the religions seem to like this angel character as they used him often. In any case, Gabriel appeared to Muhammad in a mountain cave near Mecca and taught him the opening versus of what would become the Quran (the Islamic Bible). Muhammad continued to get these revelations for three years and then God showed up and told him to start preaching. Guess what? No one was ever around to witness any of these visions, revelations, or dialogues.

To give a little background, Muhammad lived in an area that still believed in many gods – in his preaching, he informed the people these gods did not exist. He told them he had talked directly with Allah, who he believed was the one true god, and therefore they were all wrong in their beliefs. The people did not share his beliefs and did not appreciate his preaching and constant criticism.

As a result, they forced him and his followers to flee. He picked northern Ethiopia as his destination since it had a Christian king who was kind and tolerant of people's beliefs. While in Ethiopia he claimed to have miraculously gone on a one-night journey to Jerusalem where he met with Abraham, Moses, Jesus, and other important prophets. He then said he ascended to heaven and God gave him five daily prayers for Islam, which he brought back to earth. This night trip was quite a journey for 600 CE as it is 2,630 miles or 4,230 kilometers by land. This must have been like using a Star Trek transporter or maybe he channeled Harry Potter's magic. For some reason, he ended up back in Ethiopia the next morning and had to travel (without the transporter) to Jerusalem again. It obviously took a lot longer than one night. The first trip was a miracle but the second trip not so much.

After leaving Ethiopia and traveling to Jerusalem, Muhammad eventually made his way to Medina, which is located in western Saudi Arabia north of Mecca. Although he kept trying to get back to Mecca, the people still didn't want him living with them. So, he built a substantial army and fought his way back to take over the city. During his time in Medina and Mecca he fought many battles and at one point even took control of Medina, killing all the non-Muslim males and enslaving all the woman and children. Throughout all this fighting and praying, the angel Gabriel continued to appear and an army of angels helped Muhammad's army win a battle. No one saw the angels but of course Muhammad claimed they were there helping him win. Once again, none of this was written down until one to two hundred years later. It is unbelievable to me that no one questioned why these prophets and gods, who were supposed to be so enlightened and had god helping them, could not write or did not write anything down. Have I said that before?

These supernatural visions and dialogues continued throughout history associated with religions, and they weren't just stories written in bibles. As an example, the Catholic religion has many saints claiming to have had these experiences.

> In 1205 CE Saint Francis of Assisi reported Jesus told him to repair his house.

> In 1208 CE Saint Juliana of Liege had visions of Jesus telling her to start a solemn feast for the blessed sacraments.

> In 1251 CE Saint Simon Stock saw the Blessed Virgin Mary and she gave him a brown scapular, which essentially was a brown woolen tunic that the Carmelite nuns began to wear as their habit. (Amazing you can even receive supernatural fashion advice!)

> In 1366 CE Saint Catherine of Siena saw Jesus, who encouraged her to start taking care of the sick and the poor. This claimed encounter did have a noble outcome.

And the list goes on and on...

One more noteworthy supernatural experience that led to the formation of another religion was claimed by Joseph Smith, founder of the Church of Latter-Day Saints. In 1820 CE, Joseph Smith claims to have seen God the Father, and Jesus in a grove of trees near his house in rural upstate New York. He then described seeing God on a throne with angels and intense bright light, brighter than stars or a noon sun. He also said he saw twelve other people or spirits follow God as he ascended back to heaven. He proceeded to have a series of these visions over time giving him divine instruction, which of course no one else ever experienced or could prove. These divine instructions he imagined were the basis for his new religion.

So how do we explain all these visions and voices claimed by religious leaders? Taking a critical thinking approach to these many encounters leads you to realize they are all unprovable, far-fetched, and for me unbelievable. Instead, I see four possible rational explanations for these supernatural experiences the prophets, demi-gods, and saints claim to have experienced. The first possibility is they suffered from a mental illness such as schizophrenia or narcissism. The second possibility is they simply lied and invented their story in an effort to gain influence, prestige and power with their tribe. There are many people who have been or are very convincing liars, especially if their audience is starved for spiritual leadership or is gullible. Look at how many religious leaders have swindled their believers out of money in almost all religions. A third possibility was they were hallucinating on a psychedelic substance. And the fourth possibility was they had a natural psychedelic experience.

The first explanation to discuss is mental illness, including schizophrenia and narcissism. Schizophrenia is when people interpret reality abnormally, resulting in hallucinations, delusions, and disordered thinking. Religious delusions are very common in schizophrenics since religion is one approach used to understand the world and give meaning to our lives. Schizophrenics suffer terribly from coping in life and sometimes this leads them to have delusions they were sent by God as a prophet to right the world. Some schizophrenics claim they are actually Jesus or Muhammad. In order to be able to lead others, a person with this mental illness certainly would need to have a very mild case. Without any understanding of mental illness, it makes sense that back thousands of years ago, if that person was also very charismatic and could function well enough to take care of themselves, then people would actually believe their delusional claims.

Narcissism might be a more viable mental illness for starting new religions since narcissists live in a fantasy world that supports their delusions of grandeur. Since reality doesn't support their grandiose view of themselves, narcissists must live in a fantasy world propped up by distortion, self-deception, and magical thinking. Many narcissists are very functional and can be quite persuasive to people who are looking for someone to lead them or help them make decisions about their life. This happens even in current times, as there are many leaders with narcissistic traits in politics and business.

The second possibility is these people claiming to have had supernatural encounters is they made it up – they simply lied about their experiences to gain power and influence. This one is easy to accept or understand as there are television evangelist leaders who seem to be doing the same thing today. Swindling gullible people or people who are desperate for hope, is one of the oldest crimes against people in the history of mankind.

The third possibility for these supernatural experiences was they were hallucinating on a psychedelic substance and while in this mental state they created some of the earliest spiritual beliefs. Ancient people most likely had hallucinogenic experiences from eating various plants when they were out hunting and refined these experiences over time. We know this from current experience with drugs containing dimethyltryptamine (DMT), LSD, and Psilocybin. Ingesting hallucinogenic drugs can cause users to see images, hear sounds, and feel sensations that seem real but do not exist. We also know that some people who have taken hallucinogenic drugs often feel renewed, and experience a sense of awareness and creativity they did not have before taking the drug.

The reasons we know ancient people were hallucinating, is based on both coincidental proof and actual proof. The coincidental proof is seen in the creativity of cave rock art paintings found in both France and South Africa. Although discovered in these different areas, the images or art found on the walls are very similar. The geometric shapes, along with pictures of animals, people, and therianthropes (people heads with animal bodies), are the same as what people on LSD often draw after their hallucinogenic experience in current times. We also see these same geometric shapes in ancient Egyptian, Greek, and Indian art, while therianthropes were also part of Greek religions.

Actual proof of hallucinogenic religious experience was discovered in the 1972 CE excavation of the Gonur Tepe archaeological site, located about 60 kilometers or 37 miles from Mary, Turkmenistan. This site consists of a large early bronze-age settlement dating from 2400 BCE to 1600 BCE. Gonur Tepe is the largest ruin in the Murghab River delta region where over 150 ancient settlements have been found. In this site the archaeologists have located temples with fire altars similar in design to the Zoroastrian religion. In addition, they have found dishes and implements such as mortars and pestles along with ingredient remnants used to make a hallucinogenic ritual drink called Soma or Haoma. The traces of substances found were:

— Peganaum Harmala – wild growing flowering plant with medicinal and hallucinogenic properties

— Phallaris Grass – a grass containing DMT

- Ephedra – a shrub with little flowers used as a medicinal herbal stimulant
- Cannabis – a plant used for relaxation

It appears the priests assembling these ritual drinks were quite skilled at the chemistry of using and mixing these plants in different strengths for different purposes. The priests made this drink by extracting the plant juices with a mortar and pestle and then mixing it with other ingredients such as honey, milk, and pomegranate juice.

The reason these priests prepared and used Soma or Haoma in their sacred rituals was to alter their cognition or behavior for the purpose of stimulating spiritual development. What Soma gave them was light, strength, beauty and music in their minds. It was also a guide to wisdom as they imagined encounters with beings from outside of the human dimension. They had visions and discussions with angels, elves, divas, and gods. In fact, they often saw gods and goddesses in the smoke. Finally, these ritual drinks gave them a sense of bliss or ecstasy and knowledge of immortality. These experiences are often thought to be the origins of people believing their soul is part of the universe and immortal. We know these ancient people experienced these visions through documents of Vedic and Avestan (sacred book of Zoroastrianism) writings and hymns. As an example, a Vedic poet wrote, "We just drank the Soma, we have become immortal, we have come to the light, we have found the gods."

Once Gonur Tepe was discovered it became obvious the use of these spiritual drinks and spiritual ideas spread in two directions as Gonur Tepe was directly north of both Iran and India and it was also part of the silk-road trade routes. The southwest migration of these ideas moved into the Iran area and most likely was the source of the Zoroastrianism religion. The region's spiritual drink was and is called Haoma. As discussed earlier, the Zoroastrian religion influenced Egypt and was also the basis for the largest monotheistic religions of Judaism, Christianity, and Islam. The basic tenant of the Zoroastrian religion is the duality of goodness or light, and evil or darkness. One of the main psychedelic religious experiences is seeing tremendous, blinding light even when you are in complete darkness.

The eastern migration traveled to India through Afghanistan and here their ritual drink was called Soma, which is still part of the Hindu religion. Soma in India, similar to Haoma in ancient Iran, is thought to be an elixir of the gods, a plant-based drink highly valued for its exhilarating and hallucinogenic effects. The Hindu's even have a god or deity called Soma as the master of plants, the healer of disease, and granter of riches. The only difference between Soma and Haoma was the India region required the use of different plants, as the Haoma plants did not grow in the India region. The Indians used blue and white lotus and water lilies, which contain DMT. The best place to get Soma was in Kashmir, which is one of the reasons why this area was called the "valley of the gods." It is also believed some

Soma was made with hallucinogenic mushrooms when the lotus flower was not available. Almost all of the ancient gods of Hindu, as well as Buddha, are shown holding blue or white lotus flowers.

Much of religion revolves around intense blinding light, which is usually the first thing people see when hallucinating. Similar to having a positive hallucinogenic trip, people often describe seeing blinding light after having a near death experience. Both people hallucinating and people having a near death experience are often pulled toward a tunnel of light and see angels, or gods, deceased relatives and loved ones. They all expressed they wanted to keep going but were pulled back. The biblical prophets and Christian saints often talked about being drawn to a circular light surrounded by angels. These visions are where the idea of a halo around a holy person's head originated. The Egyptians even believed this light was their spiritual home and oriented their architecture to point toward Sirius, the brightest star visible from any part of earth (not to be confused with Sirius Satellite Radio).

Although people have these vivid experiences under hallucinogenic substances, science has not been able to determine what is actually happening to the human mind causing these visions and voices. What is undeniable, the trips on DMT and other hallucinogenic substances give people a glimpse of a completely different perception of reality.

The fourth explanation for these supernatural events was having a psychedelic experience without the use of substances such as LSD, psilocybin, and entheogens. There are several ways to accomplish this mental state currently in use today to achieve ecstasy, bliss, and a sense of immortality that may have also been used in ancient times. One way is through a breathing technique while lying down with your eyes closed. Called "holotropic breathwork", it induces a non-ordinary state of consciousness like a vivid waking dream. Another way is through sensory deprivation isolating you from everyone else on earth as well as your own senses. This experience eventually induces a deep meditative state that can result in feelings of euphoria, hallucinations, and even out of body experiences. Those hallucinations can involve seeing surreal images or hearing imaginary music. People experiencing this state often don't recognize the music or the voices. This state often boosts originality, imagination, and intuition.

Another way of inducing a psychedelic experience is through "motion after effect" illusion or MAE, sometimes called the waterfall illusion. If you stare at a waterfall and then look at a stationary object it will appear moving because your eyes have grown accustomed to watching motion. If this is done in an extreme way, it creates hallucinations. There is a video that does this currently on the Internet. In Toronto, Canada there is a vortex tunnel in the Museum of Illusions. This is a bigger version of the MAE that you can walk through.

These techniques all generate a state of intense wellbeing in humans, causing them to feel positive emotions such as great ecstasy, wonder and awe. It is possible these ancient religious founders and saints experienced their hallucinations in caves, on mountaintops, in deserts, or staring at water in motion. They may have also believed these visions to be real even though they were just in their minds.

It is amazing to me that in modern times, so many people continue to maintain these supernatural events happening long ago were factual and real. As I said before, just because a story is passed along for hundreds or thousands of years does not make it true, it just makes it old folklore. Again, if any of these types of experiences were told today by someone claiming them to be true, we would not hesitate to help them find mental health support. We would also not believe anything they communicated to be real. So then ask yourself this question - why would you believe the same unbelievable story from someone who lived hundreds or thousands of years ago? The people of that time period had no closer connection to spiritual or supernatural beings or phenomenon than we do today. The word ancient does not mean wisdom or insight, it just means really old or long ago. In addition, these ancient people were less informed about how the world works, their understanding of science was minimal, and they had no concept of the enormous scale of the universe. Yet with all the knowledge, access to history, information, and wisdom we have today, people still believe in these supernatural events, myths and legends.

It's important to recognize the significance of so many of the well-known spiritual world beliefs originating with these stories related to communications directly with gods or angels. Whether they were the result of mental illness, hallucinations or lies, many people continue to accept them as real. It is really dangerous in today's world to confuse people by making them believe fiction is real. Consider all the latest fictional things people are convinced to believe today such as conspiracy theories, the earth is flat, and the holocaust never happened. Convincing people to believe in magical religions encourages beliefs in things that do not exist. Answers given in response to questions about all religious beliefs include: you need to have faith, don't question - just believe, or mere mortal human beings cannot understand these truths. In other words, it is made up fiction. Incorporating this fiction into beliefs and then encouraging people to be very cruel to others in the defense of these beliefs, is extremely destructive in today's society. Unfortunately, this is true in all religions and we are seeing it across the world.

Chapter 10

I Know Math, So How Does 1 + 1 + 1 = 1?

While my religious education wasn't lacking for well-meaning intentions, what was lacking was getting logical answers to innocent questions that would make sense to my young impressionable brain. Although not because of any conscious decision on my part, during those youthful years I continued to plod along with the status quo, even though I was never able to get plausible answers to what I thought were obviously simple questions. In the last chapter, we looked at rational justifications to explain the narratives regarding supposed direct communications with God. For me as an adult, yes, those explanations I could understand, rather than believing these encounters actually happened as claimed. Ok, but I still had questions regarding other beliefs that were not quite so logical to defend. One such simple question was why do Roman Catholics believe in three Gods: The Father, the Son, and the Holy Spirit, but then they only count them as one God? Remember, Roman

Catholic is considered to be a monotheistic religion, believing in only one God. So how did that make sense? Even to me as a kid, this seemed like a fairly logical question given my newly learned mathematical skills in addition. I knew that if you added one God plus one God plus one more God it didn't equal to just one God as they maintained. Ultimately, after fumbling to come up with a reasonable justification for this math challenge, the priest's answer to my confusion was offensively dismissive, contending that we as humans couldn't possibly understand it. His explanation was that simple, it was just a mystery - the divine mystery of the Holy Trinity. What a clever religious marketing strategy – believers would get three Gods for the price of one God. Well okay, but that really wasn't a satisfactory answer to my question. But I got it – I was expected to set aside semantics and my math skills and just believe in this "mystery" of the Holy Trinity, where three gods would be considered to be one god. It's a mystery. It's magical. Just believe. I later came to realize this non-answer answer was code for when the religious people really didn't have an answer because the concept was simply made up by people thousands of years ago. That's the conundrum of the foundation of many religions – teaching people to be satisfied with not understanding the world. Asking them to set logic aside and just believe. Just believe.

Of course, I wasn't going to let this one go. This was one concept I would need to dig into a little deeper to get at its roots. As to this particular question of counting Gods, it is interesting that during the 500 years around when Jesus Christ lived and the bible was written, there were many polytheistic religions. Believing in multiple deities or gods was prevalent in the Roman Empire including Greece, as well as in the Far East and Persia. Zoroastrianism and Judaism were two of the only big religions believing in a monotheistic religion at that time, which evolved to be the foundation for Christianity. One God was plenty for them. In fact, the Jews were referred to at this time period as "the one God people". From my perspective, the Judaism people hedge a little on their one God concept, similar to other religions, since they have supernatural characters in their religion such as Abraham, Moses, Noah, Daniel, and the angel Gabriel, to name a few. Not seen as full gods, but certainly demi-gods that talked regularly one on one with god, and performed miraculous events.

When it came to religious beliefs, polytheistic religions tended to be a little more open-minded and considerate in the treatment of people of different cultures having different beliefs, even those they had conquered. As if "open-minded" and "considerate" are words that can be associated with conquerors. Conquering aside, they were more accepting of allowing the gods of these people to be added into their own pool of deities. How generous of them. Why not? The more the merrier when it came to gods! On the other hand, monotheistic religions acted much more sanctimonious, always preaching that their religion was the right one. They had no tolerance for the conquered peoples' religion, let alone allowing outsider's gods into their righteous religion. Sorry, we have all the gods we need and that number is exactly one! As Christianity was expanding and conquering, to entice the early Roman people who had believed in many Gods to buy into the Christian religion, the Roman leaders and the Christian priests came up with the concept of bundling three Gods in one to make it more appealing. They must have convinced the Roman common people that they were getting their monies worth by getting three gods in one. This most likely made the conversion to Christianity more acceptable since they were accustomed to believing in multiple gods. That is only part of the story - the full story is even more interesting as to how the Christians ended up with the three in one belief.

It began with the Roman Emperor Constantine in 312 CE. He is often thought of as the founder of Christianity as we know it today, but he actually didn't officially convert to Christianity until he was baptized on his deathbed. In fact, during his life, Constantine believed in the Sol Invictus religion (the God of the Unconquered or Invincible Sun), which was the official Roman religion beginning in 274 CE. Although Sol Invictus was essentially a monotheistic religion, the Roman leaders allowed the popular Roman cults or mystery religions at the time, to exist alongside the early Christian believers and other Judaism sects. What you may not have realized was much of the theology of Christianity was formed from these mystery religions. Basically, what Constantine did was combine the three most popular religions during this time period (Sol Invictus, Mithraism, and Judaism Christianity), in an effort to increase his power through both politics and religion across all the Roman Empire territories.

To explain how these other two popular religions, Sol Invictus and Mithraism, were combined with Judaism Christianity, it's first necessary to understand a little about each. The main one, Sol Invictus, is pretty easy as it involves solar worship and recognizes Sol Invictus as the one and only god, basically the Sun god. This religion originated in the Syrian area and became very popular in the Roman Empire in the second and third centuries. Emperor Aurelian 270 CE to 275 CE elevated Sol to the highest rank among all gods. The other one, Mithraism is the worship of Mithra, another sun god, but he also included justice, contract, and war in his responsibilities. It seems odd based on today's thinking, to combine contract and war in Mithra's job description, but at that time it made sense. Whenever two armies agreed to stop fighting, they validated the new contract for peace with a joint meal, giving thanks to Mithra. He was also honored as the patron of loyalty to the emperor. This well-known god had been around for a long time, as he originated in Iran before Zoroastrian. The belief in this god spread south into India becoming recognized as the Vedic god Mitra. Similarly, in India this god promoted contracts and friendship.

What's odd was most people in the Roman Empire believed they were monotheistic god believers, even though they had a few other gods around. This thinking was also associated with followers of the Judaism Christian cult. During this time, some Judaism Christians believed Jesus was a demi-god while others believed he was a full god. They were also tolerant of Sol Invictus as the main god, who coexisted alongside their religion for hundreds of years. Although this sounds puzzling and inconsistent, it was and still is prevalent in both Hinduism and Christianity. Both of these religions still believe in one monotheistic god. The Hindu's have one god with many attributes or god forms, and the Christians have three gods that count as one god. Although, in a way, each of the Christian gods have distinct attributes similar to the logic of the Hinduism multiple god approach.

As mentioned, Constantine wanted to merge all the different cults into one for the sake of unity and power. Similar to today, membership in these cults provided people with a sense of belonging and friendship, which Constantine knew was important. He wanted to make sure this merger of cults would be familiar enough for everyone to be acceptable. There were a number of main cults following Sol Invictus and Mithra that were combined, each with their own primary membership demographics. Naturally, with the combining of the different cults, a variety of beliefs, rituals and customs practiced by them were adopted as well.

The Isis cult focused on the goddess of love and primarily appealed to the lower middle class in seaports and trading towns. They believed in Sol but had Isis on the side. To obtain initiation into Isis you had to confess all your sins up until the time you were baptized. This baptism ritual washed away all your sins so that your life would be better, since you were now committed to the savior god. This is almost identical to orthodox Christian teaching, only they use Jesus instead of Isis or Sol.

The Mithraism cult appealed to officials in service of the emperor, soldiers (both low and high rank), imperial slaves, and influential freedmen (most likely looking for a promotion by honoring the emperor). Mithraic ceremonies usually mimed death and resurrection. They also had a sacred meal of bread and water as part of the rite. Their belief was they had been redeemed by the shedding of eternal blood as evidenced by a song they sang. Since the song is in ancient Latin, I'll just explain the song's story. The story goes like this; Mithra created the world by sacrificing a white bull that turned into the moon and Mithras's cloak became the sky with planets and stars. From the bull's blood sprang grain and grapes and his genitals provided the seed for forming all creatures on earth. The Mithraism people believed in the immortality of the soul, a future judgment, and the resurrection of the dead. Again, some of these beliefs were incorporated into Christianity. For instance, an example of one Mithraic hymn shows how close it was in meaning and belief to Christian hymns. It begins; "Thou hast redeemed us too by shedding the eternal blood". If you just substitute Jesus into the song, it works for the Christians. If you are familiar with Christianity, you know these believers are partial to death and resurrection references similar to the Mithraism believers.

Another ritual belief the Christians adopted from the Sol Invictus cult was the celebration of Christmas. In the Sol Invictus cult, their greatest festival was held December 17 to 24 at the time of the winter solstice. With scientific knowledge, we now know the winter solstice is December 21 or 22 in the northern hemisphere and June 20 or 21 in the southern hemisphere. Okay, so they were close in the northern hemisphere, but gave no thought whatsoever to the southern hemisphere. Anyhow, since daylight begins to increase after the solstice it was regarded as the rebirth of God and the renovation of life. Mithraism had a similar festival on December 25th for the same reasons as Sol Invictus and to celebrate Mithra's birth, which made it convenient for Constantine to merge these festivals into one. So, December 25th was picked, as this holiday date was close enough for both cults to accept and no one cared as long as the festival was fun. Until this time, the Christians were celebrating Jesus' birth on January 6th, but since December 25th was such a major birth festival, it was easy to change to this date for the Christian religion too. In the spirit of unity with Constantine's edicts, this made everyone happy!

Sol Invictus, Mithraism, and the Isis cult all practiced the baptism ritual where they poured water over people's heads to wash away their sins. This ritual or baptism rite was then easily adopted by the newly formed Christian religion. The Mithraism baptism rite also included a halo around the priest's head. The halo idea had been around a long time as a way to represent that a person or God was holy or a great ruler. It was popular in ancient Greece and Rome and is still popular in Hinduism, Buddhism, Christianity, and Islam in pictures and statues. Mithraism went beyond pictures and statues and actually did this in real life in early Roman rituals. This was literally done by shaving the priest's head, coating it with a protective ointment, then putting a circular metal receptacle filled with alcohol on his head and lighting it. Voila! The flame would shine around his head in a dark room - hopefully he didn't get burned, or perhaps just a little. How bizarre! But the Christians loved it, putting halos on all their most holy people in pictures and statues, however they resisted lighting the priest's head with fire or at least they don't do it anymore.

Another belief Constantine established in 321 CE was to make Sunday the sacred day and a day of rest to honor the sun. In Latin this day was called "dies solis" or in English day of the sun. It was easy for Sol Invictus and Mithraism believers to adopt Sunday as the day of rest since they already held Sunday as sacred. The other cults including Christianity did not seem to have any issue with following this edict either. Until this time, the Judaism Christian cult held the Jewish Sabbath on Saturday as sacred. This change was fine with the Christians as it allowed them to disassociate from their Judaic origins. They wanted to be more unique than other sects of Judaism, who continued to keep the Jewish Sabbath on Saturday.

Talking about Saturday and Sunday, as an aside, have you ever wondered why we have a seven-day week? Interestingly, our seven-day week was not based on astronomy, but was arbitrarily invented by the Babylonians. They named the days of the week after the sun, the moon and the five planets they could see in the sky (Mercury, Venus, Mars, Jupiter and Saturn), which is the reason behind having seven days in a week. I suppose if they could have seen eight planets, we would have had a ten-day week, which would have made for a very long work week between weekends. The original names for the seven days of the week are still used in the Romance languages (French, Spanish, Italian, Portuguese and Romanian), which were derived from Vulgar Latin. The English language days of the week don't follow this exactly since the Anglo-Saxons sprinkled in some god names from Teutonic mythology into their naming of the days of the week. For example, in the French language Friday is Vendredi named after Venus, but in English it was derived from Frigg's Day, which was in honor of the wife of Odin representing love and beauty in Norse mythology. The English speakers only kept the day names of Saturday, Sunday and Monday (Saturn, Sun and Moon) consistent with the original Babylonian names and changed the other days of the week to mythical god names. I'm surprised the Christian, Judaism, and Islamic one God people did not have a major objection with these English language day names coming from mythology.

Let's get back to the original discussion of three gods in one. Consider Constantine's dilemma. He needed to combine all these religions and cults, and sought out a way to combine the gods as well. One of his main problems was the controversy that swirled around Jesus Christ – should he be considered a full God or a lesser God? Many believed during that time period Jesus Christ was not really a full God because he had a physical beginning and was therefore subordinate to God the Father. He was considered to be a demi-god, or a minor deity since he was the offspring of a God and a human. Demi-gods could be mortal or immortal, often attaining divine status after death. Some people believed Jesus Christ was this type of God. However, others believed Jesus Christ was a full god and considered him to be on the same level as God the Father/Sol/Mithra and the Holy Spirit. In an effort to resolving this conflict, Constantine sponsored the Council of Nicaea in 325 CE held in the city of Nicaea, which is located in current day Turkey on Lake Iznik south of Istanbul. Here the council would simply take a vote to decide what Christians were to believe about Jesus. Incredible – a simple vote! This important pillar of Christianity would be decided by a vote, not by some reputed decree handed down directly from God himself as taught in religion class.

As a little background, the concept of Jesus Christ as the Son of God and also being viewed as a savior, wasn't an original or new concept. There is a similar account involving another ruler becoming a savior. During 165 BCE to 130 BCE, Menander was the king of a large empire in the northwestern regions of the Indian subcontinent. His empire covered parts of current day Iran, Turkmenistan, Afghanistan, Pakistan, and northern India. He conquered even more tribes than Alexander the Great and is noted for becoming a patron of Buddhism. With self-proclaimed prominence, he had coins made that recognized him as the Savior, the King of Kings, and with a direct link to the divine as the Son of God. Just like that - a self-proclaimed savior! A little hubris perhaps? Ultimately, Menander was very influential in establishing this concept of a ruler being treated as a savior, providing a gateway into the next life for his believers. A savior god saves human beings from death, evil, and sin. These religions always assume human beings are sinful people and need to be saved to get to heaven or to the next life after death. I can't help but wonder why religions always want to make people feel bad about themselves so their god can save them. It's almost as if they want everyone to be self-loathing.

With Menander in mind, fast-forward a few hundred years later to the Nicaea Council. The bishops here wanted to do something similar to how Menander was viewed and so they took a vote to decide if Jesus Christ would be considered a full God or a lessor demi-god. The vote passed in his favor – Jesus would forever be considered a full God. Yeah Jesus! To resolve the conflict of adding in another full god after claiming to only believe in one God, the council invented the concept of the Holy Trinity.

People had previously been told there was only one true God and it was blasphemy to believe in more than one. And then along came Jesus. Could he actually be another true God? Remember, few people were literate during this time period and would not dare question their religious and state leaders. To stop arguments about the status of Jesus and to keep the peace, many religious and political leaders of the time chose to go along with this three-in-one concept. Yes, based on the council's vote, Jesus would be treated as an equal and full true God and the people at that time bought into it. Of course, Constantine was very happy with this agreement as it merged all the religions into one. Sol, Mithra, and Yahweh became God the father and the Christians had Jesus as an equal god, the Son of God, while still only recognizing one God. But wait, that's just two gods – we still need to add a third god to the equation.

So, where did that third God of the Holy Trinity, called the Holy Ghost or Holy Spirit come from? The Holy Spirit was needed because he was referenced in several of the bible stories, doing tasks such as impregnating Mary, helping John the Baptist baptize Jesus, as well as helping out Jesus' apostles after he ascended into heaven. In addition, the Holy Spirit was included because this God was familiar to the people at that time. And as you probably guessed, this God was not an original Christian invention either. This Holy Ghost god is traceable to the very early periods of society when people believed that wherever there was motion, there was a God, or the active manifestation of God. This manifestation took the form of wind, breath, water, and fire.

The Holy Spirit was also visualized in both ancient Greece and Rome as a dove and accompanied Aphrodite and Venus the goddesses of procreation. In Rome and throughout the empire, it was common to see statues of Venus with a dove resting on her hand or head. The Roman people of this time period believed in the legendary spirit in the shape of a dove called Shekinah, which literally means "god's dwelling place" in Hebrew. The Holy Spirit associated with the goddesses of procreation was key to impregnating woman to explain how gods were created through immaculate conception. This included the Holy Ghost impregnating Mary, the mother of Jesus – this story fit well with what people even in the first century believed about Venus and her companion holy spirit in the shape of a dove. This concept is also one source of the Christian idea to have the Holy Spirit descend at baptism to signify rebirth.

There you have it - by proclamation, the Nicaea Council pronounced Christians would now have three Gods in One; The Father, the Son, and the Holy Spirit, but would continue to count them as one God. It turns out this concept of the Holy Trinity was not magical at all – in fact it was just a creative invention done by the Council of Nicaea in 325 CE.

Naturally, not all bishops were in support of this concept. Several bishops didn't buy into this newfangled belief including a very influential Alexandrian Priest, and as a result these non-supporters were all subsequently exiled for their defiance with the majority ruling. Not only did the Christians follow what was voted on in Nicaea in 325 CE, but also over time they actually were known to kill people who dared to challenge these doctrines. It's hard to believe the level of intolerance of some religions especially when the leaders at that time knew these doctrines had been merely invented by them.

This Nicaea Council was also responsible for setting the date for Easter (the resurrection of Jesus), as well as defining the authority of bishops and funding them, which significantly strengthened their power. Additionally, Constantine had all Christian orthodoxy destroyed and thereafter financed the writing of the Christian Bible. There was not much to destroy because back in 303 CE the emperor Diocletian had already destroyed any and all Christian writing that could be found at that time. As a result, Constantine's bible could be written as he and his writers saw fit since very little knowledge of original Christian writing was available. This version is the bible Christians still use today, which was written in the mid-300s CE. Think about this, the New Testament bible was written over 300 years after Jesus Christ lived. How accurate do you think it was with regard to the details of his life, but also about what he may or may not have taught?

I can only shake my head at the incredulity of the explanation I received as a young kid; that the only way to explain one God in three divine persons is to say it is a mystery that mortal men cannot understand. A religious mystery - I guess this was an easier way to explain this belief as they did not want to draw attention to the fact that this concept was just voted into existence by mere mortal men. Now you know that the concept of the Christian Holy Trinity as three gods in one was in fact invented in Nicaea, Turkey. And that it was not, as I was asked to believe, a supernatural phenomenon handed down by God that mere mortal people could not understand. It was just an invention that certainly included some flaws in the logic. How many hours have people spent pondering this so-called mystery over the last 2,000 years? It would have been so much easier if the church leaders had just said, "Sure, we made this up."

Nevertheless, people have continued to believe the three-in-one mystery for a very long time. The Nicene Creed came out of this council for all Christians to repeat as to what their beliefs would be going forward. Interestingly enough, this same creed is still repeated at the majority of Christian services and Catholic masses to this day;

"We believe in one God, the Father, the Almighty… We believe in one Lord Jesus Christ, the only Son of God…We believe in the Holy Spirit, the Lord, the Giver of life…"

I guess they thought if people kept repeating it over and over again, they would believe it. A little brainwashing strategy perhaps?

Chapter 11
The Devil is in the Details

My spiritual journey continued through the years where I began to recognize what was factual and what was simply made up when it came to religion. Facts were easy to trust – they were provable, verifiable, scientific and real. All words in which I could have confidence. On the other hand, religion and spirituality is asked to fill in the gaps that science doesn't understand. Just believe. Just have faith. For me, those words were much harder to defend. To reiterate a point made throughout this book, it's hard to defend religious phenomena that no one can really know with certainty – quite simply, it should be admitted that some things are just plainly made up. No matter how strong the belief, no one can really claim to know with certainty the legitimacy related to many areas of religion.

We already saw how rational justification could provide an explanation for the origination of some beliefs, such as those arising from direct communications with God or Gods – mental illness, intentional lies, or hallucinations could rationally account for these visions and voices. Or how other beliefs such as the concept of the Holy Trinity were simply invented and voted into the Christian dogma by mere mortal men, such as those making up the Council of Nicaea in 325 CE. The discussions regarding beliefs so far have been related to God, but they also apply to the opposite – the beliefs related to devils and where they reside in hell.

During my sophomore year of college, the movie *The Exorcist* was released. I remember it well - watching this movie when it was first released in theaters while on a road trip with my university track and field teammates. By today's standards, this movie probably doesn't pack the same punch as it once did, but at the time it was released, this was a very scary movie. Who can forget Linda Blair's performance as the young possessed girl, Regan MacNeil, the central character of *The Exorcist* – especially in that levitating scene, with her head spinning around, and green goo spewing from her mouth? Creepy stuff – certainly scarier for some versus others. It was particularly frightening to those teammates who truly believed there were actual devils lurking amongst us. Of course, as one of the young athletes who didn't share this opinion, we couldn't let this go – we found it fun to torment and scare these teammates. In hindsight, this probably wasn't a very compassionate thing to do - these guys were truly terrified and most likely had vivid nightmares from both the movie and our not-so-funny practical jokes. However, it was hard for me to comprehend that some people categorically thought devils were real. Not just evil people who were characteristically horrible and no-good. I'm talking about genuine supernatural beings that actually take over people's bodies. What I also found interesting during this time period was the Catholic Church had this same belief and continued to preach devils were real. Priests were even sometimes called upon as exorcists to remove devils from individuals. Pope Francis, in the homily of one of his masses leading up to All Saints Day and All Souls Day in 2014 CE, is quoted as saying, "This generation, and many others, have been led to believe that the devil is a myth, a figure, an idea, the idea of evil. But the devil exists and we must fight against him." To this day, the Catholics in fact still have exorcists saying prayers over afflicted people with the intentions of driving out the demons. Personally, I didn't share this Catholic belief of devils and exorcism – but, seeing this concept on display in the big-screen movie theater, my confidence in the legitimacy of the religion I grew up took a tumble. Yes, my doubts in this religion were beginning to add up.

So where did this idea of devils or demons originate? Throughout time, these evil creatures I'm referring to have been called a variety of names - the devil, Diabolus, Satan, Lucifer, Beelzebub, or Mephistopheles. They are usually depicted as blue, black, or red, some with horns and some without horns. What they all had in common though – they were imaginary. Almost all religions today include reference to devils, but the Zoroastrian religion was probably the first to introduce the idea of a devil. As I mentioned in an earlier chapter, this religion began in 600 BCE in current day Iran and it shares many central concepts with Judaism, Christianity, and Islam. Zoroastrianism believed good and evil were two opposing forces in eternal struggle. Initially this was just a conceptual belief or philosophy and not a physical thing or person. However, it is a logical leap that the people preaching and teaching this religion eventually needed a devil for the evil side of this equation, you know, to make it easier for people to understand. The evil spirit they eventually invented was called Ahriman, accompanied by his band of demons, called Daevas. Their job was to cause dissension and promote immoral behavior.

Judaism evolved out of Zoroastrianism and also initially didn't have a devil being or creature. The Israelites had an opposing force to God for most of its early history similar to Zoroastrian, but around 400 BCE they turned this force into a being. As an analogy today, this is similar to the dark force in Star Wars, which has the very powerful old evil guy leading the evil charge. The Israelites created their devil in the shape of a snake which would then be included by the Maccabees in the Judaism Bible. This is the same snake devil in the Adam and Eve story that tempted Eve to take a bite of the forbidden apple in order to gain all knowledge of God and become immortal. In this story, Eve was unfortunately vilified as a weak, easily tempted human being, who let Satan talk her into eating the knowledge apple. She was then further vilified as an evil manipulator by persuading the handsome, smart, strong, and upstanding Adam to take a bite too. And yes, that last sentence was sarcastic for those of you that just don't understand sarcasm. As a result, they were both cast out of the Garden of Eden to suffer for all eternity as mortal beings (alas they could never become gods). This is our fate as well thanks to Adam and Eve eating an apple. It's no wonder women have been treated so badly throughout history since they have been portrayed as evil in the Abrahamic religions starting from the very beginning of creation.

Christianity was one of the next new religions, which evolved by adding a New Testament Bible to a revised Judaism Hebrew Bible. The Christian Old Testament Bible is similar to the Judaism Hebrew Bible and both include the devil in snake form. Not to be outdone, the Christian religion also introduced a devil in one of their New Testament Bible Jesus stories. As the story goes, Jesus went out in the desert after being baptized by John the Baptist or the "Immerser" and didn't eat for 40 days. This is one serious diet and could be called the Jesus-in-the-desert diet! In theory, as long as Jesus drank water, he could have survived without food for 40 days in the desert but of course he would be in a severely weakened state. Also, no one knows how long he actually wandered in the desert because back then the phrase "40 days and 40 nights" was used to just imply a long time. We say similar things today that aren't taken literally such as; that will take forever, or it's a million miles away, or he has more money than

God. At any rate, during this no-eating time period, Jesus in his weakened state was tempted by the devil to turn away from God and in return he would get all the riches of the world. Of course, Jesus rejected the devil and passed the test. Interestingly, the Christian New Testament Bible does not really provide a description of the devil in detail, leaving this to the reader's imagination. Around the 800s CE Christian artists often portrayed the devil as a naked man-like creature with hairy legs, hooves, a tail and horns, brandishing a pitch fork for extra effect. I suppose these images were much scarier than a snake.

The modern visualization of hell and the devil were thought to have been inspired by Dante's inferno, which was described in the first part of *Dante's Divine Comedy* poem written in the 1300s CE. The word "inferno" is the Italian word for hell. In reading this story, the first thing you will realize it is neither very funny nor even mildly humorous – definitely not what comes to mind when you think of your typical comedy. The word "comedy" in literature does not imply humor in any way – it only means that it has a happy ending. In this story, Dante traveled through the many different levels of hell and eventually saw heaven filled with the souls that had already gotten there. And the happy ending - he experienced their unbelievable love. Yes, it definitely qualifies as a comedy, well in literary terms anyway. Some people mistakenly think this poem was inspired by God, because it has the word "Divine" in its title, however this is not the case. Initially this piece of literature was called *The Comedy of Dante Alighieri* - people admired it so much they started calling it "divine"; similar to someone saying, "that dinner was so divine!" (To get the right impact, it helps to read that last line with a privileged, aristocratic accent!)

Inspiration of this highly admired poem did not come directly from God; rather Dante's hell was structurally and conceptually based on ideas of Aristotle. These ideas centered on how to live a good and virtuous life using ethics and morality as a guide. Mirroring Aristotle, Dante's message was that we all control the choices we make in life and we will be rewarded or punished for these choices. In addition to incorporating Aristotle's philosophy, Dante also added Christian symbolism to this poem.

This story began with Dante being lost in a dark forest where he was attacked by three beasts. He was rescued by the Roman poet Virgil, who Beatrice had sent to save him. Beatrice symbolized blessedness and salvation. Dante had a childhood crush on Beatrice and viewed her as the ideal woman, but he never had a relationship with her, only in his dreams. Very sad for lonely, love-struck Dante, which may explain why he wrote about hell. Together, Virgil and Dante began the journey into the nine circles of hell because Virgil insisted this was the way they needed to travel to reach salvation. This journey took place from the Christian holy day Good Friday (when Jesus was believed to have been killed by being crucified), through Easter Sunday (when Jesus is said to have risen from the dead).

The nine levels or circles of hell in order, starting from the beginning, were Limbo, Lust, Gluttony, Greed, Anger, Heresy, Violence, Fraud, and Treachery.

The first circle of hell, Limbo was where all the nice people went who were unbaptized Christians. I imagine this level of hell must be very crowded – after all, approximately 70% of the world today is not Christian. In addition, before Christianity was even invented, logically 100% of the world was not Christian and therefore, they all would have landed in Limbo. So of course, this is where all the early Greek philosophers including Socrates, Plato, Aristotle and Virgil, lived for eternity. The Roman Catholic religion also has another holding place similar to Limbo called Purgatory, which is for all the moderate sinners that were baptized Christian and need to burn in punishment for a period of time before they can reach heaven. The really bad sinners just go directly to hell to be with the devil. Although *Dante's Divine Comedy* is just a story, the religious concepts included in this story of Limbo and its counterpart Purgatory are good examples of the totally made-up nature of religions bordering on absurdity. In addition to this Roman Catholic religious belief, many other religions have a similar idea of a state of existence between heaven and hell.

During Dante's time period, there were other depictions of hell but they were mostly underground and hot. The Greeks had Hades, which was where wicked spirits lingered in an underground twilight existence ruled by the god of the dead. The Hebrew Bible story came up with a fiery torment called Gehenna, which was a cursed place of fire and smoke. All of Dante's levels of hell were horrible, but it's worth mentioning that in his depiction of the various levels, he chose to include both fire and ice. Some levels included flames, while others had ice. I assume this is where the expressions, "you'll burn in hell" and "when hell freezes over" both originated.

Dante described the Heresy level with flaming tombs and the Violence level with boiling blood and fire, as well as burning rain and sand. The freezing cold levels of hell were Gluttony, with never ending icy rain, and the final level Treachery included a frozen lake. The devil (called Satan or Lucifer) portrayed as a giant demon with three faces resided in the core ninth level and was trapped waste deep in a barren, frozen icy lake at the center of the world. In this poem, the freezing of hell was caused by the flapping of Lucifer's bat-like wings. Generally during this time period, hell tended to be located underground, whereas heaven was up in the sky. The knowledge of what was beneath the ground all the way to the center of the earth was unknown until the late 1600s CE when Sir Isaac Newton made the first observations regarding the density of Earth's core.

Contrary to what many of us were taught in western schools, educated people realized the earth was round as early as 300 BCE with calculations made by Pythagoras and supported by Aristotle. Eratosthenes, a Greek mathematician living in Alexandria, Egypt as an adult around

245 BCE, was the first to accurately calculate the earth's circumference. He also mapped the first method of latitude and longitude. So, Dante knew the earth was round and envisioned his hell as cone shaped going down into the earth with increasingly tighter circles, but he did not know the consistency of the underworld. It is understandable that Dante would have both fire and ice in his circles of hell as he would not have known that the core of the earth is extremely hot and primarily made up of superheated iron and nickel and is now thought not to be liquid or solid but in a state called superionic. Dante was however very influential in visualizing hell as a very inhospitable place full of monsters, despair, barrenness, devils with wings, cannibalism, and disgusting substances. This is the document where many of the visualizations of hell and the devil came from in paintings, sculpture, and today's stories.

So, are there really supernatural devils lurking among us? I can't tell you with 100% certainty if they exist or not. But it is important to be aware of the origination of the idea of devils, as well as the influences on the way we portray them. Beliefs related to devils quite simply were made up – they were imaginary. Certainly, there is evil in the world, but I have serious doubts that it is being caused by supernatural devil spirits influencing people like you see on cartoons or in movies. You know, the devil on one shoulder and the angel on the other. People make decisions all the time – some decisions are considered kind and loving causing happiness, while others are cruel and hateful causing pain and suffering. I suppose it is easier to blame bad behavior on someone or something else such as a devil, rather than take responsibility for your own actions. This is most likely the underlying reason why many people believe in these supernatural evil creatures. Plus, these characters do make stories and movies much more interesting – you always need conflict or a bad guy to make a good story.

Artistic depiction of Dante's Hell.

©Shutterstock

Chapter 12

Church Service – Rated R for "Intense Graphic Violent Images"

Children are so vulnerable and impressionable that we go to great lengths to protect them from anything we consider to be remotely detrimental to either their physical or mental well-being - from seat belts, to bike helmets, to electric outlet covers so they won't accidentally electrocute themselves by sticking a fork in them, to baby gates so they won't accidentally fall down a flight of stairs, to the film rating system so they won't accidentally watch *The Texas Chainsaw Massacre*. No, it certainly wouldn't be appropriate either to expose our precious little ones to fantasies about torture, a corpse rising from the dead, magic spells, drinking blood, and snacking on a human body. Oops, I think I may have just inadvertently described what I had been exposed to in my religion classes and in church as a very young child in regards to some of the main pillars of the Catholic religion. Frankly, some of the familiar rituals and symbols associated with the church might even warrant an "R Rating" for their "Intense Graphic Violent Images!" And yet they seem perfectly normal and commonplace in the church setting. I couldn't help wonder how this happened – where did these things originate and how did they become so acceptable?

Yes, I was once one of those very vulnerable and impressionable children. As devout Roman Catholics, my family always attended the mandatory weekly mass on Sunday morning - it was inevitable that I would be exposed to some of those dubious pillars. Obviously, it didn't take long for me to notice - right there in front of me was one of them, hanging prominently front and center of the church we attended for my vulnerable young eyes to stare at in horror for the entire hour-long mass. The crucifix. That three-dimensional cross was so life-like, complete with Jesus' suffering face, a stab wound in the side with blood dripping out, nails stuck through his hands and feet, a dribble of blood down his foot, and a crown of thorns on his head causing more blood trickling. I'm experiencing a nightmarish, therapy-inducing reaction just writing that description. As such a sick and twisted image, I highly doubt the church would even be able to qualify for a G movie rating if there was such a rating applied to churches. And yet there it nonchalantly hung, just an ordinary part of the décor. The Catholic Church's explanation for this staple is that it's there to remind us of how much Jesus loved us that he would allow himself to be tortured and crucified. Not exactly the warm, fuzzy feeling usually associated with the word "love."

Interestingly, the first symbols of Christianity were not crosses or crucifixes at all, but doves, a fish shape with Greek letters, anchors, and the shepherd – now those symbols certainly seem a little more suitable for families and children. These continue to be used today, each with their own Christian meaning. As we discussed, doves are often associated with the Holy Spirit. The early Jewish Christian sect also liked the fish symbol because Jesus' disciples were fisherman and Jesus supposedly fed people with bread and fish. The Greek word for fish (Ichthys) was put inside the fish symbol as they made this word into an acrostic (word puzzle using the letters in a word to be the first letter of other words), which stood for "Jesus Christ Son of God, Savior," in Greek of course. Now it is commonly referred to as the "Jesus fish" and is often seen on car bumpers. Another symbol adopted by early Jewish Christians was the anchor, which symbolized hope in the future existence for all those who believed in Jesus. They also used a shepherd image as it portrayed Jesus as the Good Shepherd who lay down his life for his sheep. Christian leaders often preached that the common people should be like sheep, blindly following their shepherd. But none of these symbols are as powerful and iconic as the crosses and crucifixes, representing the focal point of the Christian beliefs.

About 200 years after Jesus was executed, the first symbolic crosses started appearing, however these crosses were empty. Crucifixes, which added the graphic dying figure of Jesus to the cross, began to appear about 200 years later than that and became more common in the sixth century. When Catholics and Protestants split in the 16th century, the two groups took different approaches to their religious symbols. Protestants preferred to use a simpler cross without the figure of Jesus, while Catholics stuck with the crucifix, making it a staple in their churches. I recently came across a joke (not to imply this topic is in any way funny) that said, "If Jesus Christ lived today, people would be wearing little electric chairs around their necks instead of crosses." Christian people are very proud of their cross jewelry, not realizing that wooden crosses were used to torture and savagely kill people in ancient Rome for political crimes against the empire. When viewed through a critical thinking lens, wearing a symbol that represented torture, cruelty, and death to many people in ancient Rome, not just Jesus, seems perverted and most likely ill informed.

In addition to staring in horror at the graphic crucifix in church, another of the nightmare-inducing Catholic beliefs that I struggled with as a child was the transformation of bread and wine into the actual body and blood of Jesus Christ for us to eat and drink. Catholics believe that during the consecration of the mass, the priest through transubstantiation (basically done by uttering a few magic words) miraculously changes the little crispy wafers, referred to as "hosts", into the actual body of Jesus Christ, and wine into his actual blood. Not just symbolically, but the *actual* body and blood! This is quite the magic trick - or as the Catholics claim, a Eucharistic miracle. A miracle? Sure, that's another way religious people explain things that can't be explained. So, after a few magic words by the priest, I was treated to a nibble of Jesus' body and a small gulp of his blood. Okay, when described in that way, it certainly does sound really creepy, not to mention violent and cannibalistic. Even as a kid, I remember this all seemed farfetched, regardless of the whole miracle explanation - watching the Priest utter a few magic words, I couldn't understand because they were in Latin, that would transform the host and wine into actual human flesh and blood. If you think about this literally it is really disgusting and gross. Here it comes again – me, as a vulnerable, impressionable kid, being cautioned that the only way I was going to get into heaven was to be a true believer and I needed to continue to go along with these teachings. But once again, try as a might I still had my doubts. Interestingly, the Protestant Christians didn't buy into this miracle theory either – they view the bread and wine (some denominations use grape juice because they are opposed to wine) merely as symbols of Jesus Christ's body and blood rather than the real deal. Which if you think about it is kind of sick too, just not as much.

As an adult, when you step back and look at the dying figure of Jesus Christ nailed to a cross and the changing of bread and wine into his actual body and blood for us to eat and drink, these do seem incredibly violent, cannibalistic and disturbing. Imagine a peaceful being from another planet looking at these symbols and rituals of the true Christian believers. How very frightening it might seem to them. Yes, the same applies to our vulnerable and impressionable children. Frightening! And yet, these are seen as just normal – just another ordinary, run of the mill part of the religious experience.

So, have you ever wondered why there was such a focus on death and eating the body and blood of Jesus Christ? Where did this belief come from and why was this important over 2,000 years ago? Get ready for another history lesson.

We can see evidence that human beings offered animal and human sacrifices to make amends for wrong doing or to win favor with a deity as far back as the bronze age and maybe even earlier. It is believed the original Jews also adopted this practice for a period of time. While generally repulsed by the idea, they understood that human life was the most valuable material for sacrifice and the ultimate offering to a deity. Based on archaeologist findings and writings, it is estimated that at least 25 cultures practiced human sacrifice. Some of these cultures were located in the Asia and Middle East areas where the largest religions in the world originated. It's apparent all of these religions were influenced by animal sacrifice and possibly human sacrifice practices. The point is, although by today's standards it's seen as very gruesome and inhumane, there's no doubt it was a widely accepted practice for many, many years.

There are many examples of human sacrifice throughout history. One example of the Ancient Romans practicing human sacrifice to win back favor with their gods was after they were defeated at the Battle of Cannae in Southeast Italy in 216 BCE. Apparently killing some people as an offering to the gods made them feel better about this lost battle, although it's highly doubtful this would have helped them win the next battle. There's evidence of human sacrifice also around 1000 BCE in Greece. West of Athens at Mount Lykaion where the altar of Zeus is located, the Greeks sacrificed humans as an offering to Zeus. In China, human sacrifice was practiced for thousands of years, although it appears they stopped around 221 BCE after the unification of China by its first emperor. Ancient Egypt human sacrifice occurred around 3000 BCE but was phased out by 2500 BCE. The city of Ur in modern day Iraq had a great human sacrifice death pit dating back to 2000 BCE. This is also the town where Abraham, the person documented in the Old Testament Bible and Hebrew Bible, was born and raised before moving to what is now the Israel area. He is estimated to have lived in Ur sometime between 2100 BCE to 1800 BCE. So, most likely the story of Abraham offering his young son Isaac as a human sacrifice and being stopped by a messenger from God before he completed the death was a way to teach people to stop performing human sacrifice. During this time period it was admirable that Abraham understood this to be wrong. However, he does still make a sacrifice on the altar to God, but uses a ram as an alternative to human sacrifice modeling a much more humane approach for his tribe to emulate. The assumption that he had a better chance of stopping human sacrifice by offering this alternative approach was smart as it worked. The Jews ultimately stopped human sacrifice but continued to sacrifice animals to God by following the story of Abraham.

During the time period of Jesus's life, some human sacrifices may have still been happening and we know animal sacrifices were still very popular. It therefore makes more sense why the death of Jesus was later interpreted by the early followers of Jesus (who were largely Jews) as the ultimate and final sacrifice to atone for the sins of all mankind. It was in their understanding, the climax and fulfillment of all the animal sacrifices in Judaism. In the 21st century we don't have many human or animal sacrifices to God, so these stories from 2,000 or more years ago seem irrelevant to our lives, not to mention very violent, revolting, and strange. As a result, the religions using the Old and New Testament Bibles give these stories other meanings in addition to their original purpose of convincing people to stop sacrificing human beings and animals to their Gods.

Like Abraham, it was important for Jesus to also convince people there was an alternative to sacrificing people and animals. His philosophy was that drinking wine and eating bread as an offering to God was significantly better than burning an animal or a person. There was also a similar belief in Greek mythology at this time period - if you could eat and drink the food and liquids of the gods, this would give you immortality. In Greek mythology however, deities were the only ones who ate ambrosia and drank nectar, which were the food and liquids of the gods. However, if a mortal person were to eat or drink these, they would get the magical property to provide them with immortality as well. So naturally, it was made to be a serious offense to steal either ambrosia or nectar and consume it. If you did this then you would be condemned to an afterlife in the underworld. Jesus changed this belief by not only making it okay, but also encouraged people to eat his body and drink his blood in the form of bread and wine. This provided the magical properties of immortal spiritual life similar to Greek mythology.

Magic and mystery – interesting how these stories have become part of the narrative surrounding the origins of many of the main religious pillars. But wow, this sure sounds like something that could have come straight out of a children's fantasy book like *Harry Potter*. Remarkably, many evangelical Christians actually ban their children from reading the Harry Potter books – could it be that the subject matter hits a little too close to home? Children love to believe in magic, and religious leaders often encourage their followers to be innocent and trusting like children. Accordingly, religious leaders expect their followers to believe in religious magic with unquestioning blind faith, and therefore may perceive other non-religious magical stories as threatening.

Chapter 13

If You're Happy and You Know it, That's a Sin!

So far, most of the focus in this book has been on the origins of religions and beliefs. Of course, over time many things experience change – cultures change, people change, ideas change, even religion changes. Many of those changes happen so gradually – barely discernible, they just seem to morph over time. It doesn't happen often, but sometimes significant changes in attitudes and beliefs can be identified as having been influenced by a single very influential and powerful individual. And their lasting impact on society may or may not be always positive as we'll learn in this chapter.

Attending college is a perfect opportunity in a young person's life to change by maturing, gaining knowledge and having new experiences. During my years in college, I continued to follow (or maybe it was just going along with, buying into, or pretending to follow) the Roman Catholic religion into which I was born and raised. Although I attended weekly mass service and still found it as boring as ever, the music at the contemporary church on campus was a dramatic improvement, making the entire experience significantly more bearable. As is typical of a college experience, my world started to expand as I met new people who came from different areas with different backgrounds. Sharing meals, sharing living spaces, as well as sharing ideas opened my eyes to quite a variety of people's different priorities, feelings, opinions and concerns. It was interesting to discover what made them tick – what caused someone to behave a certain way.

I was one of those people who seemed to get along with everyone. I accepted people for who they were – I respected their differences and accepted their views on life. I didn't feel the need to try to change them and I certainly expected they would treat me the same way. I was taken aback then by the actions of one particularly aggressive group, the college born-again Christians, who constantly felt the need to peddle their religious fanaticism in my direction. Perhaps I subconsciously gave them the impression that my soul needed saving. It didn't take long for me to come to the realization that some, but not all, of the people in this group who considered themselves to be extremely religious, unfortunately also turned out to be some of the most self-centered, mean-spirited people I came across. They were extremely opinionated, judgmental, and intolerant of people with different beliefs. Or maybe they were just the loudest and most vocal. I had a sneaking suspicion that many of them had tremendous guilt about their past questionable behaviors and so it seemed as if they just substituted one fanatical behavior for another, becoming religious zealots. I tried my best to withhold judgement about their personal beliefs and what to me came across as narrow-minded points of view. They were confident they were going to heaven in the afterlife due to their 100% commitment to Jesus Christ, proclaiming him to be their lord and savior, and quoting bible scriptures. But I didn't appreciate when they felt the need to proselytize to almost everyone they encountered, assuming others to be inferior as non-born-again Christians. I had always believed that God loved everyone. Instead, the message I got from watching and listening to them seemed to be more about who God does not love.

As you probably have deduced, I have had many odious experiences with people fitting this description - maybe you have too. Honestly, I did try my best to withhold judgement! But for all their efforts, their spiels never worked on me. Rather than being inspired, I was more alienated by their religious rhetoric. I heard it said that religion is like a pair of shoes… find one that fits for you, but don't make me wear your shoes. Amen to that!

Another important critical thinking life lesson I learned in college came from my favorite Economics professor. His lesson was that people who did not do any research or studying and do not know the answers to questions but still think they know everything and are always right are significantly more dangerous than people who just admit they do not know. To make his point, he gave test questions with only true or false answers that were scored very creatively. Each question counted for one point if you got it correct, however, if you got it wrong you received minus two points, and if you put no answer, you got zero points. As you can imagine, some students got percentage test scores in the 20-30% range. This testing approach really made you think about how well you knew the subject matter before answering as it was better to leave the question blank if you were not sure. The learning being, if you do not know something it is much better to admit it then to think you are knowledgeable. I find this to be true in life too. Unfortunately, the extreme religious zealots fall into the camp of, "I'm so convinced I'm right and everyone must believe what I believe even though I haven't critically investigated the answers to the life and death questions I'm so sure of."

Although I don't plan to get into the psychology driving the extreme behavior of these religious zealot born-again groups, there is much historic precedent for it. There are many examples of some of the cruelest actions taken against other human beings in the name of Jesus Christ, God, Muhammed, Buddha, and (insert any other God or Prophet name here). Cruelty and intolerance – all in the name of religion. For some reason, there seems to be a strong desire of religious zealots to persuade you to believe what they believe even though they have done no critical thinking research as to the origins of these beliefs. This has been true through history as religions strengthened in numbers and geographically. The zealots supported the goals of religious leaders, which revolved around increasing influence and power. One way to accomplish these goals was to establish new beliefs they claim had been endorsed by God, and then force their community to conform to this thinking. They did this initially by using an intellectual persuasion approach, but then they added physical pain or even death if people were reluctant to accept their proselytizing. Using a critical thinking approach, we can look back in history and find an early "born again" Christian who actually was the model for the current behavior of people who fit this profile.

The first well known extremist "born again" Christian was Saint Augustine of Hippo who lived from 354 CE to 430 CE. He had a huge influence on the culture and beliefs of western society that continues today. He's considered a saint in the Catholic Church but as you learn more about him, this is somewhat shocking since he was far from a kind and loving human being. He was born a Roman African from the current day area of Algeria in northern Africa and was among the last of the classically educated men from the ancient Roman Empire. As an early Christian theologian and philosopher, his writings influenced the development of Western Christianity and western philosophy. Augustine believed and preached that anything causing a loss of rational control was bad or sinful. He came to this conclusion based on religious influences and experiences in his life. During Augustine's time, he was influenced by the philosophy of control, which was very important in Stoic, Buddhist, and Christian beliefs. The overriding philosophy was; to be truly happy you must not allow yourself to be controlled by the desire for pleasure or the fear of pain. The life experience that had an impact on Augustine's thinking was he had been very promiscuous as a young man, having sexual intercourse with many women. Additionally, he had a lot of guilt for all the abhorrent, mean-spirited things he did growing up which led him to become "born again." Sound familiar? However, once he decided to be "born again" he began writing and teaching that sexual intercourse was evil because it caused pleasure and a temporary loss of control. It seems Augustine's philosophy could be summed up with one phrase - if you're happy and you know it, that's a sin!

Augustine even took his beliefs about sex a step further - he argued all human beings are born with original sin because their life begins with sexual intercourse and they are born through a woman's vaginal canal. Augustine positioned this as very dirty and evil - as a result, he argued that all unbaptized people would be condemned to hellfire for all eternity. So naturally, an infant needed to be purified as soon as possible after birth to rid itself of the filth of being born from a woman who had engaged in sexual intercourse. And he doesn't stop there with his anti-sex crusade. Augustine goes further asserting that women drive sexual passion in men, and therefore, a woman's embrace is sordid and indecent. This thinking contributed significantly to western beliefs that sexual topics were dirty, uncovered women were dirty, and that a woman's purpose was primarily to reproduce.

In addition to physical relations being evil and transmitted to a newborn child, Augustine also preached that everyone is born with an inherent urge to do bad things and disobey God. He also added that everyone born inherits the sin of Adam when he disobeyed God's command not to eat the forbidden fruit. As infants, Christians are baptized not only to free them from original sin transmitted to them from past generations and by the birth process, but also to welcome them into the faith.

Growing up I always had wondered what caused original sin and why it was that you were able to simply wash it away with magical holy water. No one ever explained why you had original sin - I just assumed it was like getting cooties (children's term for an imaginary germ). Not until I was an adult, did I realize through reading about Saint Augustine that original sin was related to the process of reproduction. Hard to believe this belief still exists today. Okay, now we know the origin of people believing that just the act of being born requires baptism to save you from going to hell, but why does the magical holy water keep you out of hell? This remains a mystery to me except that the guys who wrote the religion claimed it would work. I also wondered who started the baptizing business. The

Christians award this prize to John the Baptist but like many religious rituals or thoughts this one was done long before and emulated by the Christians.

The Jews utilized the baptism ritual or ritual bath in the first century to cleanse themselves after touching a corpse or a leper. After they performed these tasks, they were considered ritually defiled and could not enter or participate in holy temple. It was therefore necessary to wash away these impurities through the baptism ritual. This Jewish baptism ritual evolved to be used in converting gentiles to Judaism, which also included circumcision for men or boys.

Both John the Baptist and Mithraism deserve credit for influencing the ritual of baptism in Christianity. John the Baptist lived during the time of Jesus Christ and was part of an ascetic Jewish desert sect called the Essene tribe, which is best known for creating the Dead Sea scrolls. This sect used baptism as a purity ritual along with obeying God's commandments. They believed both were needed to be pure. And as I mentioned earlier Mithraism also had a baptism ritual, which Constantine combined with the Judaism Christian cult ritual into his one merged religion, Christianity.

Baptism, as with many other rituals, got its earliest start as a very common-sense activity. Maintaining a clean body has always been a beneficial practice for staying healthy. We also know it is critical to wash your hands after handling a sick or dead person to avoid getting sick yourself. Early people probably realized this through trial and error but did not know it was bacteria that you were removing from your body. As a result, the best way to get people to wash their hands and take a bath, aka full body baptism, was to have God require it to get to heaven. This most likely is also the origin of the western saying, "Cleanliness is next to godliness". Saint Augustine and the Christians turned this common-sense activity into a cure for sins rather than just a healthy respect for cleanliness.

Getting back to Augustine - how was he able to exert such influence on western society? Although Augustine was not an aristocrat since his father was only a petty official in Carthage, Tunisia, he did participate in the Roman privileged class because of his education. He was a very persuasive person and also a deep thinker. His writings about himself are considered to be the first genuine autobiography and his questioning of his own behavior, the beginning of the modern science of psychology. Augustine is also considered to be one of the theological fathers of the Protestant Reformation due to his teaching on salvation and divine grace.

Augustine's success can be attributed to the influence of Virgil and Cicero, the two most influential educators in ancient Rome during his time. Both of these men were especially instrumental in helping develop Augustine's charisma. It was no secret - Augustine loved Cicero! So much so that Augustine's persuasive techniques actually came from studying and modeling Cicero. He also modeled his language and style after his other idol, Virgil. When Augustine became a bishop, he delighted his congregation with rhyming the Latin language similar to what a talented Baptist preacher or evangelist does today. He created a verbal show for his congregation that was new and enticing. Both Virgil and Cicero were loved by the Latin world, with Cicero ranking just below Virgil on the divinity charts. Virgil was a great teacher of language and writing style and lived from 70 BCE to 19 BCE. He is considered to have been the greatest ancient Roman poet. His most famous work was Aeneid, which describes the founding of Rome by Romulus and Remus. His works influenced western literature such as Dante's Divine Comedy, in which Virgil appears as Dante's guide through hell and purgatory. Augustine was able to take the style of Virgil and enhance it with an African swing. He is thought to have started what would become the people's Latin of the Middle Ages, which was a more simplified, rhythmic, and rhyming language than ancient Latin.

Although Augustine was influenced by Virgil's style, he also embraced the teachings of Cicero. Cicero was a great teacher of argument and lived from 106 BCE to 43 BCE. His influence on the Latin language impacted the history of prose, not only in Latin but also in European languages up to the 1800s CE. His writings even had an influence on the structure of the United States' government. He was a formidable orator, lawyer, statesman, translator, and philosopher. Augustine modeled himself after Cicero and as a result became very skilled at influencing people and winning arguments. One of the main reasons why we know so much about Cicero is he wrote everything down. Cicero did not "speak from the heart", but instead was very calculating. He was always focused on how to achieve his goal through argument and was extremely clever. He was a genius at manipulating people and getting what he wanted. Augustine learned how to do this by modeling Cicero and as a result became very influential himself.

As mentioned earlier, Augustine was thought to be one of the first born-again Christians. He lived his life in the same manner as many born again people of today. He was self-loathing because he had been a thief as a boy, treated his overbearing mother poorly, and had sex with many women including a peasant woman he shamefully loved until he sent her away with his child. He left her and his son because he was educated and a higher-class level than a peasant. He then got engaged to marry a 12-year-old heiress, but during the engagement period decided to become a celibate priest instead, calling off the marriage. From his actions, it's apparent that Augustine was a very selfish and cruel person.

Although his mother believed in Catholicism, Augustine initially rejected this religion and followed Manicheism until he converted to Catholicism. He was strongly influenced by Manicheism, which was often referred to as the religion of light. This religion believed there was always a struggle between a good spiritual world of light and an evil material world of darkness. This religion was founded by Mani, an Iranian prophet, who declared himself to be an apostle of Jesus Christ but also the reincarnation of different religious figures such as, Buddha, Krishna, Zoroaster, and Jesus. Between 200 CE and 600 CE this religion was in strong competition with Christianity but never achieved the political support needed to overtake it. In Persia, where it was stronger, it was eventually overtaken by Islam in the 600s CE. Nevertheless, Augustine incorporated the Manicheism notion of a struggle between good and evil into his Christian teaching. He preached that people could obtain grace from God through the sacraments of the church to help them combat this evil. However, one Christian group at the time, called the Donatists, did not believe an unworthy priest could confer the grace of God through the sacraments. Since Augustine would not accept any criticism of his teachings, he had them arrested, imprisoned, beaten, tortured and eventually executed. So, in addition to being the first born-again Christian, Augustine is also credited with influencing the Catholic Inquisition as the future popes modeled their persecution of non-believers after him.

For all his greatness, Augustine was an evil cleric and used state sponsored cruelty to punish anyone who dared oppose him, although he was full of mercy for those who feared him. He also magnified the belief that to be saved from evil or to be worthy of salvation, you needed to be self-loathing and inflict punishment on yourself. There are many religions that seem to foster this attitude which I find toxic, but people like Augustine and John the Baptist along with his Essene sect seemed to love it.

Many of the foundations of modern Christianity and western society's culture can be traced to Augustine's teachings and influence. Unfortunately, most of them have arguably had a negative impact on mental health and living a happy life. For example, the damage Augustine did to our view of both the human body and sexuality is unhealthy and harmful. Ask yourself, would your creator be so ashamed of the human body creation that it needed to be covered up or be perceived as shameful? I'm not advocating running around naked all the time but our prudish views of the human body and sex could use an overhaul to be healthier and less guilt ridden. We should not be made to feel guilty by religious doctrine when we are just living our lives. All things considered; I am at a loss to understand why this guy was made a saint.

As you probably guessed I am very guarded when I encounter a proselytizing religious person, as they often tend to give the impression of being very selfish and cruel with little or no tolerance for other people's beliefs. Their words and actions were often about whom God does not love. I stopped being fooled long ago by the flowery religious words they utilize. As a result, I preferred to observe how people treat others and how they behave to assess if they are truly loving and kind human beings. I always felt the old adage is true, that actions speak louder than words. Oh, and if you're happy and you know it, just stay happy and pass it on to others.

Chapter 14

This Calls for a Celebration

There is much to love about the celebration of holidays. Some holidays are celebrated with joyful festivities, gatherings with friends and family, thankful reflections, religious importance, songs, gifts, and ooh – the food! While other holidays are more solemn in nature, often observed through fasting, prayer and repentance. Whether joyous or somber, many holidays are saturated with superstitions or traditions, sometimes to the point of being overblown, which can lead to anxiety and unhappiness. Understanding where, when, and why holidays originated makes it easier to put them in perspective, hopefully alleviating some of the angst they may cause. Realizing how many holidays and traditions have been clearly invented long ago and then influenced arbitrarily over time to what we currently believe, gives each of us the go-ahead to reinvent them to suit our own lives. In other words, we can make these holidays be what we want, which allows us to focus more on the celebration of life and less on the burden of outdated traditions and superstitions. If you can achieve this than you truly are thinking both critically and independently, and one of the benefits is a much more enjoyable and stress-free life.

This chapter is devoted to exploring a few of the main religious holidays celebrated around the world; their origins, links to pagan festivals, ties to secular observances and related traditions, rituals and customs. Acknowledging there are countless other holidays, here are the handful of holidays I selected to discuss as examples:

Christian holidays:

— Christmas (from winter festival to Jesus' birthday to Santa Claus)
— Easter (from spring growing season to Jesus' resurrection to colored eggs and chocolate bunnies)
— Halloween (from harvest season to honoring those who have died to trick-or-treating, and its relationship to Buddhist All Souls Day or Chinese Ghost Festival)

Islam holidays:

— Eid al-Fitr (breaking of the fast, end of Ramadan)
— Eid-al-Adha (festival of sacrifice)

Hinduism holidays:

— Diwali (festival of lights)

- Holi (festival of color)

Judaism holidays:

- Rosh Hashanah (agricultural new year, celebrates the birth of the world)
- Yom Kippur (day of atonement)

Buddhism holiday:

- Wesak (3-in-1 holiday: original Buddha's birth, enlightenment, and passage into nirvana)

But first, a look at the significance of calendars and numerology ...

Before jumping into the holidays, an explanation of the lunar calendar used by many religions to set their holiday dates will provide a little insight, as the timing of these holidays is often integral to their meaning. A lunar month is the time between our observed new moon phases, which on average is 29 days, 12 hours and 14 minutes. As you probably are aware, it is not the same period of time each month due to the moon's orbit, its distance from the earth and relationship to the sun. The lunar calendar's new year starts with the first new moon, which on the Gregorian calendar occurs between the dates of January 21st and February 20th. As an example of how this impacts holiday timing, you will discover that several holidays occur in the seventh lunar month, which falls in August or September rather than July, which is the Gregorian calendar's seventh month. The seventh lunar month is later than July because the lunar calendar begins almost a month or more after the Gregorian calendar's January 1st starting date.

Since ancient religions did not know the earth orbited the sun, they kept track of time by the moon. Of course, mathematically, 12 lunar months does not equal a year, so over time it becomes very inaccurate at measuring solar years. Eventually the royal astrologers realized the 12 lunar cycles were out of sync with the seasons, which follow the solar year, and started adding a month periodically to the annual calendar as early as 432 BCE in Athens, Greece. These early calendars were refined over time and eventually were switched over to our current Gregorian calendar, in which one year is based on the orbit of the earth around the sun. Of course, we know this calendar is also not totally accurate either, so every four years an extra day is added to stay in line with the orbit of our earth around the sun. This is called leap year, but as you'll learn later in the chapter, even that's not totally accurate as certain leap years need to be skipped just to keep us on our toes.

Many religious beliefs and customs still follow the lunar calendar in view of the fact that people believe they were initiated by the god or gods they worship, which made them very hard to change. Unfortunately, these gods were not very scientifically adept and therefore, not aware of the earth revolving around the sun. In addition, for 3,000 years, lunar calendars have guided farming activities in Asia and the Middle East by documenting what happened to the weather every half of a lunar period or approximately 14 or 15 days. To guide them, they divided the year into 24 periods, with four seasons of exactly three lunar months each. This actually seemed like a good tool to predict changes in the weather, except that it was not very accurate – every year it was off by 17 days because the solar year has 365 days and not 348 days based on 12 lunar periods. Similar to other ancient religious beliefs, this flawed acceptance of weather patterns based on a lunar calendar proclaimed by gods or all-knowing ancestors, was only applicable to the climate zone of approximately 50 degrees latitude to 30 degrees latitude. Apparently, the gods and ancestors did not care about the rest of the world or maybe it was assumed there were other gods responsible for those areas. In addition, as is happening more and more these days, climate change is wreaking havoc with weather patterns by changing the length of the seasons, which makes the ancient guidance used for farming even more inaccurate. However, for your informational curiosity, the following is a listing of the 24 ancient lunar-based periods as developed by ancient ancestors or gods. As a note of warning – they are very, very ambiguous!

Spring

1. Beginning of spring
2. Rainwater
3. Insects awakening
4. Spring equinox
5. Fresh green
6. Grain rain

Summer

7. Beginning of summer
8. Lesser fullness
9. Grain in ear
10. Summer solstice
11. Lesser heat
12. Greater heat

Autumn

13. Beginning of autumn
14. End of heat
15. White dew
16. Autumnal equinox
17. Cold dew

18. First frost

Winter

19. Beginning of winter
20. Light snow
21. Heavy snow
22. Winter solstice
23. Lesser cold
24. Greater cold

 Many people think these ancient gods and ancestors had superior insight into the world, but after we employ a critical approach to this thinking, we realize their understanding of the world was very limited. They only observed what they could physically see and then they made the rest up to explain what we now know from scientific discoveries.

 Since the largest religions were mostly invented in ancient times, many of them today still follow some version of the lunar calendar. For example, the Jewish religious year, dating back to 3760 BCE, begins in autumn and consists of 12 months alternating between 30 and 29 days since the average moon orbit around the earth is 29.5 days. They measure time in 19-year periods, with an extra month added in years 3, 6, 8, 11,14, and 19 to sync up with the seasons. This system is close to being accurate but still off by a few days. As you have noticed, most religions seem to be stuck in the past - even when science can explain things to make them more accurate and useful, religions refuse to change due to their deep-seated beliefs that these things were somehow developed by God(s), albeit always with Northern Hemisphere god(s).

Another example is the Islamic lunar calendar, which dates back to July 15, 622 CE, thought to be the date when the Prophet Muhammad moved from Mecca to Medina. This religion's calendar is similar to the Judaism calendar of 12 months alternating between 30 and 29 days, however no effort has been made to sync the lunar calendar and seasons together by adding leap years or extra months. As a result, it does not even come close to the current Gregorian calendar. This religion is not concerned about staying connected with agriculture or seasons and so there is a difference of 11 or more days every year versus the Gregorian calendar. The Islamic religion has been more rigid than other religions, especially compared to the Christians, by not altering their method of measuring time. The Christian religion had an advantage from its outset due to the heavy influence of the Roman Empire, which just happened to have the most accurate calendar at that period of time. Although Islam started much later than Christianity, they hated the Roman Christians and would kill them as non-believers of Islam, called infidels. Of course, they were not going to adopt their calendar, even if it happened to be more accurate. This is why the Islamic calendar is so inaccurate today and obstinately, is the reason behind their continued refusal to change.

The Christians, on the other hand, follow the Gregorian calendar or Christian calendar because their religion was started and endorsed by the Roman Empire. Although this calendar was not religion based, it was revised over time by the Catholic Church making it easier for Christians to adopt this more accurate calendar. Prior to Christianity being invented, Julius Caesar proclaimed the Julian calendar as the official calendar in 46 BCE. In the mid-300s CE, the Romans, along with their newly adopted Christian religion, continued to follow the Julian calendar until Pope Gregory 13th had it revised in 1582 CE. This new calendar eventually became known as our current Gregorian calendar. The reason for this revision was to make the calendar more accurate in measuring the earth's revolution around the sun. The Julian calendar added a day every four years, which was close in achieving this goal, but not quite right. This is when the leap year calculation got more complicated. To explain, the revision creating the Gregorian calendar stipulated a day would be added every four years, except for the years in that four-year cycle that were not evenly divisible by both 100 and 400 (For example, 1900 CE fell in the four-year cycle and is evenly divisible by 100, but not 400 and so it was not a leap year. With this stipulation, the following years are not leap years – 1700, 1800, 1900, 2100, 2200, 2300, 2500, 2600, etc. Complicated! Make sure to keep this in mind if you think you'll still be alive in the year 2100!) Ultimately, this Gregorian calendar based on science was found to be the most accurate measurement of annual time. Since the calendar had no spiritual or religious meaning to Christians, it was therefore easier for them to adopt it compared to other religions. This is a great example of when science is used, results are more useful and accurate versus relying on religious superstition and myths.

The Hindu calendar is based on both the moon and the sun. Months are based on the moon cycles and the beginning of the year is determined by the spring equinox. To sync the solar calendar with the lunar calendar they add a month every third year because the 12 lunar months are short by approximately 11 days every year. This calendar is still used for purposes of holidays and traditions. However, the approach became very cumbersome for everyday life and was also measured differently all over India. On March 22, 1957 CE with the spring equinox, Indians reformed their calendar to the Gregorian calendar for secular activities and continue to follow this calendar system, except for religious holidays, which continue to use the original Hindu calendar.

The official Chinese calendar is also the Gregorian calendar, but similar to India, this Asian culture still uses the lunar calendar for celebrations and traditions. In many Asian countries they use both systems concurrently, so you might get to celebrate your birthday twice in one year, a big bonus for getting more presents. The Chinese lunar year starts with a new moon between January 21st and February 20th. The new moon comes every 29.5 days and so they add a month every 3 years to sync with the seasons. Once again, this shows that the ancient gods and prophets were not very knowledgeable when it came to seasonal calendars and measuring a solar orbit around the sun, confirming even they were fallible.

In addition to the significance of the lunar calendar related to religious holidays, the use of numerology supporting religious superstitions was also significant. Beginning thousands of years ago, people began assigning spiritual significance to numbers. When a coincidence with a number was found, that number was embraced and all kinds of meaning were assigned to it. If no coincidence was found, people just deemed it to be random and they disregarded that information. For example, if three birds are on a branch looking into your window you could assume this is the holy trinity watching over you. Of course, if a fourth or fifth bird were to join the group, this would just be considered to be birds on a branch. Or because people believe bad things come in threes, if two bad things happen, the assumption is another bad thing is about to happen (or maybe they just forgot to count a bad thing that already happened). Religious beliefs sometimes follow this same logical or illogical way of thinking as they rely heavily on superstition.

As mentioned earlier, there are a number of religious holidays that happen in the seventh lunar month, such as the Buddhist All Souls Day, also referred to as the Chinese Ghost Festival. What was so special about the number seven? The number seven is considered to be important because it is the sum of the spiritual number three and the material number four. Ancient people found all kinds of reasons that the number three was very mystical and spiritual. For instance, in ancient Babylon, the three primary gods were Anu, Bel, and Ea - they represented heaven, earth, and the abyss. The Egyptian sun god had three main activities each day, which included rising, midday and setting. Plato thought the three corners of a triangle were very special and mystical. The Hindus and the Christians invented the holy trinity with three gods in one – Brama, Vishnu and Shiva; and God the Father, Son, and Holy Ghost.

As a result of all the religious significance and attention attached to the number three, we now have a number of folklore and superstitions reinforcing this as a spiritual number. Such as three wishes, three guesses, three little pigs, three bears, three Billy goats gruff, the little mermaid needed to find love by her third day as a human, bad things happen in threes, they even decided to have Jesus Christ die at three o'clock on the third day, and on and on and on. Hey look – even that last phrase included three on's!

Where three was considered a spiritual number, alternately, the number four was considered to be a material number for several reasons. There are four elements - earth, air, fire, and water. And there are four seasons (unless of course you live on the equator and then it's just hot, hot, hot and hot – yes, I used hot four times!). There are also four points of a compass and four phases of the moon (new, half-moon waxing, full, half-moon waning - I don't know what happened to a quarter moon or a crescent moon but it wouldn't add up to four so these were discarded as not important). Interestingly based on today's science, there are actually eight phases of the moon (new, waxing crescent, first quarter, waxing gibbous, full, waning gibbous, third quarter, waning crescent), which pretty much destroys some of the ancient symbolism attached to the number four.

Learning the origins of the meaning attached to numerology is interesting. Although it is somewhat humorous when you realize a number such as seven is considered significant simply because it is the sum of three plus four, which seems to be really weak reasoning. The point is that in ancient times and even now, people can assign any spiritual meaning to anything they choose. And yet, numerology is still alive and well, continuing to influence many people's beliefs. It's unfortunate and sad that these superstitions sometimes invade everyday life to an obsessive degree causing anxiety and stress. This is why it is so important to keep all of these beliefs in perspective and yes, always use critical thinking skills.

And now on to the holidays...

Christmas

Regardless of religious or non-religious affiliation, most people around the world are at least somewhat familiar with the Christian holiday of Christmas. Christmas has its roots in Saturnalia, a Roman pagan festival, which honors the god of agriculture and harvest. Historically, this festival was held during the seven-day period from December 17th to the 24th and was extremely popular - so popular in fact, all work stopped; even work done by enslaved people. This festival was connected to the end of the winter sowing season, which is the reason for the timing, as well as its association with the agriculture god. As mentioned earlier in the book, the Mithraism cult celebrated Mithra's birthday on December 25th, so to combine the parties, the Roman political and religious leaders moved their main holiday to December 25th even though Sol was a bigger deal than Mirtha. They also made December 25th Jesus's birthday celebration and called the combined holiday Christmas. Emperor Constantine dictated this was to be the new holiday celebration and date, making it official. Apparently, no one questioned him since he was the emperor – plus, he most likely sold the new festival as being bigger and more enjoyable for everyone.

Before the Roman Empire, the ancient Greeks had their own god of agriculture and harvest who was called Kronos. (Note: This god is not to be confused with the PlayStation 4 video game "Battle Worlds: Kronos" or the online slot machine games by the same name. It appears the video game builders also had a fondness for Greek mythology gods, or at least the Kronos god!) The Greeks depicted Kronos as an old man holding a sickle or curved sword, ready to harvest grain at a moment's notice. Kronos was very powerful as he was the son of Uranus (Heaven) and Gaea (Earth), however he was not a very popular god. And yet the people believing in Greek mythology gods still celebrated the harvest by worshiping him. This harvest festival was similar to what eventually became the Saturnalia festival, so in actuality the Christmas holiday season can even be traced all the way back to the ancient Greeks.

The Roman's god of sowing seed was called Saturn (Latin: Saturnus). Compared to the Greek god Kronos, Saturn was significantly more popular, stylish and impressive. The remains of Saturn's temple can still be seen in Rome, Italy with eight columns from the temple's front porch still standing in the ruins of the Roman Forum. He was so popular he even had a day named after him, Saturday, which in my opinion is the best day of the week.

Saturnalia was the merriest festival of the year and over time morphed into the Christmas holiday season we currently celebrate. Similar to today, most work and businesses were suspended, and back at that time, enslaved people were even given temporary freedom to say and do what they liked. Additionally, certain moral restrictions were eased such as gambling, singing, playing music, feasting, and socializing. Easing of morals sure sounds a lot like the current day office parties. Of course, in today's society people tend to get into trouble during these festivities and have to face the consequences in January. I wonder if the ancient Romans were genuinely more forgiving of these temporary lapses in judgment than we are today? And one last feature of this merry festival - people also gave each other gifts. At least we now know who is to blame for holiday gift giving stress – it was the ancient Romans!

The gift giving in ancient Rome, however, was not as extravagant or pressured as it is now with the Christmas holiday. The most common gift the Romans gave was wax taper candles, which signified light returning after the solstice. The winter solstice, or the shortest daylight day of the year, occurs on December 21st or 22nd in the Northern Hemisphere, after which the amount of daylight begins getting longer. Doesn't it seem odd this holiday is set up exclusively for the Northern Hemisphere? By the way, if Christmas is truly such a sacred day honoring the birth of Jesus Christ who brings light to the world as evidenced by the days getting longer, it only seems to apply to the Northern Hemisphere. I suppose the God 2,000 years ago didn't know about the Southern Hemisphere or was only a God designed for the Northern Hemisphere. Don't you think a God would at least acknowledge the difference between the Northern and Southern hemispheres' timing of the winter solstices? In the Southern Hemisphere, the days actually start getting shorter after this date with the summer season in full swing forcing Santa Clause to dress in his swimming suit rather than boots and a coat. Obviously, the ancient Romans were not aware of, or were really unconcerned with, the Southern Hemisphere - otherwise people living in the south would be celebrating Saturnalia or Christmas at the end of June since their winter solstice is June 20th or 21st.

One of the ancient Roman traditions that is beautiful to see continuing in today's holiday season was the appreciation for the significance of lights. Today, seeing all the candles and little twinkling lights on display during December enhances the romance, warmth, and specialness of this holiday season. The Romans must have thought so too. The Romans decorated their homes with greenery and wreaths and even changed the style of clothing they wore. I can't help but wonder if they had anything akin to an ugly Christmas sweater!

Similar to today, wishing everyone good cheer was popular back in ancient Roman times. Everyone greeted each other with "Io Saturnalia", with the "Io" being pronounced as "yo". Many just shortened their greeting to "Io, Io, Io", dropping the religious reference to the god, Saturnalia. In current times, most people seem to enjoy wishing everyone good cheer during this holiday season as well, and recently there has been a new emphasis to be more inclusive in our good cheer wishing. However, it's surprising that some devoted Christians at times are agitated or express anger when others greet them with "Seasons Greetings", "Happy Holidays", "Happy Hanukkah" (making sure they say it by clearing their throat), or "Happy Kwanzaa", instead of "Merry Christmas" or "Happy Christmas". It's as if they fail to remember more than two thirds of the world's population doesn't share their same belief in Jesus and therefore his birth on Christmas means nothing to them. "Happy Holidays" seems to be a more tolerant and inclusive greeting. There is precedent, as was done in ancient times, to drop the religious god reference to this holiday and just focus on the joy. So, if you want to be historically correct in your holiday wishes and non-denominational, consider wishing everyone "Lo", although this may infuriate those Merry-Christmas-wishing police. Could be a fun, unique and really short greeting for your next holiday card!

Now that we know the roots of the Christmas holiday, you might wonder how and when it became connected to Jesus' birthday. First of all, the earliest Jewish Christians did not celebrate Jesus' birth, and by the way, we really don't even know the exact month or date on which he was born. Around 200 CE, in the Egyptian area and some of the area east of Egypt, it was decided that Jesus' birth was on January 6th. Then around the same time period, a Roman Christian historian, Sextus Julius Africanus decided Jesus' immaculate conception was March 25th. He chose this date since this is when he believed the world was created in 5509 BCE. Considering that we now know the earth was formed about 4.5 billion years ago and we have evidence human beings existed approximately 300,000 years ago, it appears Sextus was not even close in his calculation, but let's not let facts get in the way of a good story. He didn't actually calculate anything since he just copied the Byzantine Empire's estimate of the earth's creation on September 1, 5509 BCE and then revised it to March 25th. He arrived at this date by counting backward nine months from Jesus' newly decided birth date of December 25th making the conception and birth story appear to be feasible. When the Roman Empire adopted Christianity as their national religion, they assigned this date as Jesus' birth date as well. As previously mentioned, Emperor Constantine combined the Saturnalia and Mithra holidays, which were pagan religions and now considered evil, with the Christmas holiday in order to keep everyone happy – besides, it was such a fantastic and fun holiday regardless of what you believed. Over time the Eastern Christian Church caved in as well, replacing January 6th with the newly agreed upon December 25th as his birth date. They then changed January 6th to denote the arrival of the magi in Bethlehem and thus the time period from December 25th to January 6th became known as the twelve days of Christmas, hence the song. Everything worked out great for all, even though this is still a totally contrived holiday with the dates altered to fit the story. In view of that, we all have the power to change or improve the holiday anyway we desire - just like the ancient people did. Make it be whatever it means to you – and celebrate it however and whenever you choose. In my own family, to accommodate everyone's schedules and wishes, we pick whatever date (generally in December) works best for all to celebrate the holiday – the most important part for us is just being together as a family.

A major nonreligious feature of the current Christmas holiday tradition celebrated all over the world is the arrival of Santa Claus. We just saw the leap from the ancient Roman Saturnalia to linking the holiday with Jesus' birth, but how did Santa Claus get connected to this holiday? Our current Santa Claus originated with a man named Nicolas living in the early 300s CE on the coast of the Mediterranean, in present day Demre, Turkey. Wait, what about the North Pole? That comes way later. Nicolas inherited a fortune when his parents died. He was a very religious guy and became a priest, and since he was wealthy, he was able to move up in the church to become a bishop. He used his money to help adults and protect children, which were his noblest attributes. Because the Council of Nicaea (325 CE) was close to where he lived, he was thought to have participated in it and to have had input into inventing Christianity. He died December 6, 343 CE, and as a result of all this great work and kindness to others, the Catholic Church made him a Saint. He became very popular in Europe, especially with the Dutch, and for centuries Europeans have commemorated his death on December 6th.

The evolution from Saint Nicolas to Santa Claus didn't begin until after the American Revolution in the United States. In New York City, Saint Nicholas was marketed as the patron saint of the city in remembrance of their Dutch roots, with a church being dedicated to him. As a reminder, New York was originally inhabited by the Manhattan Indians until the Dutch took it from them and called it New Amsterdam. Then the English took it from the Dutch and renamed it New York after the Duke of York. However, they still wanted to remember the Dutch roots, so Washington Irving portrayed Saint Nicholas as an elfin Dutch person with a clay pipe in his satire, "Knickerbocker's History of New York" published in 1809 CE. As background, Washington Irving was a popular short story writer who published works such as "Rip Van Winkle" and "The Legend of Sleepy Hollow". In this fictional story, Saint Nicholas was portrayed as the patron Saint of New Amsterdam (New York City), described as a jolly old Dutchman, nicknamed Santa Claus, who parked his wagon on rooftops and slid down chimneys with gifts for sleeping children on his feast day of December 6th. The word Santa Claus comes from the Dutch word Sinterklaas (a word contraction of Sint Nikolaas).

Santa Claus evolved further in 1810 CE, when the artist Alexander Anderson created the first American image of Nicholas for the New York Historical Society. He showed Nicholas in a gift-giving setting with children's treats in stockings hanging at a fireplace. In 1821 CE, a book titled, "The Children's Friend Number III" had a poem that formed the main story of Santa Claus. This poem had Santa flying over chimney tops in a sleigh driven by reindeer. It was written by Arthur J Stansbury, a 1799 CE graduate of Columbia College who later became a licensed Presbyterian Minister. He was an accomplished writer who wrote and illustrated books for children and also wrote congressional debate reports for twenty years. His illustrated story introduced the notion of Santa rewarding good behavior while punishing bad behavior. In this poem, the children's toys were described as safe, with specific warnings against crackers, cannons, squibs, or rockets – because of course, you didn't want anyone "to blow their eyes up, or their pockets!" Books in the poem were described as "pretty to store their minds" - obviously a much better gift choice. The picture accompanying the poem even included a bookshelf in the sleigh picture for these literary gifts. This poem also refers to Santa Claus' arrival on Christmas Eve, instead of December 6th.

It was later in 1823 CE when the poem, "A Visit from Nicholas" became popular, more commonly known today as "The Night Before Christmas", significantly reinforcing the Santa Claus tradition and more strongly connecting Santa Claus to Christmas Eve rather than December 6th. In the 1920s CE, Norman Rockwell and other illustrators began showing Santa as a jolly, red-suited, pleasantly plump man. This image was refined further in the 1950s CE to the image you see now in America, commonly associated with the Coca-Cola advertisements.

Around the world, Santa Claus is known by a number of different names. One Internet website lists a whopping 124 different names, although the most familiar are Father Christmas, Saint Nicholas, Saint Nick, Kris Kringle, or simply Santa. All these familiar characters originated in the western Christian culture, with all of them bringing gifts of toys and candy on Christmas Eve to well-behaved children and either lumps of coal or nothing at all to those children deemed to be naughty. Of course, if you're not Christian, or you happen to be poor and therefore can't afford to buy your kids anything, sadly you're out of luck, as this holiday was not designed with you in mind. Although this tradition of giving gifts to children has well-meaning intentions, it can be a source of cruelness or sadness. This can particularly be true for the many non-Christian or poor people living in societies where the holiday is celebrated with extreme enthusiasm and lavishness. It's important to make sure the children who do not benefit from Santa's gift-giving are not unintentionally made to feel bad about themselves, given that this tradition is focused on those who have disposable income. If an impoverished child received no gifts on Christmas morning, they would naturally assume they were "bad" or did something wrong. How sad! For these reasons, Santa Claus should probably not be portrayed as "real", even to children, as the stories about him, were made up. It's important to consider the negative effect on mental health of children that can result by deceptively portraying the myth as real or from making them feel bad about themselves. However, the Santa Claus stories are certainly fun and exciting, but perhaps they should stay in fantasyland, even for children.

Easter

The next biggie in the list of Christian holidays is Easter. For Christians, Easter celebrates the resurrection of Jesus Christ on the third day after his death by Roman crucifixion. Or for some, it just celebrates when you eat chocolate bunnies (ears first, of course) and children hunt for plastic eggs filled with treasures hidden in the yard or house. The origins of the Easter holiday include a mix of pagan festivals, Judaism, and also of course, Jesus Christ's resurrection from the dead.

Since pre-historic times, people have celebrated the equinoxes and solstices as sacred times. It makes sense since so much of survival was dependent on the weather, cycles of the sun, and agricultural growing seasons. So, it also makes sense that the spring festivals, with the theme of new life and relief from the cold and brutal winter, would later become connected to Jesus having conquered death by being resurrected after the crucifixion. Christians would use this story as emphatic proof that Jesus was indeed a real god.

As previously discussed, it was during the council of Nicaea in 325 CE, that the participating people voted on making Jesus a full-fledged god. Also decided by this council, was that Jesus' resurrection from the dead would be observed on the first Sunday following the first full moon after the spring equinox on March 21st. If you're like me, I always needed to check the calendar in any given year to find out the date of Easter, wondering why Easter was sometimes celebrated in March and sometimes as late as April 25th. Well, the reason is the Council of Nicaea's men confusingly combined moon cycles with the equinox. These guys made it a three-way complexity by combining the Judaism Passover moon cycle, the pagan spring equinox (Northern Hemisphere only), and the requirement of Sunday church attendance. If you're confused as well, here's the math as to how this calculation works.

Satisfying all those three parameters, the earliest you could have Easter would be March 22nd provided the full moon fell on this date and it also happened to be Sunday. The latest you could have Easter is April 25th if the full moon were to occur on March 21st, the spring equinox. In that situation, the next full moon wouldn't occur until 28 days later (there are 13 lunar months to a year by the way) or April 18th. And if this date happened to be a Monday, then Easter would be delayed seven more days so it could fall on a Sunday, in this case April 25th. Once again, in the name of religion, anything can be invented, provided you make the claim it had been originated from a god.

Prior to the Council of Nicaea's decision and complicated three-way scheduling calculation, the Christians observed the Crucifixion of Jesus on Passover, which was and still is, 14 days after the first full moon of spring. The resurrection was then observed on the 16th day. As a reminder, the early Christians were still a sect of Judaism and therefore the last supper of Jesus in actuality would have been the Passover Seder or Jewish ceremonial meal. This Seder meal celebrated the escape from Egypt by the Hebrew speaking people into the Israel area. In the 1200's BCE time period, the Egyptian Pharaoh and his army had enslaved these Hebrew people in Egypt, but despite living in misery, they continued to reproduce at an alarming rate. In response, the Pharaoh commanded all the newborn males be drowned in the Nile River to curb this population explosion. Despite being extremely brutal, this approach was not successful – understandably, it also became very unpopular with the Egyptian people. As a result, this killing policy was stopped and the enslaved population continued to grow, becoming an even bigger threat for the Pharaoh and his subjects. Eventually, the Pharaoh thought it best to allow them to escape into the Israel area. The Passover Seder is a celebration of this escape to freedom out of slavery.

Once again, basing holidays and their meaning on the sun cycles of the Northern Hemisphere makes no sense to those people living in the Southern Hemisphere. In the Southern Hemisphere, Christians celebrate Easter on the same time line as the north where the celebration is based on renewal, new growth, and increasing light, even though for them in the south it is the autumn time period, with shorter daylight as they head into the winter season. Of course, they still can enjoy the chocolate bunnies and colored eggs. To reiterate a point made previously, you would think using a critical perspective that an all-knowing God would acknowledge the earth had different seasons in the Northern Hemisphere versus the Southern Hemisphere.

In the mid to late 300s CE the Christians adopted four traditions associated with the Easter celebration that included the reading of prophecies, confirming Jesus was a god, baptizing and confirming all the converts to Christianity, and holding the Easter mass. Easter celebrated the resurrection, visualized as light coming out of darkness, which represented death. To reenact this visually in a ceremony they invented a Paschal candle to be lit during the Easter mass. You still see these today in many Christian denominations with the lighting of a large white candle marked with the letter P.

How did we get from that religiously focused holiday to the fun stuff like colored eggs and chocolate bunnies? Colored eggs originated because the Catholic Church forbid the eating of any meat and animal-based products, which included eggs, during Holy Week (the week before Easter Day). However, no one notified the chickens or was able to get them to temporarily stop laying eggs for the week. The solution was to color the eggs laid during this time period as a way to make sure nobody ate them. On Easter Day, all these colored eggs could now be eaten, without the threat of damnation from Jesus and the church. Overtime it was creatively decided these eggs would signify new life emerging from the eggshell, similar to Jesus rising from the tomb. You have to love this innovative thinking!

In modern times most people have no idea of the history behind the coloring of eggs and eating them on Easter, only that it was tradition and fun. Some people think the traditional Easter egg hunt represents the search for Jesus's tomb with the eggshell representing the tomb. The switch to plastic eggs most likely began for hygienic reasons since no one wants to find a stinky rotten egg in August that had been extremely well hidden since Easter. Of course, the tradition of putting money or candy inside the plastic eggs was added for extra motivation, making for a better treasure hunt. I'm not sure if the early Christians would be appalled by this new tradition or think it was fun. It certainly has very little to do with the original intent of outlawing egg eating during Holy Week by the Catholic Church. In today's world, this seems a bit random which is probably why over a period of time the rules were modified – today's rules for Catholics during Holy Week forbid only meats, but now allow fish, eggs and milk.

So, that's the story behind the colored eggs, now what about those delicious chocolate bunnies? We can thank the Protestants in the 1600s CE for introducing the chocolate Easter bunny tradition, which somehow over time led to yellow marshmallow chicks, candy eggs, all kinds of candy, and even little toys. The Protestants absolutely loathed the Catholics, so out of spite they came up with Easter traditions of their own. They decided to have a bunny or rabbit lay the eggs and then they decorated and hid them for children to find. I know it's a stretch to have the bunnies laying the eggs, but remember, in the name of religion you can make anything up and people will believe and support it. Despite the peculiar concept of bunnies laying eggs, people in the

United States loved this idea so much they converted it into the tradition of leaving baskets of chocolate bunnies and toys for children on Easter morning, similar to the Santa Claus approach. It was awesome for sales and profits of the candy companies and made this holiday into a commercial bonanza. Religion can be great for business.

Around the world, Christians celebrate Easter in similar fashion, but this holiday is not called the same thing everywhere. In fact, its various names reflect the history of where this holiday originated. The word "Easter" is named after the Anglo-Saxon English goddess of spring, called Eostre in England and Ostara in Germany. Other countries preferred the Jewish route for naming Easter. The Hebrew word for Passover is Pesah or Pesach, so the Greek festival is called Pascha, the Italian festival is Pasqua, Danish is Paaske, and in French it is Paques. Christian's believe Easter is the ultimate holiday for their religion, but I'm sure very few of them knew it was named after a pagan god in English or the Jewish Passover in other languages.

This is yet another Christian holiday with a foundation in the Northern Hemisphere's growing season and sun cycle, celebrated by pagan religions for many years before it was converted into a Christian holiday. It also has strong roots to the Jewish religion, which as we know was the foundation of the Christian religion. A major flaw in the timing of this holiday indicates once again, the god of these religions showed no interest in acknowledging the people living below the equator.

Halloween

Halloween is another popular holiday originally based in religious beliefs, which many people still consider to be part of their religion today. Over time this holiday has become more secular in nature, especially in the United States, celebrated by dressing up in costumes, children getting candy, and sometimes with the side benefit of adults getting alcoholic drinks while accompanying their kids on their trick or treating treks. The trick-or-treating tradition is most popular in North and South America, but it certainly is gaining popularity around the globe – mainly because it's fun!

This holiday, now called Halloween, got its start over 2,000 years ago as a Celtic festival called Samhain, primarily celebrated in the geographic regions of current day Ireland, Scotland, England, and Northern France. Similar to most festival holidays, it was associated with the growing season and cycle of the sun in the Northern Hemisphere. It was celebrated on November 1st, when the harvest was complete and the days were gradually getting shorter.

Human beings have always wondered what happened to people's spirit when they died, so they often invented stories as part of their religious beliefs to help explain it. The Celtic people were no different from other ancient people. They correlated death with the time period when it got dark and cold in the Northern Hemisphere around November 1st. It makes sense, since it marked the end of the growing season, the crops were dead, it was getting colder, people were inside more, often getting sick, and sadly as a result many died. To this day, heading into November every year in the Northern Hemisphere, many people start feeling somewhat depressed thinking about the coming of winter - perhaps the Celtic people also experienced the same thing.

The Celtics thought that on the night before November 1st, the boundary between the living and the dead became blurred, with the souls of the dead returning to earth. To ensure these spirits would not harm them, they would dress up like the people that died that year, or in animal heads and skins. They would also light bonfires to keep the ghosts from causing trouble and damaging their crops. In addition, these fires were used to sacrifice crops and animals to the Celtic gods in hopes they would protect them.

The Roman Empire, before adopting Christianity as its official religion, also had a festival in late October to recognize people who had died. When the Romans conquered the Celtic area, they combined their festival with the Celtic Samhain festival. As Christianity was forced upon the Celtic people, over time this festival became a problem for Christian doctrine. The Pope realized he needed to replace these festivals with Christian alternatives to entice the people to follow the Christian beliefs. As background, the Christian All Saints' Day, or the feast of all martyrs and saints, had been originally celebrated on May 13th from the late 300s CE to the 700s CE. In the 700s CE, Pope Gregory III moved All Saints' Day to November 1st to honor all the saints and martyrs that had died. In this way, the night before that day could replace Samhain with people now dressing up in costumes as saints, angels, and devils more in line with Christian teaching. They did continue to have big bonfires and parades; I am assuming because not only was it a tradition, it was also festive. So, where did the word Halloween originate? Well, All Saints' Day was called "All-Hallows" in Middle English, with the night before then being called "All-Hallows Eve". These names eventually evolved into Halloween.

The reason Halloween trick-or-treating became so popular in the United States was due to the Irish and Scottish immigrants bringing their traditions to the United States in the mid-1800s CE. Originally in the 800s CE during the Samhain festival, the poor Celtic people asked for money for food and ale (during this time period ale was a good substitute for water which was often polluted). As this festival was transformed into a Christian festival, the poor people would visit wealthy family homes and offer to exchange prayers for soul cakes. The wealthy believed that if the poor people prayed hard enough for them, it would help them get to heaven. As this belief waned, during the 1500s CE young people in Ireland and Scotland went guising to get a treat such as fruit, nuts, or coins. The term "guising" meant they performed a song, recited a poem, told a joke, or some other trick, in exchange for a treat. All these activities were still designed to pay homage to the dead.

Overtime, these traditions were adopted in the United States. The phrase "trick-or-treat" came from a Canadian newspaper story in the 1930s CE and eventually caught on in the United States. Until the 1950s CE, in the United States pastries and coins were popular giveaways for young people who were dressed up in costume. The concept of performing a trick in exchange for a treat was lost, with the children only wearing costumes in their quest for treats. During the 1950s CE, factory wrapped candy became a more popular offering as parents feared strangers could tamper with treats that weren't store bought and wrapped. Candy had become more convenient and affordable as well. Unfortunately, this also may have contributed to tooth decay and cavities, as well as childhood obesity, but that's a discussion for another time.

In Roman Catholicism, All Saints' Day continues to be observed on November 1st, commemorating all the people who made it to heaven. Of course, the major sinners went directly to hell and the unbaptized went to limbo. There is not a Remembrance Day in Christianity for these condemned people as far as I know. In association with Catholic's All Saints' Day, they also have All Souls' Day, which is observed on November 2nd for all the souls that were baptized but did not make it into heaven because they had committed minor sins or infractions – these were the residents of purgatory. If you recall, purgatory is the place invented for people somewhere between heaven and hell. The way to think about this is purgatory is a low burning area, while hell is a very high burning area. All Souls' Day is an occasion set aside for Christians to pray for those people who are in purgatory to help them get into heaven. I'm not sure how anyone can know who of the deceased made it to which spot. But it would be very insulting if your soul made it to heaven and people still had doubts about your soul and continued praying for you to get out of purgatory.

Saint Odilo of Cluny is recognized as the guy who started this day of commemoration for the purgatory residing souls. He was the abbot in charge of the Benedictine monastery in Cluny, France and died in 1048 CE. During Odilo's rule, this monastery, located north of Lyon, France became the most famous in Western Europe. Odilo was highly regarded as a very kind, compassionate, and gentle person. That said, although he was a nice guy, his All Souls' Day invention was not in fact new – it seems he may have copied the idea from another ancient religion, specifically the Buddhist All Souls' Day.

In Buddhism, All Souls' Day was, and continues to be, a major summer folk festival observed on the fifteenth day of the seventh lunar month, which primarily falls in August or September. It is sometimes called the Chinese Ghost Festival. The seventh lunar month timing was selected because the spiritual number three and the material number four come together to equal seven. This was when they believed the spiritual world combines with the physical world and as a result souls were thought to be roaming the earth during this time period. Amazingly, people today still believe this to be true, especially in Asia.

This festival originated in ancient India dating back to sometime between 550 BCE and 350 BCE and was based on a story about a disciple of Buddha named Maudgalyayana (try to say that three times fast).

As the story goes, he gained power through meditation and eventually was able to discover his mother and other ancestors were unfortunately reborn into hell in one of their reincarnations. He was very sad about this situation and asked Buddha for help to get his deceased mother and other deceased parents out of hell. Buddha said he would help them but only if they happened to be born into hell over their last seven lives (obviously the Buddhists also gave spiritual meaning to the number seven). Buddha further told Maudgalyayana to offer food, drink, and shelter to the spirits of his ancestors at the end of the monsoon season, which typically occurred on the 15th day of the seventh lunar month. There are many variations to this story but all of them are based on the same idea of remembering and helping dead ancestors. Once again, the timing of this religious festival is very specific to this area of the world and does not recognize the total earth.

The belief in this ancient Indian festival was introduced into China by an Indian monk named Amoghavajra, in the early 700s CE. This was approximately 1,000 years from when Buddhism started, around 400 BCE. This festival and ceremony then moved into Japan and other Asian areas as well. In Japan, two altars are made for their deceased ancestors - one for the nice dead ancestors, and one for souls who were not very nice and now have no peace. Nice or not nice? Imagine the debate among family members deciding in which group their dead relative belonged. The Christians followed the same pattern and have one feast for saints and martyrs and one for the not so nice deceased souls. The key issue with all of these beliefs is we do not know with certainty what happens to us when we die. That's why religions have invented all kinds of scenarios and stories to explain the unknowable and position them as fact or inspired by God. Critical thinking teaches us to be...critical of these stories as nothing more than someone's imagination.

People in Asia, primarily Buddhists and Taoists offer food, money, treats, and entertainment to the ancient spirits on their ghost day. Likewise, the western Halloween holiday also has its roots in this thinking. Even though in the west, most people have no idea why they dress up in costumes, some scary and some silly, and beg for candy. The only thing they know is this is fun and they always did it since they were small children, but assign no meaning to it other than getting the candy and eating it. So, the next time you dress up for Halloween or give out candy, remember where this behavior originated almost 2,400 years ago but be sure to still have fun.

Islam Religious Holidays:

Moving away from the Christian and Ancestral holidays, let's look at a few of the Islamic religious holidays. Islam has two religious holidays that are publicly recognized. There are additional holidays, but they are not considered to be official in all Islamic sects.

Eid al-Fitr

The first official holiday is called Eid al-Fitr, which is Arabic for festival of breaking fast. It marks the end of Ramadan, the holy month of fasting and is celebrated during the first three days of the tenth lunar month. Ramadan always falls on the ninth lunar month, which moves around the Gregorian calendar and seasons. It falls 10 to 11 days earlier each year, because twelve lunar months are about 11 days short of a solar year. Therefore, over the span of 33 years, it falls in every season before coinciding with the same time period in the Gregorian calendar. The 33 years is approximate since it is still a few days short of a solar-based year of 365 days (obviously mathematically short as 33 years times 11 days equals 363 days).

For some reason, religions see it as important to impose sacrifice and martyrdom into their beliefs. They seem to think people need to suffer in order to feel better about themselves. Compared to other religions, Ramadan may lead the pack on this accomplishment of imposing sacrifice. In most Christian denominations, the practice of giving up things of your choice during the 40 days of Lent as a way to get ready for Easter is not even comparable to the Ramadan level of suffering from fasting.

The Ramadan ritual of fasting during daylight hours of an entire month can be traced back to the Prophet Muhammad during the ninth lunar month in the 600s CE, which occurred in August and September. So why did he do this and why are Islamic people still following this activity today? Well, the word "Ramadan" literally means "intense heat", which refers to a really hot summer month. Remember, Prophet Muhammad lived in the desert of Saudi Arabia where it is incredibly hot in the summer, especially during the daylight hours. In fact, Mecca and the area around it is one of the hottest places on earth. Apparently, during the hottest month of the summer, people preferred to stay inside their houses from sunrise to sunset because it was too hot to be out in the desert sun. Of course, air conditioners had not yet been invented, so it was still hot in their houses too. In Prophet Muhammad's situation, he went up to a cave on Mount Hira near Mecca to escape the heat, which was a very smart move. He stayed there for a month since it was cooler, out of the sun, and also extremely isolated from people, allowing him to meditate without interruption. He was brought food and water when the sun went down and Ramadan reenacts this situation. According to the story, he was meditating in the cave when the Angel Gabriel appeared to him with the first installment of the Quran, which is now the holy book of Islam. At its core,

Ramadan is a celebration of this supernatural event. Can you imagine today if a military leader went up to a cave for a month and then came back and said he had a nice chat with an angel. Would you believe him? Would you follow him? I suppose if your life was threatened, you would go along with it and this is probably what happened in the 600s CE. As mentioned earlier, it's curious that people in religions who have these visions are always alone during the event and the event isn't recorded in writing until hundreds if not thousands of years later.

During Ramadan, you must restrain yourself between dawn and dusk from all food or drink, any sexual activity and all forms of immoral or evil behavior. Does this wording imply that it is okay to be immoral or evil after dark during Ramadan? Also, why does sexual activity always seems to get on these religious lists of no-no's? Sex certainly seems to be a top-of-mind topic for religious leaders, thanks in part to the misogynistic Saint Augustine. Anyway, once the sun goes down each day during Ramadan, people can eat and drink as usual with family and friends, often beginning with eating dates or apricots and water or sweetened milk. This is what Muhammad liked to do, so the religion follows his preferences for eating and drinking.

The main benefit of Ramadan, according to the Quran, is that God forgives your past sins if you observe this holy month with fasting, prayer, helping the poor, and avoiding evils, including sex. The one part of this requirement that is physically harmful is the prohibition of drinking, even of water, during the daytime. Fasting can actually be beneficial, but not drinking water and causing dehydration over any period of time has proven to be damaging to your body. The God behind this idea obviously was not concerned about human physiology and the need for water for brain function, flushing the body of toxins, and keeping cells healthy. Forcing people to dehydrate by not drinking water all day is a really harmful idea and tradition. On the other hand, the Ramadan tradition of helping the poor is very positive and of course not doing evil things especially to others is just plain good common sense. These things should be done all the time, but a reminder once a year is certainly worthwhile. It is not known exactly why the early founders of Islam decided sexual activity was evil and by extension that woman needed to be covered up. It could be they needed the men in their armies to stay focused on fighting and killing and away from woman and loving or tenderness. Islamic beliefs were used as the justification for the armies led by Mohammed to conquer new territories and expand his new empire.

The actual holiday called Eid al-Fitr comes at the end of the fasting holy month and is celebrated over three days with a festival. During these days, children wear new clothes, women dress in white, and special pastries are baked. In addition, gifts are exchanged, graves of relatives are visited, and people gather for family meals and to pray in mosques. All religions seem to like dressing women in white as a sign that they are virgins or pure, since sex, remember for some reason is considered to be evil. It appears Islam is no different - following the holy month, when there was not supposed to be any sexual activity, the women were now considered to be forgiven by God for engaging in sexual intercourse before Ramadan, and thus could now dress in white as a new virgin. It seems odd the men are not required to dress in white as well. It obviously is not considered evil for men to have sex. However, the traditions of this holiday, of getting together with family and friends, sharing meals and focusing on giving, are very positive and worth preserving.

Eid-al-Adha

The second big holiday for Islam is called Eid-al-Adha, which in Arabic means festival of sacrifice. It begins on the tenth day of the last month of the Islamic lunar calendar and continues for three or four days. Similar to Eid al-Fitr, this festival will occur in all seasons over a 33-year cycle. This festival marks the end of the Muslim five-day pilgrimage to Mecca, Saudi Arabia, called the Hajj, following a route Muhammad once walked. All Muslims are obligated to make this physically demanding pilgrimage at least once in their lifetime to wipe away their past sins and get closer to God. However, Muslims all over the world still celebrate Eid-al-Adha even if they did not go on a pilgrimage. During the three- or four-day festival, the wealthier people sacrifice a sheep, goat, camel, or cow and then cook and share the meat with friends, neighbors, and the poor. The animal must be sacrificed in a halal way, which means permissible or acceptable by Allah (aka God). They decided the animal must be healthy when it is killed, which must be done in a way to limit suffering, oh, and you must say a prayer as you kill it. I'm not sure who determined what God's method of killing an animal entailed, but it does seem very reasonable, although vegetarians may not agree. The reason why this festival focuses on sacrificing an animal is because it is a reminder of when Abraham sacrificed a ram instead of his son Ishmael (in Judaism, and Christianity it was Isaac being sacrificed, or maybe Abraham couldn't remember the name of which kid he was sacrificing). Thinking about this critically, it is more likely that this story was just fabricated to teach people not to sacrifice human beings. Anyhow, people love the story and some people even fast before this celebration. They also visit friends and family, sharing meals and exchanging gifts, in addition to donating food and money to families in need. The nicest thing about this holiday is the tradition of giving to not only family and friends, but also people in need and of course getting together for a shared meal.

Hinduism Religious Holidays

A variety of holidays and festivals are celebrated across the Hindu lunar calendar with fasts, vigils, offerings to deities and feasts. Hindu festivals are known as Utsava, which in Sanskrit literally translates to removal of worldly sorrow, but in practice translates to merriment and pleasure. Although there are a number of holidays and festivals, the two main religious holidays in Hinduism are Diwali, the festival of lights, and Holi, the festival of color.

Diwali

Diwali is the most popular Hindu festival of the year and can be compared to the level of popularity of Christmas and Thanksgiving in the United States. This festival is also celebrated by other religions such as Jainism, Sikhism, and Buddhism. The traditions and reasons for celebrating this holiday differ among these religions and even Hindu's vary in their celebrations for different reasons depending on the region of India. However, common among all these religions and Hindu regions is the primary focus of celebrating victory of light over darkness, knowledge over ignorance, and good over evil. The word Diwali or Divali was derived from the Sanskrit term "dipavali" meaning row of lights. As a reminder, Hinduism is the oldest major religion in current day tracing its origin to Vedism with their records written in Sanskrit.

Diwali lasts for five days, with the third day being the main day. Like most religious holidays, this one was most likely linked to the growing seasons - in this case, the harvest festival and the coming of winter, similar to Saturnalia (now called Christmas) in more northern climates.

The holiday timing is based on the lunar calendar and occurs in October or November, following the last harvest (in Northern India) before winter. This is the time when people prayed to Lakshmi (spouse of Vishnu) for wealth and good fortune in the coming year and to survive the winter season. Diwali begins just before the arrival of a new moon between Asvina (which is the seventh lunar month) and Kartika (which is the eighth lunar month). The third or main day of the festival always falls on a new moon. Hinduism in India follows the lunar calendar and focuses on the seasons for the timing of its religious festivals. Many people in western northern cultures assume there are four seasons, but India and Hinduism recognize seven seasons reflecting the climate in this area of the world. In the north, west, and central areas of India, spring is March/April, summer/hot season is May/June, monsoon/rainy season is July/August, autumn is late September to mid-November, pre-winter/cool season is late November and December, and winter season is January/February. The timing of these seasons is different depending on the region, but Diwali is still celebrated by everyone at the same time regardless of their location. It follows the northern area of India where Hinduism originated, with the holiday taking place near the end of the autumn season and the last harvest.

 Here is one common way Diwali is celebrated, although remember it does differ across the various sects of Hinduism and cultural regions. The first day known as Dhanteras, is dedicated to cleaning homes and purchasing small items of gold. The significance of this cleaning ritual is to encourage letting go of all last year's worries and troubles and becoming more positive and renewed or illuminated with light. The gold signifies luck, prosperity and abundance. The gold also invites prosperity into the household and seeks the long life of the husband based on one of the Hindu mythological stories. The story is about King Hima's son who was predicted by his astrologers to be killed when he turned 16 by a snake. To stop the death, the son's wife decided to put all her jewels and gold ornaments in front of the door blocking Lord Yama, the god of death, when he approached as a snake. The snake was distracted by not being able to see due to the glistening of the gold and jewels and also by the singing of the son's wife all night long. This is how she saved her husband from death and one of the main reasons why many Indian people are fond of gold.

The second day is called Naraka Chaturdashi, in remembrance of the death anniversary of Narakasura or the demon king. This is a celebration of good conquering evil. Narakasura got his wish to be immortal in the memories of people, with the celebration of his death symbolized by lighting lamps. Narakasura was the son of Bhudevi, the earth goddess. He was very powerful and became evil. Through meditation he was able to get Brahma to give him a boon (helpful gift) making him able to be killed only by his mother. Because of his evilness, the people felt he needed to be killed. They called upon Lord Krishna (reincarnation of Vishnu), and together with his wife Satyabhama, they were able to kill him. Well, actually Satyabhama (reincarnation of Bhudevi) killed him but she did not know Narakasura was her son at the time. When she found out he was her son she felt bad and made Narakasura immortal with this holiday lighting of lamps - remember he is still dead but the memory of him is immortal. Tying this whole thing together, Bhudevi is also the avatar of Lakshmi, which is why this goddess is a major deity associated with Diwali. Seems like one of those detective's evidence investigation boards with string connecting all the different characters would be helpful! In addition to lighting lamps in the evening of the second day, people also have a bathing ritual in the morning, symbolizing the elimination of evil and purification of the mind and body. They also pray for the souls of ancestors.

The third day or main day of Diwali is a new moon day making the nighttime very dark. During this day Hindu's worship Lakshimi, the goddess of wealth and good fortune, by lighting candles and diyas (small cup-shaped oil lamp made of baked clay with a cotton wick), shooting off fireworks, and visiting temples. The diyas symbolize goodness and purity and lighting them gets rid of darkness and brings everyone into the light. As you can imagine, this festival on a large scale is absolutely beautiful and very romantic. Lakshmi is a very popular goddess and is married to Vishnu, which is a big deal since he is a key member of the Hindu trinity. As a reminder, Brahma, Vishnu, and Shiva are the three gods of the Hindu trinity with Vishnu's role being to maintain order and harmony. This holiday primarily focuses on Lakshmi and the many different forms she took on to be with Vishnu in all of his reincarnation stories, including Padma (which means lotus), Dharani, and Queen Sita. Based on scripture writing, Lakshmi was born from a churning ocean of milk, seated on a lotus and holding another blossom in her hand. (Perhaps another example of hallucinations resulting from drinking soma?) One of the rituals on this day is also to give thanks and show appreciation for the things you have in your life by going through your house and lighting diyas. Basically, you go into each room and give thanks for the things you have and what they do for you. Giving thanks to inanimate objects may seem odd at first, but it does make you appreciate your life and living conditions. But it's not just physical objects that are recognized; appreciation and gratitude are also given for the people and positive aspects in your life.

The fourth day known as Goverdhan Puja recognizes Krishna's defeat of Indra, the king of the gods. Even though Indra was basically a good god, he became overly impressed with himself and had the farmers and villagers pay homage to him all the time instead of working. Krishna (avatar of Vishnu) told the farmers and villagers that duty to family was above all else and work was a form of worship. For this reason, they all went back to work, which angered the arrogant Indra. Since he controlled the weather, he sent torrential rain, storms and floods to punish the people. The people asked Krishna to help them, so with his little finger he lifted up the mountain called Govardhana and told them to go under it for protection. On seeing this tremendous feat, Indra was humbled, asked for forgiveness and sent the sunshine back to the people. At this point Krishna accepted his apology and put the mountain back in place. Nowadays this day is often recognized as the beginning of the fiscal year for businesses and celebrates the nobleness of hard work, righteousness and duty.

The fifth day called Bhai Dooj, celebrates the bond between brothers and sisters. On this day, sisters pray for the success and wellbeing of their brothers and brothers lavishly give gifts and goodies to their sisters. This day celebrates family ties with a special focus on the appreciation of siblings.

In general, Diwali is a time for visiting, exchanging gifts, wearing new clothes, feasting, feeding the poor, lighting diyas, and setting off fireworks. Like many holidays, people most enjoy getting together and sharing meals with each other. However, it's important to remember the core beliefs are generally based on mythology, and although the stories are entertaining, they should not be believed to be real or factual. Nevertheless, the holiday celebrations are filled with many nice traditions and good intentions including showing gratitude and focusing on improving yourself in the new year.

Holi

The other big holiday in the Hindu religion is Holi, which celebrates the coming of spring - it is known as the festival of colors. It occurs on the day of the last full moon at the end of winter, which is typically in March or late February. Similar to Diwali, this festival celebrates the triumph of good over evil, but it differs in that it also focuses on forgiveness and making peace with everyone around us.

The evening prior to the festival begins with a bonfire and is known as Holika Dahan (burning of demon Holika). The bonfire represents the burning of Holika, who was the sister of the evil god Hiranyakashipu. Hiranyakashipu asked Holika to kill his son Prahlada, because the son worshiped Vishnu. As the story is told, Holika, wearing a fire-resistant cloak, tricked Prahlada into sitting with her on a pyre. When the fire started burning, the cloak miraculously flew over to Prahlada, and instead Holika was the one who burned to death. Shortly after this attempt on Prahlada's life, Vishnu showed up as half man and half lion and killed the evil Hiranyakashipu. The bonfire is set every year to signify the end of evil.

The next morning begins the carnival of colors - people come out into the streets to play with colors by drenching each other with colored water from water guns and water balloons or smearing powdered colors on each other. The origin of this tradition comes from Krishna having blue skin as a result of being poisoned by the demon Putna's breast milk when he was an infant. As he grew older, he wanted the girls to like him, even though he was blue. His mother suggested smearing colors on all the girl's faces so everyone would be equally colorful and accepted. As a result, on this day everyone is treated the same regardless of caste, gender, status, or age. In the streets, the celebration often includes off color (no pun intended) language and behavior. However, at the end of the festival everyone cleans up and goes back to normal society behavior.

As you would expect, Holi celebrations include special foods and drinks. A few foods that are eaten include Puran Poli, a thick roti filled with dal, and Gujiya, a sweet fried or baked dumpling. The main drink is Thandai, which is a cold-milk topped with almonds, saffron and spices. Many people also drink bhang, which is a Thandai drink laced with crushed cannabis leaves. Bhang resembles a green smoothie made out of hot milk and finely ground cannabis leaves, but tastes of spices and herbs such as saffron, fennel, and garam masala. Hindu's drink this to honor Shiva, get closer to God, meditate better, and focus on being honest, truthful and fighting away evil. People claim this drink also cures nervous disorders, skin diseases, and wounds. On the downside, as a word of caution, it can also give you a terrible hangover headache if you drink too much. Presently bhang is a substitute for the ancient India ritual drink soma. However, bhang does not impact your consciousness like soma, as it does not have the psychoactive substances that soma had in ancient times. The soma drink in the ancient Vedic culture in India was a hallucinogenic sacred drink.

The Vedic culture wrote that people consuming soma gave them immortality, visions of them being brought into the light, and finding the gods. Drinking Bhang reenacts this ancient ritual of drinking soma, but in a much tamer way - it also loosens you up for a very entertaining and happy Holi celebration. Let's hear it for Bhang!

Judaism holidays

Now, let's explore a few of the Judaism holidays, where they came from and how they are celebrated today. Certainly, Judaism is a relatively small religion as measured by the number of followers; nonetheless, it is important as the foundation for both Christianity and Islam with roots in the most ancient religious thinking of the Babylonians. The main holidays for Judaism are Rosh Hashanah and then ten days later, Yom Kippur. These holidays recognize the religion's roots, and as you'll learn are much more solemn and repentant in nature rather than celebratory.

Rosh Hashanah

Rosh Hashanah is Hebrew for "beginning of the year" and like many of the other religious holidays related to the growing seasons, this one falls on the first day of the agricultural new year called Tishrei. This holy day begins on the first day of the seventh month, which usually occurs in September or October. And yes, you probably figured it out – this religion also uses the lunar calendar, which is how the seventh month ends up in the Northern Hemisphere's autumn season. It also marks the end of the harvest as well as the start of the new agricultural year. Once again, this only works in the Northern Hemisphere, as influenced by a northern god that does not acknowledge the growing seasons of the equator or Southern Hemisphere.

Rosh Hashanah is also known as the day of remembrance of when God created the world (or at least the northern half, or maybe just the northern section around the middle east since this god did not know the world was round and thus excluded North and South America as well). Basically, Judaism is celebrating the birth of their particular world. On this holy day, the Jewish people also recognize their responsibilities as God's chosen people. Sort of a "we're number one" chant combined with a "we also need to provide a good example to all the people God deemed to be inferior to us" message. It's like a sibling claiming, "Dad likes me best and I'm in charge!" It's quite an arrogant and privileged attitude promoted by this religious belief, along with the added recognition of the responsibilities that come with being superior.

This holiday starts with some people fasting the night before followed by the blowing of the ram's horn called a "shofar" in the early morning. This horn blowing reminds the Jewish people of Moses' spiritual awakening on Mount Sinai. The horn is also supposed to awaken the Jewish people, reminding them to examine their relationship with

God for a very good reason. Besides celebrating the birth of the earth, this holiday also starts the ten days of Awe, the period of time between Rosh Hashanah and Yom Kippur, which ultimately determines one's fate. Jewish law teaches that God judges all creatures during the ten days of Awe, with the good and righteous being rewarded with ongoing life, while the evil and wicked are given death. Yikes! This religion is deadly serious, no pun intended! The people falling in the middle or between good and bad have ten days to repent and hopefully get moved over into God's life column. As a result, the Jews consider Rosh Hashanah and the days after it as a time for prayer, doing good deeds, reflecting on past mistakes and making amends with others. The intentions of this period of time are very positive, albeit a bit harsh with the threat of death. If you've read the Hebrew Bible or the Old Testament, you know that the Jewish God Yahweh is portrayed as a brutal and cruel god to anyone who crossed him, misbehaved, or treated his chosen people badly.

The judging of people by God was not a new concept to the Israelites. Before Judaism was invented, the Babylonians living with the Israelites also had a day of judgment each year. They believed their gods got together in the temple of Marduk to determine the fate of every individual. Marduk, the national god of Babylon in the Mesopotamian religion, was the god of thunderstorms and the predecessor to the Greek god Zeus, king of the gods. The Jews obviously copied this idea but converted it into having one god in judgment of every individual, versus using a group of gods in judgment. Maybe this was a mistake because you may have gotten a better deal with a group of gods as you had more chances to get at least one god to like you.

As a result of the threat of death for bad behavior, this holiday is obviously not meant to be a rip-roaring good time. However, people celebrating this holiday do get together with family and friends to share a meal together. One of the eating rituals performed is the dipping of apples in honey as ancient Jews believed apples had healing properties, and honey signified hope that the new year will be sweet. Other delicacies are also eaten such as a round challah, which is braided bread. The round shape is to symbolize the cyclical nature of life or the crown of God. One custom that some Jewish people perform is to throw pieces of bread into a flowing body of water while praying. The bread symbolizes the sins of the past year and as the bread is swept away or eaten by the birds or fish, the person is spiritually renewed and relieved of their guilt. Seems like a positive way to focus on improving one's personal behavior, very similar to New Year's resolutions. However, if millions of people were to throw bread into a stream it could result in an environmental disaster of sorts. Maybe it would be better to just visualize their bad behavior sailing down the river. Unfortunately, even with good intentions many people go back to their old ways after this ten-day period. Well, at least God won't be striking them down dead - that is, until he judges them again next year.

Yom Kippur

The next biggest holiday for Judaism is Yom Kippur, which is ten days after Rosh Hashanah. Yom Kippur is Hebrew for the "Day of Atonement" and the most solemn Jewish religious holiday. On Yom Kippur, Jewish people abstain from food, drink (including water), and sex. Similar to the attitudes of Islam and Christianity, sex is oddly perceived as a sinful activity in Judaism as well. Unless you are prepping for a medical procedure, the ban on drinking water is problematic and shows a lack of this God's understanding of human physiology. It really is important to stay hydrated, however the practice of fasting can have a positive effect on your health. In addition to the bans on food, drink, and sex, the Orthodox Jews are not permitted to wear leather shoes or apply lotions or cream on their skin, no matter how dry or itchy it feels. Some misguided person thousands of years ago must have thought this was a good idea. Oh, and back then it was oils since they did not have lotions or creams like today. And you must be wondering about the leather shoe ban – apparently, they were thought to be way too comfortable and so obviously they wouldn't be able to provide the level of suffering needed for this holiday. Inflicting pain and suffering seem to be a main tenant of almost all religions as a way to make people better.

The Jewish people spend the eve of Yom Kippur and the entire day in prayer and meditation. Friends ask and accept forgiveness from each other for past offenses - sort of like what people do in Alcoholics Anonymous. Everyone promises to improve their behavior and perform good deeds, with the purpose being to make them feel better about themselves and reduce guilt for being cruel or nasty in the past. They also believe that if people were able to forgive you, then God would forgive you as well. Remember, much is at stake here because if you don't get on God's good list and you end up on his naughty list, he will kill you. Obviously, this is a good reason for taking this holiday very seriously.

The day's service ends with the blowing of the shofar, the ritual ram horn, which if you recall was also blown ten days ago at the beginning of Rosh Hashanah. Horn blast symbolism is not unique to Judaism as other religions utilized this symbolism too. For instance, Conch shell horns were blown in both ancient Hawaiian culture and ancient Aztec Mexican culture. The conch horn blast was done to welcome the new day with the sunrise and announce the end of the day with the sunset. It was also associated with gods and the ocean and was used to announce the beginning of sacred ceremonies or to welcome dignitaries. All types of horns have been used throughout history to announce kings and queens, ensuring the common people would notice them. So, clearly horn blowing is not unique to Judaism and many religions and monarchies seem to favor it.

Yom Kippur was invented when the Israelites left Egypt and arrived at Mount Sinai, which if you remember was where God supposedly gave Moses the Ten Commandments.

The way the story is told, Moses went up the mountain for 40 days and 40 nights and received the Ten Commandments from God. When he returned, he discovered his people worshipping a golden calf - in anger Moses smashed the sacred tablets into little pieces. Sounds as if he was really in need of some anger management therapy. In response, he had his people melt the calf down, mix it with water and drink it. Somewhat strange, but that's how the story was told! He then went back up the mountain and prayed to God for forgiveness. This approach worked - God forgave him for losing his temper and forgave the Hebrew people for worshipping a golden calf. However, this was the same God who was also vindictive, having sent a plague to kill any and all Hebrew people who still believed in other Gods. At any rate, Yom Kipper was created to commemorate God's forgiveness.

Most of this story about Moses was based on mythology, although some of the particulars were based on real history. We do know that Moses actually lived, however the timing of his life is unclear. Some scholars estimate he lived in the late 1300s BCE to early 1200s BCE. We also know the Hebrew people were enslaved by an Egyptian Pharaoh and later escaped. The Hebrew people at this time were a class of people who made their living by providing services to the wealthier Egyptian people. It's likely they formed a group similar to a trade union in today's world, which resulted in them growing stronger as a united group, having greater influence on Egyptian society. Unhappy with this situation, the Pharaoh enslaved them. But as their population continued to grow and they became an even greater threat, he decided he had enough of them and let them flee east out of the current day Cairo area with Moses as their leader. This is where the story gets somewhat far-fetched with the image of Moses parting the Red Sea for safe passage of the Hebrews and then to drown the Egyptian army pursuing them (which apparently were sent because the Pharaoh changed his mind as he needed the Hebrew people returned as slaves once he realized there was nobody left to clean his palace). If you look at a map, there was very little water to cross from Cairo, Egypt into the Sinai Peninsula, as the Suez Canal was not built until 1859 CE or approximately 3,100 years after Moses lived. Also, it was not called the Red Sea, but instead was called the Sea of Reeds. Most likely these Hebrew people forded a stream or marsh that could have been dry due to wind or draught. The reason why they called this area the Sea of Reeds was because it grew papyrus (used as writing paper), which is only able to grow in fresh water. Bottom line, it was not deep water that was parted in the Moses myth - at best it was a very shallow stream or marsh.

The next part of the story gets even more squirrely. The Judaism and Christian religions accounts' have them traveling into the Sinai Peninsula to Mount Sinai, which by the way is still part of Egypt on today's maps. The Islamic religion had them traveling into Saudi Arabia to another mountain called Mount Sinai. No one really knows where their travels actually took them, but each religion decided to make it convenient to their origins. The Jewish story continued with Moses going up into the mountain for 40 days and 40 nights, while the previously enslaved Hebrew people continued to wander around the Sinai Peninsula or Saudi Arabia for 40 years. The writers of the Hebrew Bible, Old Testament Bible, and Quran all seem to be partial to the number 40. It actually was just meant to refer to a really long time. As already pointed out, religious people love to assign meaning to numbers and the number 40 is no exception. But here goes: five times eight equals 40 with five meaning grace of God and eight meaning new beginning; and four times ten equals 40 and four means creation and ten means perfection and completion - both Judaism and Islam have more number spiritual significances, but reviewing them all gets even more ridiculous. While in the mountains, Moses of course met God and he told him his name was Yahweh, which meant, "he who creates or brings into being". This is curious by the way, since the God Yahweh, as the one and only god was not invented yet. When the Jewish people later invent him, this God is described as a man God, never a woman God, since only men wrote the sacred texts. Other religions also have their version of a creator God as the one and only God - definitely this was not a new idea unique to Judaism. However, the writers of the Hebrew Bible did need to do a little history revision to the story of Moses after the fact, once Yahweh became the one and only god.

Another historical clarification to the Moses story was the golden calf the Hebrews worshipped was actually a bull and not a calf. If this story in reality happened, these people were likely worshipping and praying to an ancient Egyptian religion bull God called Hap, or Apis in the Greek religion. They were very familiar with this God as he dated back to 2900 BCE or over 1,700 years before Moses. This sacred bull deity was worshipped at Memphis, the capital city of ancient Egypt, which is about 15 miles south of current day Cairo. This is where the famous pyramids are located. The reason why it is presumed they were worshipping and praying to Hap was they likely were hungry and this God was a fertility god they thought would help increase grain yield and domestic animal herds. Realistically this activity would have been very normal for these people.

This next part of the story was mostly fictional since these Hebrew tribes were not the one-God people yet and Judaism and the God Yahweh were not invented, but here is how the story is written in the Bible. Moses decided after spending time up in the mountain by himself, that worshipping idols or believing in polytheism was the most serious sin punishable by death. So, Moses commanded the people could only believe in Yahweh because he was their leader and would punish them if they were carrying and worshiping a little bull god (the Bible says golden calf). This is the origin of why Judaism celebrates Yom Kippur and they are still fearful of Yahweh killing them if they get on his bad side. As you probably noticed, both the Judaism holidays and the Islamic holidays are very serious and solemn in nature and not as enjoyable or uplifting happy celebrations compared to the most popular Christian and Hindu holidays. Well, maybe this comment doesn't apply to the Christian fascination with the torture and crucifixion of Jesus, which were definitely brutal, or the burning of demons in Hinduism, but for the most part the rest of their holidays are enjoyable.

Buddhism celebrations

The Buddhism holiday celebrations are summarized next, and similar to other religions founded by one man they celebrate the notable events in their founder's life. In the Buddhism religion they celebrate Buddha Gautama's birth, enlightenment, and passage into nirvana. The birth part and passage into nirvana are self-explanatory. To clarify the enlightenment part, this is when the creator god Brahma from Hinduism descended from heaven and asked Buddha to teach because humans are at different levels of development. In Southeast Asia, they celebrate all three of these events on the same day called Wesak or Vesak. In other regions the festivals are held on different days and incorporate a variety of rituals and practices.

Wesak, or the all-in-one holiday, is celebrated in April or May depending on the lunar calendar date. It falls on the full moon of the lunar month Vesakha, or the second month of the Hindu lunar calendar. Interesting how ancient religions seem to favor new or full moons – nope, no half full or half empty moons for these ancient people. Wesak is observed as a public holiday in Southeast Asian countries as it is considered to be a very important religious holiday. On this day there are devotional services, people give food or money to monks, and they release captive birds. Releasing birds from cages is thought to be compassionate, which Buddhists believe will reduce bad luck or misfortune and improve health and longevity. However, this practice in modern society has gotten out of control. It has become inhumane since people capture the birds over and over again just so they can release them for good fortune. However, this practice is very disruptive as the birds are often damaged or become sick, and whatever kindness originally intended has been lost. Perhaps, this ritual should consider a change by getting involved in helping birds and animals recover from man-made environmental disasters such as oil spills, garbage and air pollution. Better yet, how about getting involved in stopping or reducing these disasters in the first place, which would be beneficial to everyone's fortune, health, and longevity.

In addition to these rituals, they also chant and do meditation reflecting on Buddhist teachings at their local temple. Families decorate their homes with lanterns, join processions wearing special white clothes, and share meals with each other. They also may send cards to each other similar to Christians sending Christmas cards to people they know. A ceremony called "bathing the Buddha" is also done. Water is poured over the Buddha statues' shoulders to remind people to clear their minds of negative thoughts such as greed and hatred. The Buddhism religion is very big on using mnemonic devices such as the water and the Buddha statue to help them focus their meditation on improving themselves. This actually is effective as our mind works best when we can visualize an idea. This is why religions use imagery like a Buddha statue and water to convey their ideas - because it works.

The one thing you can say about the Buddhists is they sure are efficient by packing all their religious celebrating into this one-day holiday, Wesak.

*

To summarize...

Holidays in all religions include some nice traditions and cultural customs that are both interesting and enjoyable. In the spirit of tolerance and inclusivity, perhaps we should share them and celebrate them with all people and not just those in our own religious group. However, beliefs in the fantasy or mythology attached to these holidays need to be recognized for what they are, which were just based on someone's imagination. Continuing to believe these stories to be real is not healthy or productive and can result in divisions in our society. Traditions that have a positive impact on our lives should be honored, while those causing anxiety and stress should be reevaluated as to their intent and purpose and changed. For example, threatening people with death and eternal damnation and making them feel guilty about anything they did to others that was not perfect, is not helpful to improvement. Rather, focusing on the positive aspects of holidays using critical thinking and then strengthening them may be more beneficial to people in helping them feel better about themselves and encourage them to treat others with more kindness in the long run. We should embrace holiday attributes that are positive, helpful, and enjoyable such as: sharing meals with each other, helping people less fortunate or lonely, being thankful and appreciative for what we have, reaching out to people who are different than us and making new friends, forgiving each other and asking for forgiveness for past wrongs, increasing romance in our life, and ultimately making a plan to improve ourselves both physically and spiritually.

Chapter 15

Another Powerful Empire Bites the Dust

When I was in my 40s, I experienced a significant turning point in my life - one that really motivated me to become more intellectually curious on topics outside of my familiar business world. I truly believe this experience made me a better person by opening my eyes to different cultures around the globe, leading me to become more understanding, empathetic and tolerant. I was inspired to delve into some of the factors that make us all different – our different backgrounds, our different cultures, and our different beliefs. I was especially curious as to where and why many of those beliefs originated including my own. To illustrate how I became inspired to learn more about history and cultures, here is my story…

At this period in my life, those middle-age years when I was focused on my career, I obtained a global general manager position with a Fortune 500 consumer products' company. In this job, for the first time in my life, I was provided the opportunity to travel the world. Exhausting and exhilarating, I literally travelled all over the world. I quickly learned, if I was going to be successful at providing global direction in this position, I really needed to get good at listening, understanding the unique cultures in each country, and most importantly learning to trust people from all around the world.

This last trait, establishing trust, required me to ask a lot of direct and sometimes uncomfortable questions. This took courage to be vulnerable in my honesty with managers I did not really know. Of course, the hard part in getting to this level of trust often required some conflict resolution first, as both parties often did not understand the other person's cultural approaches, priorities and attitudes. Through this process, eventually I developed friendships with many of these business leaders. One of the nice benefits of doing this was, we sure had some good laughs – sharing childhood experiences, explaining slang phrases that were common across our different pop-cultures, or my feeble attempts at mimicking foreign language sounds that were unfamiliar to my American ears. As a result of developing these friendships, we often talked about non-business topics during the dinners we shared. These discussions opened my eyes as I came to realize how deficient my knowledge of the arts, literature, and history was in comparison to many of these managers from other countries. I also became aware of the affect their backgrounds and knowledge base had on their personal beliefs.

As an example, during one of our casual dinners, we had a discussion on the history of American Indigenous people. Embarrassingly, even though I had lived my entire life in the United States, I realized my knowledge of the subject was very limited in comparison to these manager's knowledge level, and none of them had ever lived in North or South America. Over time I confided in a few of these new global friends that I was in awe of their knowledge of the world compared to mine, despite the priority I had placed on education my entire life, even having obtained an MBA in Business. At this point in my life, I started on a mission – I was determined to become more well-read, to catch up through reading a wider variety of non-business books, to take more of an interest in this huge world, from history to what was happening now. It was a very exciting time for me, since I was also better able to discuss thinking approaches and skills with people from all over the globe, which ultimately helped me in both my professional and personal life.

I started to have a new respect for our cultural differences and views, which was later solidified by actually living in Europe. My wife and I had the wonderful opportunity to move to Switzerland for a three-year stint for my job. Prior to embarking on this venture, we were provided with guidance to make it easier for us to adapt to this countries' culture. One of the best pieces of advice we were given was to refrain from judgment – avoid judging the differences between cultures as right or wrong, better or worse. Just see them for what they are – they are just different. We found this helpful because it's true - you can accomplish the same tasks or interact with people in many different ways and most of them work very well, even if they are new to you. By welcoming things that are "different," it certainly makes the world more interesting and can help us improve our lives by teaching us to be more tolerant in general. It encourages us to be open, ask lots of questions and learn. The key to advancing your own understanding of the world and striving to innovate is dependent on having tolerance for ideas and ways of living different than what you are accustomed. Many people I have come in contact with, even international travelers, struggle with embracing tolerance. They don't understand how being open to new ideas and ways of living can lead to a more fulfilling life and an increase in innovation. Staying as open minded as we can to new things, experiences and thinking is a philosophy in which I totally believe and embrace wholeheartedly.

As I read more and more, and continued to travel through countries on almost every continent, my knowledge and understanding of the world grew. However, the more I learned, the more I aspired to learn more. I was particularly drawn to understanding the origins of the many cultural elements I encountered – everything from the food choices to religious beliefs to government structures. These were the drivers of my intellectual curiosity- asking questions and doing the research to determine where, how, and why things originated. This revealed to me that many beliefs and behaviors were actually based on the actions and very arbitrary decisions by some powerful and influential people (predominantly men) throughout history. Some of these were positive, but unfortunately some were cruel and discriminatory, resulting in much pain and suffering over the years. This learning obtained through reading and listening also led to the realization that much of what I personally believed to be real was actually fantasy. I saw how fantasy beliefs have led to intolerance throughout history, which was detrimental for many societies because it led to economic stagnation, violence, and ultimately collapse. This is incredible to me since many of the beliefs they were fighting and killing for were based on someone's imagination and at the same time were intolerant of other's beliefs.

Throughout history, there are examples of major empires being destroyed as a result of their intolerance. Unfortunately, intolerance still exists with dire consequences today in the 21st century. Tolerance to different cultures, races, ethnicities, creative thinking, and religions is essential for survival – it's the power that drives innovation and growth. As soon as societies become intolerant and close themselves off by becoming nationalistic, violence erupts and growth stops.

One historic example of the tragic effects of intolerance was in Alexandria, Egypt thousands of years ago. Remember back in 325 CE, the Nicaea Council proclaimed Christians now would believe in the concept of three Gods in one. And it was decided those three gods would all be equal gods – God the Father, Jesus Christ the Son, and the Holy Ghost. Not just equal, but all three would have full god status. And just like that – the council debated, they voted and then proclaimed it to be so. Of course, it was never going to be just that easy. They needed to convince all Christians this is what they should, and therefore would, believe going forward – as you would expect, there were bound to be dissenters. And as was pointed out earlier, that's exactly what transpired. Some people did in fact challenge this new doctrine, including many people in Alexandria who disagreed with the voting decision to make Jesus Christ a full immortal God. These dissenters caused much consternation for both the Roman Emperor as well as the religious group that supported that decision.

So why did the Roman's care so much about what was happening in Alexandria? The city of Alexandria, founded in 331 BCE by Alexander the Great, was and still is, a major port located on the Mediterranean Sea in northern Egypt. The city grew to become one of the largest and most prosperous in the world, attracting scholars, scientists, philosophers, mathematicians, artists, and historians. But not everything was all rosy in Alexandria particularly after that Nicaea Council proclamation. As a result, Alexandria also became infamous for its religious strife, resulting in the martyrdom of the philosopher Hypatia in 415 CE, which then catapulted the Christian religion to suppress all pagan beliefs.

Hypatia (370 CE to March 415 CE) was a popular female teacher of philosophy, science, and mathematics at the University of Alexandria. She was renowned for her generosity, love of learning, and teaching expertise. She had charisma, charm, and was skillful in making difficult mathematical and philosophical concepts understandable to her students. Her influence was very strong, which became particularly troublesome as she daringly taught concepts that contradicted the relatively new Christian religion. During this time period, the city of Alexandria was culturally diverse, and was also becoming more religiously diverse, especially because of Hypatia's influence. Cyril, the Christian Archbishop of Alexandria did not like this situation and thus needed to find a way to suppress Hypatia.

According to the historical account, in March 415 CE, on her way home from delivering her daily lectures at the university, Hypatia was attacked by a mob of Christian monks at the direction of Cyril. She was pulled from her chariot, dragged down the street and into a church - it was there that she was stripped naked, beaten to death, and ultimately burned. But it didn't end there. In the aftermath of Hypatia's death, the University of Alexandria was sacked and burned on orders from Cyril, along with pagan temples being destroyed and torn down. Not surprisingly, there was a mass exodus of intellectuals and artists from the newly Christianized city of Alexandria. So how did the church respond to this horrific situation? Cyril was later declared a saint by the church, praised for his efforts in suppressing paganism, and fighting for the true faith. Hypatia's death has long been recognized as a major turning point in history, when the classical age of paganism began declining, and the Christian religion began to expand.

Tragically for the city of Alexandria, as Christianity rose in power, the city began to decline. The death of Hypatia of Alexandria has come to embody all that was lost to civilization as a result of religious intolerance and the destruction it engenders. A cautionary example of what can transpire once the rulers and people in these civilizations became intolerant and take actions underscoring their intolerance - the civilization declines.

By contrast, we find the opposite to be true as well. Throughout history we learn that tolerance for different cultures, religions, and ideas drives growth and bolsters great civilizations. One of the earliest examples of this positive impact of tolerance was the empire developed by Alexander the Great, who founded Alexandria. His empire spanned from the area where he grew up in Macedonia (Northeastern Greece) to include the entire Eastern Mediterranean area, Egypt, the Middle East and parts of Asia (Northern India). Alexander was able to conquer and integrate such a vast land by including the people and their new military ideas into his army as he conquered them. He also embraced the cultures of the various areas by adopting their dress and allowing and sharing their religious beliefs. Through his conquests, the Greek language, literature, art, architecture, and philosophy spread across this entire area.

In addition, much of the local knowledge was incorporated, resulting in a cultural hybrid known as Hellenism, which would go on to influence Christianity and the western world. Alexander began the process of culturally unifying these areas through tolerance and sharing but unfortunately, he died early in his life at age 32 of a fever. After his death, Alexander's empire immediately fragmented into warring kingdoms when they became intolerant of each other and greedy for power. Despite this conflict and the collapse of the empire, Alexander's cultural influence known as Hellenism was not totally undone and continued to live on for centuries.

Another example of how tolerance helped build a great empire, and ironically how intolerance helped destroy it, was the Roman Empire, one of the greatest empires of all time. The empire spread through all of continental Europe west of the Rhine River and south of the Danube and the islands of the Mediterranean Sea. It also included near East Asia west of the Euphrates River, and Northern Africa including Egypt. Basically, the only significant area in continental Europe not included in the Roman Empire was the Germanic area of current day Germany, Poland, and Ukraine. These people would eventually become problematic, ultimately leading to the decline of the Roman Empire.

The Roman Empire started in Rome, and from the very beginning was good at assimilating into their society the people it conquered or acquired through alliances. One of the ways they did this was by allowing people of all races and economic classes to become citizens. This was a great way to also spread the Roman culture and values. The people intermarried in many of the regions, and those from the provinces who were educated could serve in public life and reach elite status. As examples, emperors Trajan, Hadrian, and Marcus Aurelius came from Spain; Antonius Pius was Gallic (French area); and Septimius Severus was from Africa and had a Syrian wife. The Roman way of life became popular and was considered very civilized and prestigious. For instance, men wore togas instead of pants and people learned to speak Greek and Latin. In fact, the Romans offered citizenship as a marketing ploy to attract men to join the army, which worked quite well. Although the Romans were open to new innovations, there were limits to what they would tolerate. After all, their primary goal was to assimilate people willing to adopt the Roman customs, manners, and philosophy.

The Romans did reject certain practices or customs deemed to be barbaric or morally repugnant. Things that were frowned upon were poor hygiene, wearing pants instead of tunics, togas or robes, and cooking with butter instead of olive oil. I suspect the current spiritual leaders of the Abrahamic religions, including priests, rabbis, and imams are still trying to emulate the ancient Romans by wearing tunics, togas, and robes since they are still wearing them today in their ceremonies. Perhaps they aren't aware this style went out of fashion more than a thousand years ago, except for maybe at college fraternity toga parties in the United States. Considering all the options available today - pants with zippers, jeans that stretch, and of course, spandex, you'd think they would change except religious traditions tend to be rigid and inflexible. As to cooking, the Roman insistence of cooking with olive oil is a fun fact and could help in the debate over frying eggs in olive oil versus butter. The Romans thought the notion of people in the northern part of the empire cooking in butter was disgusting. I guess they didn't know that olive trees couldn't grow very well up north. Other things banned by the Roman Senate, which seem like very good decisions, were the Druid practice of human sacrifice and self-castration by the male eunuch priests that worshiped the goddess Cybele. There was also a period where they did not allow Jewish circumcision. Apparently, all these practices were appalling to them, even though they didn't seem to have a problem watching criminals get mauled and partially eaten by animals in an arena setting.

Although the Roman Empire could be brutal at times, their accomplishments in architecture, road and bridge building throughout the empire were incredible. Through an immense military, they were able to conquer and connect people and trade routes across Europe, Asia, and Africa. As a result of their tolerance to new ideas and innovation, their knowledge would grow in science, literature, philosophy, medicine, astronomy, architecture, natural history and government structure to a level that would not be surpassed for a thousand years.

I was able to catch a glimpse of some of these Roman achievements first hand by touring the Pompeii ruins, aided by a college professor tour guide. If you have a chance to travel to this area, I highly recommend visiting this archeological site, however make sure you hire a really competent tour guide. The reason why these ruins are such a treasure of information and perspective on the Roman Empire is Pompeii, which was destroyed in 79 CE by the volcanic eruption of Mount Vesuvius, is essentially intact. What is unique about the ruins of Pompeii is they have been so well preserved for almost two thousand years, buried under the ash of the volcano. The sophistication and cosmopolitan nature of this society is surprising when you see it first hand – the bustling city complete with a complex water system, market area, amphitheater, hundreds of streets, even pedestrian crosswalks. It also offers a view into the tolerance of this Roman time period. Pompeii was a multi-cultural town actively trading with Egypt, North Africa, India, and the Middle East and was a multi-racial society that included black Africans. They did have enslaved people, however there was a path for them to become freed people, similar to other areas in the Roman Empire. As proof of this, there is an ancient statue in Pompeii that included an ex-slave, the woman who originally owned him, and a friend who deceived him with an inscription recording their relationship and history. I was amazed by the sophistication of the city of Pompeii, recognizing that many of the innovations uncovered here were made possible by the Romans' practice of accepting and embracing ideas coming from so many different cultures.

So, what caused the Roman Empire to eventually collapse? There are many theories about lead poisoning in the water due to the lead pipes used in the aqueducts, mosquitoes causing malaria, soil exhaustion resulting in famine, excess decadence of the ruling class, and eventually being overrun by Germanic tribes. All of these things may have contributed in part to the decline, but intolerance to the Germanic immigrants causing them to rebel, is what finally broke the back of the Roman Empire. This happened over time beginning in the third century.

The Roman Empire suffered from repeated invasions by the Germanic tribes located in the current areas of Sweden, Germany, and Romania. These invasions were eventually suppressed and Rome permitted these people to remain socially intact in the north and east. However, they left them autonomous and did not assimilate them into the Roman culture. These people did not like imperial rule and began to desire independence since they were not getting any benefits from being part of the Roman Empire. This friction and continued attacks from the north and east caused the Romans to eventually become irritated and intolerant of these people. Thus, instead of assimilation and compromise, they began insisting on total compliance with the Roman way of life. Which is exactly the opposite of what they should have done.

In the early fourth century, Rome also began to be intolerant of other groups that would not cooperate with the empire. The Jewish Christians at this time period accounted for about ten percent of the Roman Empire population, or five million out of a total 60 million people. These Jewish Christians lived primarily in urban areas, whereas the rural people were almost exclusively followers of the official Roman Empire religion. It was difficult for the Jewish Christian sect to convert these rural people since they were very attached to their old beliefs and ways, and were reluctant to change. This difference in thinking between urban and rural is evident even in today's society and politics all over the world. During this time, the majority of Roman subjects disliked the early Jewish Christians. These people would not recognize the gods of Rome, would not offer sacrifices to them, and they were even accused of incest and cannibalism. The accusation of incest came from misinterpreting their practice of referring to each other as "brother or sister in Christ" even though they were actually living as husband and wife. The cannibalism accusation came from the secrecy surrounding the reenactment of Jesus' last supper in their homes, using words such as eating and drinking the body and blood of Jesus Christ. Furthermore, because they did not recognize Roman gods, the Roman people blamed them for all sorts of negative effects such as military defeats, natural disasters and famines. The Romans thought the gods were angry with them because the Jewish Christians would not pay homage to the Roman gods. Another group, the non-Christian Jews also denied the gods of Rome but were left alone as they were recognized as a more ancient cult. By contrast, the Jewish Christians were viewed as a new cult even though they were still Jewish, and therefore they were not granted any status or rights to violate Roman religious law. It's important to understand the Roman religious cult practices were believed to be a public way to keep the gods happy - people not participating in these practices were viewed as disloyal to the community. To add more friction to the situation, the Jewish Christians did everything possible to get the people believing in Roman cults to stop following the customs of their parents and friends. The Romans felt these proselytizing actions were threatening to the cohesion of their society. The Jewish Christians also did not respect the ancestral pagan customs, and preached of a new king to lead them called Jesus. All of these actions gave the implication they were organizing a revolution, which is also why the Romans disliked them.

Beginning in 303 CE, the emperor Diocletian had enough and began to persecute the Jewish Christians by removing them from public office and from the military. They arrested them for not making sacrifices to Roman gods, destroyed their churches, burned their written scriptures, and killed thousands of them. His goal was to restore complete unity in the empire under the Roman cult. As expected, this approach did not work, only causing more friction and further weakening the Roman Empire. This is yet another good example of the negative impact of intolerance.

Once Constantine became emperor, to calm things down in 313 CE he issued an edict of tolerance for all religions. This was only ten years after Diocletian started persecuting the Christians. Once Constantine promoted tolerance, all the various cults grew including Christianity. In fact, Christianity got a huge boost in popularity from people honoring all the martyrs who had been killed by Diocletian's regime. However, since there were so many different beliefs, Constantine felt the need to unify all the religions of the Roman Empire as a way to strengthen the empire under one belief system to fight against barbarian attacks. He decided to use Christianity as a foundation, merging aspects of the Roman cults with it to make a new stronger Christian religion. He favored Christianity because it dealt with improving yourself morally and in so doing your soul would have eternal life. The pagan religions were primarily focused on just keeping the gods happy. Since paganism was so ingrained in the people's beliefs, he needed to break down and transfer these beliefs to his new and improved Christian cult. To do this, he stripped the Roman temples of their riches and built Christian basilicas. As a result, in just seven years it was clear to everyone that Christianity was favored by the Roman Empire and the power of this religion and its bishops was strengthening.

Since the Western Roman Empire was also suffering from repeated invasions by the Germanic tribes called Goths, and the Eastern Roman Empire was growing stronger, wealthier, and more stable by trading with Asia, Constantine made the decision to move the center of the Roman Empire from Rome to Constantinople (it had been called Byzantium, but he changed it to Constantinople, and now this city is called Istanbul). His next move was to hold the Council of Nicaea in 325 CE, which was located geographically near Constantinople.

Receiving many mentions already, the main purpose of this Council of Nicaea was to establish the Christian orthodoxy. One year after this council met to establish a state religion, Constantine's next action was to confiscate and destroy all writings, art works, and statues that challenged the orthodox Christian teachings agreed to at Nicaea. The works destroyed were both Christian and pagan. To further strengthen the new state religion of Christianity, he funded the church, bishops, and established their palace in Rome. And finally, in 331 CE he commissioned and financed the writing of the Christian New Testament bible in Greek. The reason why it was written in Greek was a marketing ploy to reach more people in the Roman Empire. Most educated people in this time period were bilingual in both Latin and Greek. In addition, the Eastern Roman Empire, where they primarily spoke the Greek language was doing better than the western region. More and more people converted to Christianity as this was the state religion and the ambitious people knew they needed to follow the state religion to get ahead. Obviously, there was no separation of church and state during this time period.

Once this new bible was completed, there was now a written way to enforce Christian orthodoxy. This is why the Christian Bible is favorable to the Roman's treatment of Jesus, while vilifying the Jewish people. It was written to appeal to most of the Roman Empire. At this time period, the Roman Empire tolerated the Jewish settlements because they were thriving economically, but they did not like their independence and unwillingness to adopt Roman culture and the new state religion. The Bible was used as a propaganda tool to blame the Jewish people for the death of Jesus and it worked very well. In reality, it was the Romans who killed Jesus, along with the other Jewish rebels or zealots who were fighting for independence from 4 BC until 136 CE.

Over time, as the empire became more and more Christian, intolerance to other beliefs increased. The church and Roman officials established a campaign to eliminate paganism and all non-Christian believers, as well as the Christian believers not following the official orthodoxy established at the council of Nicaea and written in the bible. Constantine and his successors believed that religious uniformity was necessary to strengthen the empire and thus, protect it from barbarian attacks. However, the effect was exactly the opposite, causing much more animosity, which eventually contributed to the downfall of the Roman Empire.

Around 370 CE, the Huns coming from the areas of Eastern Europe, the Caucasus and Central Asia, invaded

Central Europe outside of the Roman Empire, primarily in Germanic areas. This caused the Germanic people and the Goths from Sweden to flee into Roman territory. In the past the Roman people would have welcomed these new people into the empire and encouraged the men to join the army. However, the Germanic people were disgusting to the native Roman people and for the first time, they adopted policies of apartheid against their new subjects. These Germanics were forbidden to intermarry with Romans, they forbid men from wearing pants, and they condemned the Germanic form of Christianity. Romans lynched Goth soldiers and they massacred villages of Germanic people who they considered Christian heretics. This friction caused the Goths to rise up under the Gothic king Alaric, sacking Rome in 410 CE. They then went on to overtake the Roman Empire in Gaul (primarily France area) in 419 CE. Once again, this negative effect of intolerance to both religious beliefs and an ethnic group of people caused the Roman Empire to further decline.

In North Africa, the shutdown of pagan temples and the persecution of people believing in their own form of Christianity caused rioting. Eventually the people began to support the Vandal King Genseric, coincidentally considered a heretic Christian. This oppression and lack of tolerance with the Vandals resulted in them fighting back and sacking Rome again in 455 CE. (As a side note, the word vandal or vandalism in Latin now means willful destroyer of what is beautiful. Obviously, the Christian historians wanted to demonize the Vandal's, but of course they never recognized how badly they had mistreated these people.)

By 475 CE the Western Roman Empire no longer existed as it was controlled by many of the Germanic tribes. This was true even in the Northern part of the Roman Empire as the Germanic tribes took over once the Huns' control of this area dissolved after King Attila the Hun died in 453 CE. In addition, toward the end of the Roman Empire, the Jewish people were also being treated with intolerance by the Roman Christians, with some of the people in the villages being massacred for their non-Christian beliefs. Instead of fighting back, the Jewish people just moved into Persian territory, taking with them their trading expertise. These events significantly damaged the economic health of the Roman Empire, also contributing to its decline.

The turning point for the growth of Christianity was when it was adopted as the official state religion of the Roman Empire beginning in 325 CE. This also was when we can trace the beginning of the Christian's anti-Jewish feelings and persecution. As Christians gained power and influence, they were more brutal than the people they replaced. The other religions pleaded for tolerance but the Christians would not accept any other religion, persecuting all non-Christian and also Christians not believing in the Roman Christianity orthodoxy. Their so-called religion of "love, peace, and brotherhood" looked very much like the previous religions of Rome. As a result, to avoid persecution and execution, massive numbers of people converted to

Christianity, not because they believed in the new religion, but to protect themselves from this intolerance. I had originally felt pride in being raised Roman Catholic, however I never realized what that meant except it was different from the Eastern Orthodox Catholic religion. Now that I've learned the history of the early Roman Christians, I am horrified by their intolerance and inhumanity towards others. Little by little, my pride gradually turned to regret for my earlier uninformed acceptance.

Early on during the growth of the Roman Empire, their strategy of tolerance and uncoerced assimilation worked well and built the empire. On the other hand, when the empire would not tolerate or assimilate the Germanic tribes and their different Christian beliefs, and they also stopped acceptance of the Jewish communities, the people rebelled or fled, resulting in the decline of this great empire. Since the Roman Empire is considered to be one of the greatest empires of all time, it is an important example of how an empire grew through tolerance and assimilation of new people and then what it did wrong through intolerance to cause it to decline.

My trivial example about the Romans hating the Germanic culture's customs of wearing pants and using butter are great examples of intolerance that could have instead led to innovation for the Romans. If the Romans had been tolerant to new ideas, they would have discovered that wearing pants made it easier to ride a horse for instance or allowed them to move around better when they worked.

They may have even been able to improve the Germanic pants design instead of rejecting it as barbaric. By the way, most people wear pants now and they are not barbaric - perhaps someone should point this out to the religious leaders still stuck wearing robes and togas. As to the butter example, the Romans could have asked questions to find out why the Germanic people used butter for cooking instead of olive oil, which would have been a good place to start. As we all know, butter tastes great and can be a great alternative to olive oil. If the Romans had been tolerant to new ways of cooking during that time period, who knows how many innovations in food dishes they would have developed. Although these are very petty, inconsequential examples of intolerance, they are emblematic of how people even today think and act similar to the Romans. Like the Roman's, many people's first reaction to something different is to reject it outright instead of considering it objectively and with an open mind.

I know from experience that cherishing or embracing diversity not only leads to innovation but it also is very interesting and can make your life more fulfilling. Rejecting diversity and being intolerant to new ways of living or ideas leads to the decline of society, more so now than ever. Policies encouraging protectionism, isolationism and xenophobia will eventually lead to a declining civilization similar to what the Roman Empire experienced. Unfortunately, very rigid religious beliefs often learned at young ages can interfere with the ability for people to be open minded, kind and considerate of others. Realizing that religions, at their core, are all based somewhat on imagination and fantasy stories will help people become less adamant that they are always in the right. The belief that they are right because their God told them so is not really a valid, meaningful defense. In the end, we all need to be more open-minded and work together by sharing ideas - we should also insist our leaders do the same.

As I said at the beginning of this chapter, the topic of tolerance and intolerance is as important today as it was in the Roman Empire thousands of years ago. We certainly need to learn from past mistakes. Being tolerant and inclusive is now more important than ever as we become closer and more reliant economically and socially with people all over the world due to improvements in technology, commerce, and transportation. We, as a global community, need each other to solve problems we cannot solve alone such as pandemics, climate change, and the impact technology has on social platforms, propaganda, power grids, water systems, and supply chains. We must embrace our differences, discuss them and understand them, because it is now necessary to interact more frequently with people who are often very different than us. It doesn't mean we have to accept everything or even agree with it, it just means we need to take the time and effort to listen and understand each other. Who knows, you may learn something new and go on to create a significant innovation.

Chapter 16

Does God Really Bless America?

The United States of America is arguably one of the most successful governments in the history of the world - some people have the delusional belief it was inspired and endorsed by no other than God himself. By extension, many Americans also believe the founding fathers of this nation were near God- like, almost supernatural in their powers. Although it is positive to be proud of your country, as I am, it is not judicious to believe your country is not only superior to other countries, but that it has been specifically chosen by God to lead the world. Believing God supports your country over other countries is not healthy. It nurtures the conviction that your country is always right and your way of living is the best and only way, because of course… God said so. Too much nationalism, which seems to be increasing in the world right now, is detrimental not only to peace and tranquility, but it also slows our ability to solve world problems through cooperation and innovation. Problems such as pollution driven climate change, poverty, starvation, violence toward others, slavery, drug addiction, discrimination, and oppression, to name a few – all areas of concern that definitely demand and deserve attention. The United States should not consider itself to be an island, as it needs to cooperate with other countries in order to solve global problems. The benefits of working with and learning from other countries will greatly improve its quality of life and help other countries improve theirs as well.

Although the United States is thought to be a great country, other countries also have many great attributes and ways of living a better life that we can learn from and adopt. The United States has the potential for continuous improvement but it can also decline if it becomes less democratic and intolerant. Currently, the United States of America is a significant empire, some even considering it to be the greatest in the history of the world. Objectively, it is not the greatest of all time, at least not yet if you measure empire rankings by a mix of criteria such as landmass controlled, population, strength of the military, influence on the world's wealth, and longevity. To date, based on these criteria the most powerful empires in the history of the world chronologically include:

The Persian Empire (550 BCE to 330 BCE)
It ruled over 44% of the world's population at the time and connected multiple world regions.

The Roman Empire (27 BCE to 476 CE; however, in 476 CE, the Western Roman Empire fell but the Eastern Roman Empire survived as the Byzantine Empire until 1453 CE)
It was one of the greatest empires of all time not only because of its size, but because of its influence on philosophy, religion, architecture, roads, and culture by incorporating aspects of Greek culture with their own and forming a Greco Roman culture. This empire is responsible for establishing and growing the Christian religion.

The Arab Empire or The Caliphate (632 CE-900 CE, although parts of it survived until 1258 CE when the Mongols destroyed Baghdad.)
Founded by the Muslim Prophet Muhammad, it encompassed most of Arabia by the time of his death in 632 CE. The ideological influence of Islam fueled this empire to grow to several times larger than the Roman Empire in just 100 years. Its location based in the Middle East enabled it to easily connect other world civilizations in Africa, Europe, Central Asia, India, and China, which drove innovation in mathematics, science, engineering, architecture, and art. This empire was responsible for growing the Islamic religion.

The Mongol Empire (1206 CE - with parts of it existing into the 1300s CE.)

It was the world's largest contiguous landmass empire controlling most of China, Russia, and the Middle East. The Mongols connected the east with the west using the Silk Road and were a conduit for encouraging innovation until their demise. They were unable to successfully manage this vast empire once their founder, Genghis Khan died. They were also not set up to manage this empire effectively and when the black plague hit, it shut down the trading routes, reducing their income and power significantly.

The British Empire (1500's CE to 1997 CE, when they transferred Hong Kong to China)

In the 1900's CE, at the peak of this empire, it controlled 23% of the world's population at the time and 24% of the world's land area. The British Empire is attributed with having influenced modern government design across the globe by encouraging characteristics such as individual autonomy, equality of opportunity, free trade, the rule of law, protection of individual rights, free speech and freedom of the press. This influence was not planned as it just happened over this empire's long history. Although it was one of the largest empires in history, it accomplished this feat through organizational and financial skills, rather than through its military strength.

*

Over time, the United States of America will most likely be comparable to these great empires, as it currently has one of the most powerful militaries ever amassed. It also has the number one economy in the world, with China in the second position but closing the gap. In addition, the United States can be compared to all the greatest empires in the history of the world, as it shares many of their same strengths. For example, it combines different cultures and links regions, similar to what was done by the Persian Empire; it has an attractive culture similar to the Roman Empire; it spreads its ideology across the globe like the Arab Empire; it has a military that can cause total destruction like the Mongols; and it trades globally and believes in the rule of law and individual rights like the British Empire.

Foreseeably, the United States has a long future ahead of it as a great power unless it repeats the same mistakes that led to the decline of previous great empires. Its success or failure most likely will not be caused by a god's influence, but rather is dependent on the actions of its citizens and their elected officials. However, there certainly are many American citizens wishfully believing some supernatural intervention will solve the current political division in the United States. As has been witnessed throughout history, internal division, intolerance, and disrespecting one another is eventually what has destroyed the most powerful empires. Even though the Persians were strong, they were conquered because their leadership was weak. Despite its strong military, Rome fell due to internal division and not accepting and tolerating the Germanic tribes that were part of the empire. The Arabs had a successful empire until they were taken over by people who made the Arabs subservient and poor. And finally, the British demise resulted from their over-extension by trying to control too many regions and they also did not respect the rights of their subjects causing them to rebel.

The United States is a special country and should not be considered completed, as it will always be a work in progress. The Founding Fathers knew their design of the original Constitution would need to be improved over time and that it was far from a perfect document, even though it was exceptional for their time period.

The Founding Fathers of the United States should be recognized as great people who engineered the beginning of a great nation. But they were not demi-gods as many Americans naively believe. In fact, these ordinary men were very flawed individuals. Their greatness came from combining their knowledge of history and philosophy and by working together as a team. They also argued vigorously yet still listened and respected each other. America's top Founding Fathers are recognized for both their contribution to winning the war of independence from England and establishing the Constitution of the United States. These men were intelligent and well-read, having gained their education from the top colleges in the colonies, with the exception of George Washington and Benjamin Franklin, who were primarily self-taught through extensive reading and life experiences. John Adams graduated from Harvard College, Alexander Hamilton and John Jay graduated from Kings College (now called Colombia University), Thomas Jefferson graduated from William and Mary, and James Madison graduated from the College of New Jersey (now called Princeton).

Initially this group of men did not have a vision for creating an independent nation as they were only reacting to their environment. By the way, their overall living situation was significantly worse than just being subjected to high taxes without representation as most people were taught in school. If you think about it, taxation alone is not a very strong reason to endure all the suffering and killing caused by the American Revolution. What is not usually explained in school is the colonists were experiencing horrible treatment by the British and the Founding Fathers were also aware of bad treatment by the British in other areas of the world, such as India and China. Worth noting, in the 1700s CE, India and China had the largest economies in the world, each with around 20% of global Gross Domestic Product. The Founding Fathers were aware of the British atrocities inflicted on the people of these areas and knew it would most likely happen to them as well. So yes, the American colonists were experiencing excessive taxation by England to pay for the French and Indian war, but there was much more to be angry about. The British military was abusing their power by seizing people's homes and treating the colonists unfairly and roughly. The British also were limiting growth west of the Appalachian Mountains and using the Indians to attack and murder these early settlers. And finally, the legal system was unfair. The criminal justice system for corrupt British officials and military abuses was moved to England, resulting in few, if any, prosecutions. It was also very difficult to get a fair trial in the colonies, as the British government controlled the judges. For these reasons along with excessive taxes, people started fighting against the British leading to the American Revolutionary War.

Thomas Paine was one of the more influential persons to publicly talk about forming a new independent and democratic government apart from England. He wrote a pamphlet entitled "Common Sense" and in the first three months of 1776 CE, sold 120,000 copies. Considering the population of the colonies was only 2,500,000, which included 500,000 slaves, and the literacy rate was relatively low, this was considered to be an extremely successful document. In fact, George Washington had it read to his troops as it was easily understood. It explained why the colonies needed to become independent from England and why the English royalty were not ordained by God to rule over the colonies or anyone. It's incredible to realize the early colonists understood the royalty or people with privileged ancestry were not ordained by God almost 250 years ago, and yet some people today still believe otherwise. Unquestionably, this pamphlet influenced the American people and the Founding Fathers to fight for independence, not just revolt against taxation.

After the war for independence was won and validated with the signing of the Treaty of Paris in September 1783 CE, the colonies struggled economically since Congress, which consisted of elected delegates from each state, was not able to rule effectively. At this point, the thirteen colonies only had the Articles of Confederation to run their new nation, which were written at the start of the Revolutionary War. These articles gave congress power to make rules and request funds from the states, but it did not give them enforcement power, the ability to regulate commerce, or print money. They had sacrificed far too much during the war to have their newly won independence fail, and thus they recognized the need to make changes to their government. So, Alexander Hamilton with the support of George Washington and James Madison, helped convince congress to organize a Grand Convention of state delegates for the purpose of revising the Articles of Confederation. These delegates assembled in Philadelphia, Pennsylvania in May 1787 CE for the purpose of writing the United States' Constitution.

Although they started with a blank sheet of paper, most of the Founding Fathers had a strong knowledge of history and philosophy. To help them write the United States' Constitution, they were able to draw from their knowledge of Greek and Roman history and philosophy, as well as from the wisdom of several significant political philosophers in Europe that lived during the 1600s CE and 1700s CE. Since the Founding Fathers' education included Greek and Roman history, they were well versed in where and when many of the beliefs of their time period originated. They used knowledge of the Greek philosophers, such as Plato and Aristotle, to shape their thoughts regarding the invention of a new democratic government. They also admired and were influenced by the Roman Empire's mixed government approach, which incorporated a shared design for ruling, which included both aristocratic individuals and democratic common people.

In addition to the ancient philosophers, other European philosophers influenced the Founding Fathers including Thomas Hobbes, John Locke, Jean-Jacques Rousseau, and Baron de Montesquieu. Of course, the Founding Fathers were selective in choosing the ideas they would incorporate into their new constitution from these philosophers. So, who were these men and what were their influential philosophies that are now integral to the United States Constitution?

Thomas Hobbes (1588 CE to 1679 CE) believed that written laws were the only way to effectively operate a government, but he also thought the best form of political authority was a king. Although the Founding Fathers agreed with the importance of written laws, they rejected his king recommendation. He felt the primary goal of government was to provide peace and personal security for all its citizens, which the founding fathers also embraced as their goal. Hobbes developed the idea that a government ruled effectively by law is the only protection against anarchy or as he put it "a war of all against all". He believed if you do not have laws to adjudicate disputes, everyone would fear and mistrust everyone else and as a result there could be no justice, commerce, or culture. His approach to end this unsustainable condition was to encourage individuals to agree to relinquish their natural rights to everything, and transfer their self-sovereignty to a higher civil authority. In other words, total freedom to do anything you want results in total chaos. I actually witnessed this state of chaos first hand in Haiti during the 1990s CE as there was no government or infrastructure in place until the multi-national forces came in to try and help this country establish a formal set of laws and legal system. The pain, suffering, and chaos I observed due to the absence of laws and a legal system reaffirmed my belief in the United States' Constitution and rule of law. Freedom does not mean you are free to do whatever you want; rather freedom means you are free to not be harmed by others. Many Americans do not understand this simple philosophy, which was supported strongly by Hobbes and then adopted by the Founding Fathers. In fact, on this topic Hobbes disagreed with Aristotle's political belief that human beings are naturally suited in life to residing in a city-state (or polis in the Greek language), without the need for legal controls. As a side note, the word "political" was derived from the word polis. Hobbes thought the only way for humans to live peacefully in a city-state was through the enforcement of written laws to protect them from each other. Obviously, the Founding Fathers agreed with Hobbes on this topic as the United States is based on a very formal system of laws, beginning with the Constitution.

The next philosopher's thinking that inspired the Constitution of the United States was the English philosopher, John Locke (1632 CE to 1704 CE). He had strong views that had been influenced by the founders of modern science such as Robert Boyle and Sir Isaac Newton, both of whom were his friends. Boyle is known as the father of chemistry and the developer of the modern experimental scientific method. Newton is considered one of the most influential scientists of all time and leader of the Scientific Revolution of the 1600s CE by inventing calculus, and the theory of universal gravity. Locke's political thought was based on the need for a social contract between citizens that included tolerance, especially in matters of religion. He believed the sole responsibility of the church is salvation of souls, and the ceremonies to accomplish this goal should be of no concern for anyone but the participant. He rejected the claim by kings to have been given the divine right to rule over citizens and he believed there should be no natural hierarchy among humans. He defined political power as the right of making morally based laws and then enforcing them for the public good. He contended each person is naturally free and equal under the law of nature, but each person is required to enforce as well as obey this law. His solution to eliminate injustice and violence was for citizens to enter into a contract with each other to form a higher authority that would require compliance with laws.

Not surprising, the Founding Fathers in agreement with Locke also rejected the concept of kings and nobility. They specifically included the statement in the Constitution, "No Title of Nobility shall be granted by the United States." Also noteworthy was the influence of Locke's idea regarding equality on the Founding Fathers with the well-known second paragraph of the United States Declaration of Independence that states: "We hold these truths to be self-evident, that all men are created equal, that they are endowed by their Creator with certain unalienable Rights, that among these are Life, Liberty and the Pursuit of Happiness." Unfortunately, it wouldn't be until amendments to the original Constitution were adopted many years later that those equal rights for all would be legally protected.

Another philosopher influencing the United States' Constitution was Jean-Jacques Rousseau (1712 CE to 1778 CE) from Switzerland. He believed the purpose of a civil society was to provide peace for everyone and ensure the right to own property, and as he added, "that is if you're lucky to have any." He thought this would help everyone, but especially the wealthy people. In his view, a genuine social contract provides people an independence and freedom, in exchange for true political or republican liberty. Such liberty would be realized through self-imposed laws. To accomplish liberty, society must pledge to a group whereby people give up natural rights in return for civil rights. This freedom or liberty can then be enforced by the whole group. Rousseau, however, agrees with Plato that most people are stupid (his words, not mine). Therefore, intelligent people are needed to draw up a constitution and system of laws. The continuation of this intellectual arrogance could be why today in politics, people in the United States seem to prefer candidates who are charismatic and fun loving, regardless of their intelligence level. You've probably heard the saying in support of a candidate, "He seems like he would be nice to have a beer with" as opposed to, "This politician is really smart."

Rousseau suggested the lawmakers needed to claim divine inspiration from God to persuade, in his words, "the dim-witted multitude to accept and endorse the laws it is offered." The good news is most of the Founding Fathers did not follow Rousseau's point of view on this topic and also insisted the Constitution was written using intelligence, reason, and common sense rather than God's intervention. They strengthened this view by insisting religion be kept separate from government. Rousseau argued Christianity, as a civil religion, is useless as a republican religion because it deals with the unseen world and does nothing to teach citizens the virtues of courage, strength, and patriotism in service to the state. This reasoning reinforced why the Founding Fathers kept religion out of the Constitution even though many of them had been raised in the Christian faith. Although Rousseau's intellectual superiority attitude was arrogant, governments such as the United States need to do a better job of attracting the most intelligent and accomplished individuals as leaders. Electing someone because they are charismatic and friendly are not sufficient qualifications for effective leadership.

The final political philosopher that had a strong influence on the writing of the United States' Constitution was Baron de Montesquieu (1689 CE to 1755 CE) from France. He wrote "The Spirit of the Laws" which explained human laws and social institutions that had a major impact on modern society. The authors of the United States' Constitution embraced his views on the best structure for their new government. His studies on governments found that corruption would most likely happen if a system of government did not include a balance of power structure. To solve this problem, he invented the idea of separating government authority into three major branches: Executive, Legislative, and Judicial. He thought it was key to create separate branches with equal but different powers. This is the main source of inspiration for why the United States' government is set up this way as outlined in its Constitution.

Over the last 50 years or so the balance of power structure of those three branches has been intentionally diminished in the United States. The Republican Party has been very clever and effective in dominating the Supreme Court and stacking the federal courts with judges friendly to their conservative point of view. This situation may prove to be dangerous to democracy as the Constitution always intended that the Judicial Branch be as balanced as possible in its political views for the overall health of our society. This was the goal of the Constitution - the judicial system was set up to enforce laws and interpret the constitution, not write laws. However, it should be noted that the courts have always interpreted the Constitution based on, or at least swayed by, the majority opinions of the United States' citizens. This is why a mix of judges with diversified views on this court is critical to democracy, so the court does not overly favor one political party's views over another.

Other philosophies written by Montesquieu were also adopted by the authors of the United States' Constitution. One philosophy adopted was his belief that a government elected by the people was the best form of government. Another was his belief that justice and the rule of law were the ways to ensure an orderly and predictable society. Similar to Hobbes' philosophy, he defined liberty as not the freedom to do whatever we want, but rather, to live under laws that protect us from harm while leaving us free to do as much as possible. This is why smoking laws, gun laws, and vaccine requirements make sense. Freedom must include not being harmed by others in daily life.

A final area of Montesquieu's influence on the authors of the United States' Constitution dealt with some of the same philosophies as Rousseau with regard to religion and government. Montesquieu believed it is a mistake to base civil laws on religious principles. This is because civil laws focus on the welfare of society while religions focus on the perfection of the individual. Whenever a government attempts to enforce God-based laws, we make religion an instrument of fanaticism and oppression. Even though Montesquieu and Rousseau both were adamant about keeping religion out of government, they both felt all religions in a country should be tolerated. However, this principle could be improved by adding a caveat, "…however, only if the religions are tolerant of other religions and do not cause pain or harm to others or their members."

These highly regarded political philosophers definitely had an influence on the group of Founding Fathers tasked with writing the Constitution. Yet, there were still many that thought the United States was inspired by God, and more specifically Jesus Christ. This Christian religious thinking eventually won out over time by first getting the words, "In god we trust" on coins during the Civil War in 1864 CE, and then getting them on paper money in 1957 CE. The Christian religious fanatics were also able to add the words "One nation under god" to the pledge of allegiance in 1954 CE, and in 1956 CE they changed the United States' motto from "E Pluribus Unum" (which translates to "out of many, one") to "In god we trust." Although all of these changes are diametrically opposed to the original intent of religious tolerance in the United States' Constitution, the religious fanatics were able to use the fear of atheistic communism during the McCarthyism era and Cold War to undermine the Founding Fathers' intent. It's interesting to note, in the country's history, adding these phrases revering God as a supporter of the United States is a fairly recent change which was done primarily in the 1950s CE, or more than 165 years after the constitution was written. The mentality and culture of the people who insist the United States' Constitution cannot be changed or interpreted differently than the original intent are often the same ones who are systematically trying to transform the United States to a Christian based government or theocracy. This is very unhealthy for our government, as the principles of religious tolerance and respect for different beliefs are a key foundation to peace in our society, just as the founding fathers had originally intended. Turning the United States into a Christian theocracy would be disastrous and most likely would eventually lead to the decline and collapse of this country.

In addition to the knowledge and influence of Roman and Greek history and the philosophers of the 1600s CE and 1700s CE, the structure and thinking behind the new United States' republic was also guided by Deism. Deism is the belief in the existence of a supreme being that created the universe but does not intervene in the universe. Many of the Founding Fathers believed in the philosophy of Deism even though they publicly followed the religion in which they were raised. There is evidence that the views of George Washington, John Adams, Benjamin Franklin, and Thomas Jefferson followed deist thinking. However, they learned quickly to hide their true beliefs, since politically it was necessary to give the appearance of being full-fledged

Christians. As an example, when Thomas Jefferson ran for President, he was accused of being a Francophile Atheist and also a Deist, which he quickly needed to denounce, professing to be a card-carrying Christian.

The people's belief that to be elected, a candidate needed to be an active church going Christian was true back then and still seems to be true today, almost 250 years later. What is not true however is that weekly church going people are necessarily all wonderful, kind, and compassionate people and are somehow better qualified to lead our country. What is also not true is the people who do not attend church regularly are automatically thought to be immoral human beings and therefore unqualified to lead. In other words, just because someone goes through the motions of going to church every week doesn't necessarily mean they are a moral person or a better candidate for political office.

The only Founding Fathers of the new republic who publicly promoted their Deist beliefs were Ethan Allen, publishing, "Reason: The Only Oracle of Man" in 1784 CE, and Thomas Paine, publishing "Age of Reason" in late 1794 CE. In Ethan Allen's document, he rejected that scripture had been God inspired. He also rejected the prophecies and miracles in these scriptures, the notion that God intervenes in people's lives, the holy trinity, and original sin. At that time, this publication was not widely accepted, as it was somewhat difficult to read. On the other hand, Thomas Paine's writing style was easier to read and appealed to the literate common people. His publication was popular and resulted in a small Deist movement among the population of the colonies. Paine criticized the superstitions of Christianity and vilified the priests and ministers who perpetuated these beliefs. He felt Christianity was a huge obstacle to obtaining human happiness through reason. His rationale was the Bible was violent, with its graphic narratives of cruel and tortuous executions, and God's actions in the Bible were often vindictive and cruel.

To understand the influence different beliefs had in shaping political philosophical views, it's helpful to be familiar with the basic differences between Deism and Theism. As noted, Deism is the belief in the existence of a supreme being that created the universe but does not intervene in the universe. Principally, Deists believe the creator set things up but you are on your own in deciding how you choose to live your life and ultimately, what happens to you. Theism also includes the belief in the existence of a god or gods as creators of the universe; however, these god or gods intervene in controlling the universe and have a personal relationship with their creatures. Most current day religions, such as Christianity, Islam, Hinduism, and Judaism, are Theistic religions. This is the reason people pray to God in hopes he will intervene and improve their lives. People following Theism thinking (which include most of the world's population) believe they are at the mercy of God's will or plan. If things go well, people thank God for their good fortune or success, and if things go badly, people blame God, saying it was "God's plan", or "God works in mysterious ways", or something to that effect.

By contrast, the people following Deist thinking believe God is not favoring any one person and they are on their own. Therefore, they encourage working through problems using reason, and treating people equally. Deist thinking relies on people shaping their world through moral decision making and insisting on social justice, as they do not rely on a god or gods to intervene and improve their lives. This philosophy influenced the Founding Fathers to embrace liberal political ideals, which were extraordinary for their time. Since the Founding Fathers supported rational analysis, they were very skeptical about religious mystery and doctrine, but still they advocated for religious tolerance. Compared to Theism, Deist thinking was more action oriented, whereby many of these Deist believers supported universal education, freedom of the press, and separation of church and state. The Theists on the other hand, relied on prayers to God to solve their problems and to take care of them.

In the American colonies, the Deist movement gained some support in the 1790s CE due to Elihu Palmer, who founded Deistic societies in New York, Philadelphia, and Baltimore. These groups were often radical feminists and abolitionists, believing in equality of human beings, humanitarianism and compassion. They believed all people, regardless of gender, skin color or physical appearance, should be treated equally in society. However, many of the educated elite feared the consequences of Deistic thinking in the hands of so many people. The ideas of rational thinking, which removed the threat of God's wrath and supernatural powers as a way to control people, was a real threat to both the elite and religious leaders. This fear drove the backlash against the Deist movement, especially by the Protestant leaders. As a result, Deism did not spread to the common people and remained primarily a philosophy of the educated elite, as many of them believed religions' main purpose was as a social control over the ignorant masses.

During the origins of the United States, the rational thinking of the Founding Fathers along with the public debate related to Deist beliefs, was a real threat to religious Christian leaders. This change in attitude away from supernatural religious thinking prompted "The Second Great Awakening," which was a Protestant Christian religious revival during the early 1800s CE in the United States. The movement began in the 1790s CE and gained momentum from 1800 CE to 1820 CE. By 1820 CE membership rose rapidly among Baptist and Methodist congregations led by their preachers. This movement had a strong appeal to the supernatural and continued the effort made by The First Great Awakening.

As a point of reference, the First Great Awakening was a movement devised to increase enthusiasm for Christianity during the 1730s CE and 1740s CE when people living in the American colonies were not that interested in religion. This initiative by Protestant preachers combated the European philosophical movement known as "the enlightenment," which emphasized a scientific and logical view of the world and downplayed religion. Instead, the preachers stressed the importance of scripture, faith, predestination, and the grace of God. They taught that all humans were sinners, God was an angry judge, and individuals needed to ask for his forgiveness. In addition, faith alone justified almost all actions. Perhaps this is where the phrase, "I'm a God-fearing person" came from. What's odd about this thinking is it assumes if you fear God, you are somehow a good person and going to heaven, and if not, you are evil. These preachers were very successful selling this thinking through simple and emotional communication. Their message could be summarized in five core beliefs:

1. All people are born sinners

2. Sin without salvation will send a person to hell

3. All people can be saved if they confess their sins to the Lord Jesus Christ, seek forgiveness, and accept God's grace

4. All people can have a direct and emotional connection to Jesus Christ

5. Religion shouldn't be so formal, solemn and institutionalized

With the exception of the fifth core belief, Augustine of Hippo would have loved these protestant ministers since they were preaching his philosophy. This awakening movement is primarily responsible for what is now referred to as the "Christian Evangelicals," which includes the same techniques and messages used by the most successful television and large crowd performing evangelists today. The only difference is the early preachers did not become quite as wealthy as the current day Evangelist preachers, although many of them still did very well. The business of religion was lucrative then and still is today. These preachers during the 1730s CE and 1740s CE were very effective at reinvigorating religion in America during a time when it was declining. Their entertaining, charismatic, and emotional sermons enticed people, especially those living in the southern colonies, including the enslaved people. Even Benjamin Franklin, a religious skeptic, was interested in the performance of George Whitefield and became friends with him. Whitefield, originally from Great Britain, was one of the most popular ministers touring the colonies at this time. However, not all Protestant religious groups agreed with this awakening message and style because they believed religion should be more formal and solemn, as they were in opposition to the fifth core belief. This thinking was strongest in the New England and Mid Atlantic colonies, while the southern colonies really liked the emotional screaming and trembling approach used by these new ministers. This continues today, as many of the Evangelical believers are mostly rooted in the southern United States geographic area.

Both the First and Second Awakening movements were successful at stopping the appeal of intellectual freedom, where reason would triumph over superstition, and scientific and rational thinking would be valued and tolerated. Society did not tolerate Deistic thinking or any thinking that challenged the dogma and beliefs of the Christian religion. It wasn't until after the Civil War (1861 CE to 1865 CE) that people could freely read and discuss Thomas Paine's Age of Reason publication. Even today, Thomas Paine, who was a key influential person responsible for encouraging and justifying the independence of the United States, is still vilified by some for his religious beliefs. As an example, Mark Twain is quoted as saying, "It took a brave man before the Civil War to confess he had read the Age of Reason."

Tolerance for new beliefs and actual consideration of Thomas Paine's ideas on religion improved after the Civil War. The main reason was because of Charles Darwin's book published in 1859 CE entitled, "On the Origin of Species," which explored evolution and natural selection. One of the key ideas in the book is the notion that all living species are descendants of ancestral species and they are different from present day ones due to the cumulative change in the genetic composition of a population. In other words, the population characteristics change through diversity, and a natural selection of traits is needed to adapt to a changing environment. Worth mentioning, he did not say humans evolved from apes, he said humans evolved from several human species. The knowledge that humans evolved over time and were not always the same as current day challenged the belief that God created us and no more change occurred from that point forward. Of course, this evolution took over hundreds of thousands of years, but we can even see evolutionary changes in the human population since as recently as the 1700s CE. For example, people now are taller, heavier, and more diverse in skin color and physical characteristics than when the United States was founded. Darwin's ideas caused a large-scale abandonment in Britain of the literal reading of the Bible, which also had some impact in the United States. As a result of this change in thinking, it made reading and discussing Thomas Paine's Age of Reason not as dangerous in society, at least in academic environments.

The original architects of the United States of America were able to build an incredible foundation for their country to grow and prosper by working together and resourcing their knowledge of philosophy, science, and history. Although the country as a whole flourished, many people were left behind and suffered greatly over the years, such as women, people with darker skin, and the poor. However, the founders of the United States acknowledged the Constitution and its laws would need to be improved over time, as it was not perfect. Thankfully some of the shortfalls have been corrected such as abolishing slavery, and demanding equal rights and respect for all, not just for those people who happened to be white skinned heterosexual males with European heritage. Correcting all these inequalities is still a work in progress but at least the United States is heading in the right direction. The areas included in the original thinking of the Constitution that we need to protect are the principles of maintaining a separation of church and state, and insuring the balance of power between our three branches of government; Executive, Legislative, and Judicial. The actions being done to weaken this balance through expanded Executive power and one-party control of the judicial branch is very dangerous to undermining the United States' democracy. In addition, it's essential that every person's voting rights be protected, especially the poor who have been even more marginalized in the 21st century, as income inequality has expanded.

To make sure the United States endures and prospers into the future, it needs to support a more Deist thinking approach for its government. It is up to its citizens and their leaders to proactively make this country the best it can possibly be rather than idly standing by hoping a supernatural god will swoop in and do it for them. As a country, its people need to be more open-minded and tolerant of each other. This doesn't mean they must agree on everything, but it means discussion and debate is necessary, similar to the approach used by the early founders, acknowledging different points of view based on facts, not propaganda, and learning from them. Almost everyone has similar goals for their personal wellbeing, and for humanity and society as a whole. The discussion and debate therefore should focus on how to best accomplish these goals. Very few people want to see others suffering or in poverty or feeling marginalized or unwanted, and at the same time people want to have the opportunity for personal and financial success. One of the inhibitors of discussion on these topics is unquestioning adherence to fictional religious beliefs and non-factual political beliefs, that are not helpful to having a rational common-sense discussion of what is best for society.

The Founding Fathers of the United States had a vision for a better life for everyone and they used their knowledge of history and philosophy along with common sense reasoning and debate to establish what would become a very successful United States. This approach should be embraced to address much needed improvements in our society, acknowledging this will always be a work-in-progress.

Chapter 17

And Now, My Thoughts

As far back as I can remember, I have always been intellectually curious. I was that kid – always questioning. What's that? How does that work? Where did that come from? Even questioning my priests and teachers in Catholic school, looking for explanations of what I was expected to believe about life and death and God. Over time, my intellectual curiosity only continued to grow, fueling my desire to read more and more, wanting to learn more about this marvelous world in which we live. And so, I read – about the arts, about history, about people, and yes, about religious beliefs. I found myself particularly drawn to this subject of beliefs, especially in light of the pain, suffering and mistreatment of so many in the world, unfortunately often caused by our unwillingness to see the value in every human being. Of course, I had to ask questions. Why do we choose to mistreat each other? Why do we not see every person as equally worthy of living a healthy, productive life? Unfortunately, throughout history, the answer often points to our differences – our different cultures, our different values, and our different religious beliefs. Ultimately, looking for answers is what inspired me to write this book.

That was the start – I began digging into the origins of religions, their beliefs and their effects on society. Of course, there is so much more to learn, but based on the research I've discovered so far, here is what I can confidently say I do know; all of the major organized religions are based on peoples' imaginations, some level of fiction, and they all accept stories claiming to answer unknowable questions as true, factual, and real. The earliest of religions explained nature, the growing season, weather, and death. They were heavily influenced by superstition and Gods that if not worshipped and prayed to, would destroy their lives. This thinking is still built into current day religions, despite the fact that we are now much more educated on the science of our world and how it works.

I also know these same current day religions claim they came from supernatural beings or Gods or were inspired by them, and yet I know they were all written by men thousands of years ago for the purpose of controlling and governing mostly illiterate people. These so-called "sacred scriptures" were written so that leaders could exploit their people and the natural resources of their territory, in order to expand their wealth and political power. They used their governmental power to organize conquests to obtain wealth and used religion to justify their actions. This religious justification is still apparent today. Most religions are very much anti-other religions, even though some of them have made attempts to temper this teaching. Each of their so-called "sacred scriptures" talk about converting people to their beliefs, and if this fails, destroying the unbelievers or the infidels.

And finally, I know from my research that we do not know what happens to us when we die, even though every religion has made up an answer to this question. Their answers are intended to scare people, causing many of them to disregard facts in favor of made-up stories that make them feel better. This idea, that living with fantasy beliefs is better for people to cope with life versus having the courage to acknowledge what we know and what we do not know, seems dangerous and unhealthy to me. Convincing people they will win the ultimate prize of eternal happiness by attacking or being cruel to other people who don't believe in their religion, is too strong of a weapon in today's society.

Based on my research, those are things I "know". But that begs the next question - so what do I believe? I do have a number of beliefs related to a few of religion's biggest ideologies. My mission in writing this book was to focus on the history of beliefs, rather than the philosophy of religions. Having said that, I will attempt to share some of what I believe, along with my thinking behind these beliefs. I'm sure you'll quickly see a common theme that has been repeated throughout this book – admitting I really don't know any of this to be factually true, nor can I prove it. It's just my beliefs, which if I didn't write this book, would have remained personal unless someone asked for me to share my thoughts.

*

As to the existence of a higher power in the universe and creation...
Even after all my research, and despite realizing I had been brain washed and misled by religious teachers and theologians, I still choose to believe there is some sort of higher power in the universe. I don't know this to be factually true, nor can I prove it, but I still have a belief there has to be a superior power. My rationale is based on observing both the universe and earth's natural world. The universe is amazingly vast, estimated to have a diameter of 540,000,000,000,000,000,000,000 miles (that's a whopping 540 septillion) or 869,046,000,000,000,000,000,000 kilometers, although it may be even larger. With the Hubble Telescope and the James Webb Space Telescope we are able to see thousands of galaxies outside of our galaxy, the Milky Way. These galaxies are billions of light years away from us, which is both unimaginable and awe inspiring. Within this extraordinarily humungous cosmos, on our little planet earth, indeed we are truly very insignificant. Given the vastness of the universe in comparison to our little planet earth, I logically believe there is a power or

force much greater than us, even though I do not know what it could be. I do not know this for sure, as it is only a belief with no supporting facts, but I do feel this thinking has some logical reasoning. I don't like to use the word God, as this implies a being like us. Instead, I prefer to say I believe there is a higher force or power or energy and leave it at that. My hope is this power or force is kind and compassionate, which I realize are human traits but it is all we know.

As to the question of creation, I believe there had to be some intelligent influence on both creation of the universe, including earth and human beings. The big bang theory and evolution only explain some of creation. The big bang theory states that approximately 13.8 billion years ago, all matter was compacted into a very small ball with infinite density and intense heat. For some reason, this ball began expanding and the universe, as we perceive it, began. But what put the ball there that started the universe? The other big creation theory is evolution through natural selection. This theory explains some of the changes we have observed in the development of animal species, plant species, and human beings, but it cannot be explained by evolution alone. For example, the intelligence level of humans is so far superior to other animals, birds, fish, and insects, that it had to have been engineered. Through scientific discovery we are continuously learning how our physical world works and we have made amazing progress. However, almost every scientist would admit that we are far from understanding the full complexity of our bodies, our world, the universe and how they all connect. Certainly, we do not have the knowledge or technology to design and build a human being or an animal.

As human beings, we are very complex biological-based machines that have been evolving over time. In some cases, we are taller and stronger, and in other cases, more obese and weaker, as our environment changes through improvements in medical science, changes in food quality (both good and bad), and changes in the quality of our air, water, and soil (again both good and bad). When you think about it, the original design of the human biological machine that reproduces and grows is incredible. Yes, we are learning about genetics and how cells work, but inventing organisms or humans from scratch is beyond our knowledge base. We cannot even perceive how this was done and all we can do is work with what we currently have and know. So, I do believe an intelligent power had influence in our creation, nevertheless we also have evolved over time. Once again, I do not know how human beings were created but I know for a fact that no one else knows either.

The most important thing I did learn from studying history and the major religions is that we all must be willing to admit when we do not know something. We need to have the courage to say, "I just do not know," and then leave it at that. We can believe or not believe in a superior power, but we should not get into arguments or even wars over these beliefs because they are unknowable. Killing other human beings or even fighting with other human beings merely because they do not believe what you believe or they dared to question your belief, is morally wrong and totally unacceptable in society.

Although I believe a superior force was involved in creation, I do not believe this force interferes with our lives or the health of our planet. In fact, I find the people who think a God is helping them in their life are often extremely arrogant. Most of the people who feel God is looking over them are gifted, such as athletes, musicians, actors, and politicians and by the way, they tend to be very wealthy. Think about how cruel this is to the people who are less fortunate, do not happen to have tremendous talents or are born into extreme poverty. Given all the pain and suffering in the world, if a God is actively getting involved in our lives, then this God is very evil and mean-spirited. The religious fanatics just argue the underprivileged need to pray more and believe, which is also a sad way of thinking, at least that's how I see it. Even the people who believe in reincarnation believe the downtrodden didn't do it right in the last life, so they are punished with poverty and pain in the next life. Again, a really cruel belief. This thinking must stop, as we need to look at and treat all people with respect, trusting that they are doing the best they can. Our goal as a society should be the fortunate need to help lift the less fortunate up so they can live a more comfortable, safe, and fulfilling life.

As a case in point, I find it disturbing when athletes on television in their post-win interviews give a shout-out to God or Jesus, their Lord and Savior, thanking him for their win or they point up to the sky with their finger. Do they really think God or Jesus took time out of his busy schedule to help them win? Did they pray harder than the other team? Did he like them better? Or were they more deserving? What about all the people who didn't even make the team or had very little athletic talent? I guess God or Jesus didn't like them enough to lend a hand, or maybe their prayers were poorly delivered. Of course, in the United States the athletes would never ever thank Allah or Buddha or any other non-Christian god for fear of being attacked or ostracized by fans and the media. As a result, we never hear if the athletes believing in these non-Christian religions have the same thoughts - they are being helped by supernatural powers. The point is, I don't think these athletes think about all the other people in the world that were not as fortunate as them to have superior athletic genetics. They also don't consider other people's beliefs as they just assume their belief is the right one. They may not have bad intentions, but it certainly seems that they are very self-absorbed with their own thinking. This behavior is somewhat selfish and immature, similar to how an infant perceives himself as the center of the universe. When you consider the unimaginable size of the universe and all that is happening in the world, it seems really self-centered to think that a superior force or being would take time out to prioritize helping an individual win a race, a game, or a match.

I believe we are all born into a situation with inherited abilities, and we all try to do the best we can with those abilities. It is similar to being dealt a winning or losing hand in cards. You can improve chances, but if you are given a terrible hand, it is much more difficult to succeed. Yes, I give credit to the extremely gifted for working hard and excelling at what they do, but they were also very lucky with the body and brain they inherited. They also were lucky to be in an economic environment that provided them with a better chance at success. In addition, everyone who does well in life, defined as economic and personal success and happiness, had or has someone(s) helping them. No one does it alone in this world, no one!

I refuse to believe God is supporting certain people and punishing the rest. I also don't believe a God is supporting specific governments of his choosing. The idea that God supports the United States of America over other countries is very arrogant and potentially destructive for our planet. Ask yourself why would a God punish the poorest countries in Africa, Southeast Asia, and South America in favor of helping out the United States? If you lived in Burundi or South Sudan, how would you feel when someone from the United States declares "God Blesses America?" Because if you believe that God blesses America above all, then you believe God thinks lesser of other countries and may even condemn some to a life of misery on earth. What did these people do other than be born into a very bad and poverty-stricken situation? What we do know is, by helping these people get proper nutrition and education and putting them in a more stable infrastructure and political environment, they tend to excel. God did not have anything to do with this. Even in the United States, which some religious people insist is God's "chosen country," almost 80 million people or 24% of the population strain to stay above the poverty line. In fact, 34 million people or 10% of the population are living below the poverty line. This means these people in the United States are struggling just to meet their basic needs of having enough food to eat and a place to live. The implication of this narrow thinking is their United States' Christian God only supports people who are fortunate.

The reason why I am belaboring this point is, we as a human race, need to more universally believe in the notion that we control our own destiny rather than rely on a supernatural God. The idea that a God will swoop in and help us out is not based on any facts or logical reasoning. The prophesies about God showing up and killing all the true believer's enemies and then taking the believers to heaven with him seems absolutely nonsensical. We need to stop praying to God for miracles and get to work. All of us live on this planet and no one is on an island by themselves. We as a group need to help improve the world for everyone, which includes the poor and downtrodden. By lifting the poor up, it will lift everyone up and make for a better world. There's a song, "It's Up to Us" by French singer Charles Pasi, that includes the following lyrics which I find to be very inspirational:

"You've got your hands together, hoping' for answers,
But we need your hands, to grab another man's hand"

As members of the human race, we need to focus on creating the kind of life experience that we want for everyone and that everyone deserves. However, everyone's perspective on this topic is a little different, so we need to help each other understand the perspective of the people who are suffering. At their core, I believe most mentally sound and healthy people are compassionate and kind. This is a good place to start in our attempt to gain support for positive social change and programs. First, it's important to identify what most people would like to change, such as eliminating or at least reducing:

— suffering from oppression,

— being made to feel inferior,

— starving from hunger,

— living and then dying in agonizing pain with no medical support,

— needing a place to live, or living in a filthy unsafe environment.

The first priority to help people dig out of financial insecurity has to be paying everyone a living wage for their job. If you are a business owner and you cannot pay your employees a living wage, then you do not have an ongoing concern. You do not have a business that is viable and yes, you should go out of business if you cannot pay people properly. Not paying people a living wage is just an example of slavery by another name. By the way it is appalling that most religions don't outright condemn slavery, this is because it was acceptable when most religions were started and later documented in their so-called sacred scriptures.

It's important to understand there is not a finite number of jobs or income. Yes, there are short-term localized unemployment situations, which need to be addressed, but new people, such as immigrants coming into the labor market should not be viewed as taking jobs away from anyone when looked at from a macro viewpoint. We also know as people make higher wages, they are able to buy more which causes the economy to grow creating even more jobs. In addition, more diversity and tolerance for others in the workplace drives innovation, making our world a better place. I do not believe there is a God managing our employment situation - we should not even passively be relying on God's intervention. No one can prove God has a plan for us, so we need to proactively create our own plan.

I suggest our life plan needs to be based on what we observe in our world, as this is all we have available to us. What we observe is that we influence each other, as we do not live on an island. If you are observant, you can discern when someone is cruel or rude to another person –

moreover, this behavior tends to get passed along to others. Just imagine if everyone started acting negatively toward each other, with everyone becoming angrier – the situation would continue to escalate, resulting in a very unpleasant, unhappy and potentially dangerous environment. In the same way, the opposite is true when people are kind and helpful to each other. This positive behavior also tends to get passed along, resulting in a happier and enjoyable environment. Hence, the encouragement for people to pass along good deeds. We cannot disassociate from our society, family, friends, as our behavior has an impact on other people, no matter how much we might prefer to be alone or think no one cares. Accordingly, we need to be cognizant of this basic life fact and our actions should be biased toward kindness and being unselfish.

Through this observation we recognize how we should behave for a more pleasant life. If we cause or encourage happiness through our actions, this tends to have positive aftereffects, which is a good thing. If we cause pain or suffering, even unintentionally, this will have negative ramifications, which is a bad thing. We don't need the threat of a killing or punishing God to get us to take this approach in life – by design, we were meant to act in a positive way. Unfortunately, in our current world, many people are selfish or at least self-absorbed, which also seems to be indoctrinated in current day religions. The religious teaching idea being… I follow my beliefs. I will be saved by my God whereas you will not. Too bad for you!

Essentially, you actually have to care about other people and not just yourself – this is the core principle behind encouraging and taking action to making other people's lives happier. This doesn't mean you shouldn't take care of yourself, but it means that you shouldn't put yourself first at the expense of others. Even the so-called golden rule of, "treat others as you would like to be treated" doesn't address the topic of how can I be a positive force in making other people's lives happier.

Most people know the Ten Commandments whether they care about them or not, but we now have formal laws dictating how we are to behave in society. Unfortunately, we now seem to accept, even encourage, bad or immoral behavior as long as it is not illegal or doesn't directly violate these Commandments. The view of some people is, "I will take advantage of other people to maximize my own wealth, even if it is immoral, unethical, cruel, or hurtful just as long as it is not illegal or I can get away with it." They actually see the people they took advantage of as inferior or stupid, simply because these people are kind and compassionate. Unfortunately, our capitalist-based society seems to reward these people, at least in the short term. We see business people not paying people livable wages, claiming bankruptcy in order to avoid honoring their debts, swindling others, and destroying lives with no apparent guilt of wrongdoing. How can this be good for society? We sometimes see these same people attending church, temple, or synagogue and thinking very highly of themselves. They feel God loves them above others – after all, they are so clever and he is watching out for them considering he had chosen them. These illusory religious beliefs really need a major makeover to actively denounce this immoral and unethical behavior.

*

As to the existence of a soul...

The next big question people have is related to the existence of a soul beyond our physical body. Concerning this question, the only thing I know for certain is no one has the answer to this question. We just don't know what a soul is or if we even have a soul at all. However, I personally want to believe there is a spirit beyond just genetics that is part of each of us. If you were raised in an environment of religious teaching, you were taught that you have a soul or spirit. As with most beliefs, this one started in ancient times and evolved overtime. In ancient Greece, Plato's (427 BCE to 347 BCE) theory on the soul was that it was the force in the body that provided thought, perception, and desire. He also decided the soul was immortal and existed before and after death. The next important Greek philosopher, Aristotle (384 BCE to 322 BCE) slightly modified this thinking to consider only the intellect part of the soul as immortal. The Christian philosopher St Augustine (354 CE to 430 CE) further adjusted the Greek thinking and decided the purpose of the soul was to be united with God after death. He also said the soul was the true person and the body was separate. Then St Thomas Aquinas (1225 CE to 1274 CE) reverted back to supporting the Greek philosophy that the soul was the driving force of the body and both were needed to make an individual person. As a result, over time Christian philosophers adopted the Greek thinking that the soul was immortal, created by God and infused into the body at conception. The Muslim soul belief is similar to the Christian belief. As you hopefully have realized by reading this history, all of these views have been invented by many people over the years, changing and then re-changing, however none of them can be proven and they are just theories not based on anything knowable.

Hinduism had a different idea about the soul. They decided the soul was the universal eternal self. What this means is your soul (or atman written in Sanskrit) is what makes your body function. The Hindu religion believes Brahma (the ultimate God) makes everything in the universe work and the soul or atman is part of this system. They believe your soul after death either transmigrates to a new life or attains moksha. Moksha is the release from the bondage of human life and death and unification with Brahman. Once again, people made this up a long time ago because they did not know with certainty how the human body worked or what happens to us when we die. We now know more about our body, although we still do not know what happens when we die or if we actually have a soul.

Through science we can now explain much about a person's personality and physical makeup based on genetics. Everyone is different, even an identical twin, which is the surest way to prove this fact. Although identical twins share the same DNA (deoxyribonucleic acid code), they have slightly different genes. First, a little background as to why this happens. Identical twins are formed from the same sperm and egg with the embryo dividing in two and therefore, each has the same DNA code at the very beginning of development. DNA is made up of the chromosomes that contain our genetic information, such as hair and eye color, height, bone structure, athletic ability, and personality traits. What happens to identical twins is they each pick up genetic mutations in the womb because of nutritional differences, cells developing differently and environmental differences. As a result, they are not genetically identical by the time they are born, even having unique fingerprints. The twin example, along with other genetic work, proves that much of the thinking and theories of these historic philosophers concerning a person's essence or personality can be explained by genetics rather than a soul. However, it's interesting when we observe children at a very young age who seem to have traits beyond genetics. We often say a child has an old soul or they are wise beyond their years, which is hard to explain by genetics alone.

What kind of a person we are, our essence or personality, is determined by many factors; our genetics, environment, the beliefs we were taught or brain washed to follow, family guidance primarily by our parents and siblings, peer pressure, culture, and a lifetime of learning and acquiring knowledge. However, the argument for a soul overlaying all of these personality-influencing factors breaks down when we consider people who are severely mentally ill with disorders such as schizophrenia, manic depression, autism, dementia, and Alzheimer's. All of these illnesses affect a person's thinking, feeling, mood, and behavior. If we all have a soul tied to our personality, then how is the soul affected for those people inflicted with these illnesses? In all of these mental illnesses we know the brain is not functioning properly either due to a genetic disorder, biological factors such as a chemical imbalance in the brain, traumatic brain injury, exposure to viruses or toxic chemicals while developing in a womb, or drug or alcohol abuse. Severe pain also impacts our personality as well, making us angry, cruel or depressed. We have a lot to learn about the brain - when it's not working properly, it's more difficult to discern a person's soul or essence.

What we do know is, as humans we are a very complex biologically based machine with a brain. When the heart stops, the machine shuts down resulting in no more energy to the body and brain. There is absolutely no proof that an aura or spirit exists along with our physical body. In fact, the colored auras or energy fields that psychic or guru's claim to see around people have been proven not to exist through scientifically controlled experiments. The claims by these people are false and a hoax.

If you have ever been around someone who has just died, you do feel the energy leave his or her body or at least you perceive this to happen. Some people think this is the soul leaving the body, while others just think it is the biological machine shutting down. In 1907 CE, physician Duncan MacDougall claimed to have measured the weight of souls when people died, however his experiment was proved to be faulty, inaccurate, and a total failure. To date, no one has been able to prove human beings have a soul. Again, this question cannot be answered - you can believe in a soul or spirit but you cannot say you know it exists for sure, as it is unknowable.

I do believe people influence each other based on non-verbal or non-physical actions. We all know people who have an impact on us, either positively or negatively, by just their presence. As a result of this real or perceived experience, like many people, I do feel there is some other energy attached to our body that is not physical, having an effect on the essence of who we are beyond our personality and genetics. It's an intangible thing but it seems to exist, although once again, no one can prove it. What about the severely mentally ill? What soul or spirit do these people have? A broken one? This last statement would argue that we are just a biological machine with our personality or essence determined by genetics, our environment, and upbringing. As to what I believe; I want to believe there is a spirit beyond just genetics that is part of our being. However, it is very tough to feel any confidence in this belief because; I have no idea what this spirit is, I don't know where it comes from in our early life, I don't know where it goes when we die, and I cannot explain the soul of a mentally ill person. Basically, we just don't know and logically can't justify if we have a personal essence or soul beyond our physical body.

*

As to what happens to us when we die...
The next belief relates to the big question of what happens to us when we die, which is tied to the previous question on the existence of a soul discussion. Again, like all the other questions, this one is also unknowable. On this topic I have more hope than a belief that we live on in some form after we die. It seems to me there must be something more to us than we are just born, we live and then we die. Again, I refer to observing nature for hints on this hope. For example, most of us are programmed to be rewarded for our good behavior; actions and words that cause happiness and joy for others, not being selfish, and limiting how much pain and suffering we inflict. We can even observe that the more we give, the more we seem to get in return. This return can be in both tangible and intangible forms such as knowledge, new friends, love, feelings of accomplishment, a sense of community, camaraderie, connections leading to more rewarding and higher-level jobs, and a sense of purpose.

Since we observe positive returns for positive actions most of the time in our world, this expectation must have been intrinsically built into our understanding of how to treat each other. My hope is that whatever created us chose to include this cause-and-effect relationship so we would expect to be rewarded at the end of our life if we live it with kindness, compassion, and unselfishness. Therefore, I am hopeful there is a reward for living a good life at the end. At the same time, I also believe that living this way results in a more pleasant and happier world now, so our lives are enjoyable even if there is no after life reward. The reward can be now!

But what about the people who just want to cause others pain and suffering and only care about their own happiness? I do believe the people who act this way are most likely mentally unstable. This does not mean all cruel or selfish people are narcissists or psychopaths with no conscience, however really cruel or selfish people most likely have degrees of an abnormality. I have met people in my life who are so selfish and privileged they have very little orientation to noticing or acting on other people's feelings or wellbeing. These people may only have a limited conscience gene in their personality, coupled with being raised privileged, to have such little regard for others. Many of these people are not totally evil people, because when confronted with this selfish behavior, they often feel badly – it could be they are just clueless. I would classify these people as mildly mentally unstable. I would hope all the people who cause pain and suffering would be given a do-over with a healthier brain, which relies on some form of reincarnation, otherwise I'm at a loss to make a conclusion as to what happens to them in an afterlife.

Two issues come up with not having an answer to what happens to us when we die. The first is fear and the second is questioning why are we alive? Addressing both of these issues together can help overcome mental anxiety or depression. Even though, philosophers have pondered the meaning of life for thousands of years with no successful answer. Thankfully, psychologists have written much on how to overcome fear.

Religions use fear of death as their main motivator to get people to believe their philosophies and support them. However, this fear is irrational since it is based on the unknown as we have no idea what happens to us when we die. So how do you deal with this fear without relying on made-up fantasy?

One of the best ways to overcome fear is to do what the military teaches, which dates back to the Spartans of Greece. The military's approach is to get soldiers to focus on thinking about accomplishing a task as opposed to thinking about what could happen. These organizations have their members practice these skills over and over so that they become automatic, even in the face of extreme danger. By doing this, the soldier executes their actions with very little, if any, fear. This approach also works in life. The more you concentrate on living your life to the best of your ability and being kind and generous to others, your fears will reduce. One of the best ways to improve your mental health is to focus on helping others and not always thinking about yourself. We all must have the courage to live our lives to the fullest, which can significantly reduce fear.

The second question of why we are alive cannot be answered. We don't know, and pondering this question is a waste of time. Perhaps the wrong question is being asked. The better question is: How will we live our life to its fullest? There are actually answers to this question and those answers can change throughout our life. I truly believe we have a duty to use the talents we possess as best we can. Everyone has strengths they can use and also can improve on their weaknesses. We must take advantage of the opportunities we are given with courage and conviction. This is so important because if everyone used his or her abilities fully, the world would truly be a better place. If we are lazy and don't push ourselves, society can't reach its full potential. In addition, everyone owes it to each other to use what they have to the best of their ability because people are given very different abilities through genetics and just plain luck. Since we do not know what happens to us after death, we need to stop thinking about it and focus on making our life and the society around us the best we can while we are alive. We, as a collective community, can shape our world how we would like to see it and not rely on a god to do it for us.

*

So why is now the time for reality?

All this said, I truly believe we control our world and have the ability to make our lives more fulfilling and pleasant if we use these abilities to not only help ourselves but those around us. Being unselfish is a key to achieving this goal along with focusing on causing happiness and joy as oppose to causing pain and suffering. We cannot write laws for all of this, as it needs to be what people choose to do on their own. Laws are important for stability in our society, but just because something is not illegal does not mean it is moral or ethical. The first question everyone should ask before they take a questionable action is, who will this hurt? If it hurts people, then don't do it. If it hurts the environment, then don't do it. If we all focus decision making on doing the right thing, then the world improves in the long term, even if we need to struggle a little in the short term. At least we know, in our hearts, we did the right thing. Although much of the religious beliefs we were taught are not facts but just man written imaginative stories, I still feel it is healthy to have our own personal spiritual beliefs. However, don't assume yours are necessarily right and others are wrong. It's important to be open to listening to other people's ideas and you might even learn something.

Throughout history, religious groups have armed themselves with both political and physical weapons along with using hatred and discrimination, aimed at anyone who does not share their beliefs and way of life. And it is continuing today. As examples, this includes Christians primarily in the western world, Islam primarily in Southwest Asia, Hinduism primarily in India, and Buddhism primarily in Myanmar. All these religions are persecuting others who do not believe or practice their religious fictional stories and customs. This seems absurd to me. Every one of these religious groups cannot be right. But guess what - all of them can be wrong!

So how did we get here? The early religions were invented when very few people could read and write. Primarily, only the educated ruling class and religious leaders were literate. This gave them tremendous power over the people they ruled. As I mentioned several times already, isn't it interesting that not one God and not one prophet selected by God wrote anything down about the religion attributed to them? It seems to me that if you were a god or god's messenger, you would be able to write your instructions down in every language, both present and future.

The benefit of having an illiterate society when a religion was originated permitted the ruling class and religious leaders to write anything they wanted. They could tell people this came directly from God and needed to be followed on penalty of death. What a powerful way to rule and control the masses of people. This worked best for an authoritative government having a king or emperor in power, combined with the support of a religious leader. Once these beliefs were established, over time they were passed down through the generations and never questioned in a transformative way because to do so was considered heresy. It also would alienate you from your family and the society you lived in if you chose not to believe. This remains true today in much of the world.

The three main reasons we can now challenge these beliefs are that we have improvements in literacy, education, and availability of information. As to literacy, more than 85% of the world population can now read and write and this is continuing to increase for both men and woman. This is a tremendous improvement when you consider only 20% of the world's population was literate 200 years ago. Think about how far we've come since the origins of the United States and many other countries around the world. This is an amazing gift for everyone in the world and should be used to its fullest extent. We all need to make it a priority to read more in order to learn and understand the world around us, including history, science, religion, philosophy, literature, and the list goes on. Being ignorant and not reading books should not be viewed as a positive trait or a source of pride for anyone. After all, our governments and parents have spent significant resources helping us become literate. You do not need, nor should you "just believe" a story someone tells you to be true and accurate - take it upon yourself to research it to determine for yourself what is really true. Oh, and make sure you use more than one source and make sure those sources are reputable.

The second reason why we can now challenge beliefs is the level of education has increased significantly in the developing world. The average years of education people received in the developing world has more than tripled between 1950 CE and 2010 CE. As people become more informed around the world, they can challenge their society better to improve living conditions and social interactions through innovation and policy changes. As an aside, the world economic community is now defining the development level of a country based on its Human Development Index (HDI). This index is determined by combining per capita wealth, education attainment, and life expectancy. Out of 193 countries recognized by the United Nations, approximately 51 are considered high development, 41 countries are considered low development and the remaining 101 are considered average. The country with the highest HDI is Norway, and the United States is ranked number 13 as an example.

The third reason why we can now challenge beliefs is the availability of information in both libraries and the Internet. 80% of people in developed countries and 45% of people in developing countries have available Internet access. The access to information has never been better in the history of the world in terms of both scale and access. Access to information is no longer an excuse to be ignorant. People need to combine their reading skills, critical thinking skills, and access to information to both question and improve their lives as well as the society in which they live. In addition, obtaining more knowledge and understanding of other cultures tends to lead us to becoming more tolerant, resulting in a more peaceful world. Many adults have trouble differentiating fiction from reality as evidence by the significant number of people who believe in conspiracy theories. Some of these same people also quote scripture frequently as they have no hesitation in assuming fictional stories are real, they just believe. In today's society it is so important to realize that if you have unquestioning faith, then you have no faith at all, only brainwashing. Believing in fantasy stories as real is extremely dangerous to the overall health of our world given the modern-day power of our weapons and of propaganda fueled by mass media and social media. It has become too easy to mobilize hatred using fantasy. As a result, the overall population must start using critical thinking and intellectual curiosity to question and research what they are being told. After all, our government has taught over 90% of us how to read, we need to use this gift along with all the information now available on the Internet and libraries.

I personally am embarrassed to have blindly gone along with the Christian dogma and beliefs I was taught for so much of my life. Shame on me for not doing the research to find out the origins of my own religious beliefs! As I increased my research on history and religious history, it became obvious as to the source of these religious beliefs. To now realize these and other religious beliefs were just invented ways to explain life and death and control people was demoralizing. As to getting people to embrace religious beliefs I also came to the realization that the strength of brainwashing from an early age, combined with family and society endorsement is extremely hard to break. The key to overcoming brainwashing is to question things you are told and then follow up with intellectual curiosity and research to determine if they are factual or fantasy.

So here we are today, literate and educated with access to more information than anyone could possibly consume in a lifetime. With just a bit of curiosity and some quick research, we can discover these religious truths are just mere imaginary stories. Not factual events. This is not to imply having beliefs in unknowable spiritual topics or practicing rituals or actions that help encourage positive mental wellbeing is necessarily unhealthy, bad or wrong. Having a personal belief in a supreme creative power, a soul, and life after death is our right as a human being and no one can tell us our thoughts are wrong. By the same token we cannot and should not unequivocally say we are right either. We just do not know the answer to these spiritual topics. There are also benefits associated with beliefs in rituals that help with our mental state and coping with life. Such things as meditation to calm our minds and focus our thinking, lighting candles to give thanks for what we have or remembering a loved one, singing to give thanks or uplift our spirits, and sharing meals with family and friends. These rituals are examples of activities that have been proven to work since ancient times. You can even learn about these activities and their benefits through reading and research and maybe even learn about some new rituals or traditions that you may enjoy. Our goal should be to get through each day as happy as possible but in a world where our beliefs are built on reality, not fiction.

I wrote this book because I wanted to share my research with other people who enjoyed learning history and had questions about where their beliefs originated and if they were based on facts or fiction. My hope is you will better understand the origin of your beliefs and as a result, no longer just blindly believe these stories to have been factually based. One of the benefits of eliminating the dogma, fiction, superstition, guilt and tension inflicted by religions are it results in reaching a more peaceful state of mind. I now appreciate this process of coming to an awareness regarding my own beliefs was a necessary step to becoming a wiser and more knowledgeable person. Once I came to this awareness, I apologized to my children for subjecting them to religious dogma during their early years, thus breaking the generational passing on of religious myths. On a positive note, my children were doing their own research as they got older and obtained a much more robust education in history than myself. As a result, they began more aggressively questioning all the fiction and myths in religions much earlier than I did in my life. Thankfully, my unintentional brainwashing of beliefs did not damage them too much. I hope you have the courage to internalize what we know and more importantly, what we don't know about the universe, creation, and our lives. Dreaming up answers to important questions that are unknowable and believing you are definitively right is not a solution. Quite the opposite - it is destructive. We need to face what we don't know and admit it. Now is the time for you to embrace your own intellectual curiosity and embark on your own spiritual journey. Now is the time for reality!

Reference Sources

Alighieri, Dante, & Anderson, Melville Best, The Divine Comedy, World Book Company, 1922

Aristotle's Political Theory, Stanford Encyclopedia of Philosophy, 2017

Arnhart, Larry, Darwinian Conservatism, The Evolution of Heaven and Hell: Aristotle and Contemplative Life, 2010

Baigent, Michael, Leigh, Richard & Lincoln, Henry, Holy Blood, Holy Grail, Bantam Dell, a division of Random House, Inc, 1983

Bekhrad, Joobin, This Obscure Religion Shaped the West, BBC Culture, 2017

Cahill, Thomas, How the Irish Saved Civilization: the untold story of Ireland's heroic role from the fall of Rome to the rise of medieval Europe, Nan A. Talese, Doubleday, 1995

Choudhury, Raja, Soma: the psychedelic origins of religious experience and the third eye

Chua, Amy, Day of Empire, How Hyperpowers Rise to Global Dominance – and Why they Fall, Doubleday, 2007

Confucianism as a Religion, Factsanddetails.com, 2019, and Wikimedia Commons, 2016

Das, Subhamoy, Hinduism for Beginners, Indian Arts and Culture, Learn Religions.com, 2019

Diamond, Jared, Guns, Germs, and Steel, The Fates of Human Societies, W. W. Norton & Company, 1999

Duignan, Brian, Diwali, Encyclopedia Britannica, Inc., 2021

Everitt, Anthony, The Rise of Rome, The Making of the World's Greatest Empire, Random House, 2012

Frankopan, Peter, The Silk Roads, A New History of the World, Bloomsbury, 2015

Graves, Kersey, The World's Sixteen Crucified Saviors: Christianity before Christ, Cosimo Classics, 2007, original published 1875

Greek Mythology.com 1997-2019

Haass, Richard, The World, A Brief Introduction, Penguin Random House LLC, 2020

Harris, Sam, The End of Faith, Religion, Terror, and the Future of Reason, W. W. Norton & Company, 2004

Harrison, Jane Ellen, Themis: A Study of the Social Origins of Greek Religion, 1927

Hillerbrand, Hans J, Encyclopedia Britannica, Easter Holiday, 2021

History.com Editors, Halloween 2021, A&E Television Networks, April 27, 2021

History.com Editors, Rosh Hashanah, History A&E Networks, 2021

Jacobsen, Thorkild Professor of Assyriology, Mesopotamia, Encyclopedia Britannica, Harvard University, 2021

Janick, Jules, The Origin of fruits, fruit growing and fruit breeding, hort.purdue.edu, new crop, origins, 2005 Purdue University

Jewish Virtual Library, A project of AICE, Judah the Galilean, American Israeli Cooperative Enterprise, 2022

Knowledge of Reality Magazine, 1996-2006, Issue 22

Konig, Franz Cardinal, Zarathustra Iranian Prophet, Zoroaster, Encyclopedia Britannica, 2021

Lama, Dalai, Beyond Religion: Ethics for a Whole World, HarperCollins, 2011

Mark, Joshua J. "Hypatia of Alexandria" Ancient History Encyclopedia, 02 Sep 2009. Web. 05Mar 2019

McKeever, Amy, Diwali is India's most important holiday – and a celebration of good over evil, National Geographic history and culture, November 12, 2020

Montesquieu, Baron de, translated Nugent, Thomas, revised Prichard, JV, The Spirit of Laws, D Appleton and Company, 1900, original 1748

Noss, David, S, Grangaard, Blake, R, A History of the World's Religions 14th Edition, Routledge, 2017

Paine, Thomas, Age of Reason, G. E. Wilson, 1794

Paine, Thomas, Common Sense, R. Bell, 1776

Petruzzella, Melissa, Assistant Editor of Encyclopedia Britannica, "History of the First Council of Nicaea", Dec 2018

Richard, John, Pollard, Thornhill, Greek Mythology, Encyclopedia Britannica, 2021

Rosh HaShanah, Reform Judaism.org, Union for Reform Judaism, 2021

Ruthven, Malise, Fundamentalism, The Search for Meaning, Oxford University Press, 2004

Saini, Angela, Inferior: How Science Got Women Wrong- and the New Research That's Rewriting the Story, 2017

Saloff, Darren, Deism and the Founding of the United States, Divining America, Teacher Serve National Humanities Center, 2021

Srinivasan, Amrutur, Hinduism for Dummies, Core Beliefs of Hindus, Wiley Brand, 2021

Stocker, Michael, The Schizophrenia of Modern Ethical Theories 1976 paper on ethics

Strauss, Valerie, why is Christmas on Dec 25? The Washington Post, Dec 25, 2015

The idea of the Holy Ghost, Issue 22, Knowledge of Reality Magazine 2020

Weatherford Jack, Genghis Khan, and the Making of the Modern World, Penguin Random House, 2004

Wikipedia Theophany, Wikimedia Foundation Inc July 9, 2020

World Development Indicators, The World Bank Group, Data.worldbank.org, 2022

Zinn, Howard, A Peoples History of the United States 1492-2001, HarperCollins, 2003

About the Author

Dan Friedrich is a retired business executive with 40 years of experience in North America and Globally with several Fortune 500 consumer products companies. During his business career he was successful at building businesses using critical thinking skills to develop strategies, tactics, and processes. This skill of combining information and ideas from many sources using critical thinking and then communicating the solutions succinctly made him uniquely qualified to write "They Told Us to Just Believe". He was raised Roman Catholic and followed this religion most of his life but through his passion for reading history he learned that the historical stories behind these religious beliefs were not what he was led to believe. Through his research and global travel, he also became more tolerant and interested in other cultures and beliefs. As a result, he wanted to share his learning with his children and others to help people think more clearly about what they believe, which in the long run will lead to a better, kinder, and less selfish society. He has an MBA from Western Michigan University and lives in Connecticut with his wife Susan, who was instrumental in helping him edit this book. He is also the father of three adult children and has three grandchildren.

www.ingramcontent.com/pod-product-compliance
Lightning Source LLC
Chambersburg PA
CBHW060450030426
42337CB00015B/1531